Representing Communities

Ruth Sanz Sabido
Editor

Representing Communities

Discourse and Contexts

palgrave
macmillan

Editor
Ruth Sanz Sabido
School of Media, Art and Design
Canterbury Christ Church University
Canterbury, UK

ISBN 978-3-319-65029-6   ISBN 978-3-319-65030-2   (eBook)
DOI 10.1007/978-3-319-65030-2

Library of Congress Control Number: 2017949471

Cover credit: Andrew Tallon

Printed on acid-free paper

This Palgrave Macmillan imprint is published by Springer Nature
The registered company is Springer International Publishing AG
The registered company address is: Gewerbestrasse 11, 6330 Cham, Switzerland

For Donald

ACKNOWLEDGEMENTS

The project *Representing Communities: Discourse and Contexts* emerged from the organisation of the annual MeCCSA conference that was held on 6–8 January 2016 at Canterbury Christ Church University (Canterbury, UK). I am grateful to Felicity Plester for her interest in the proposal, and to Martina O'Sullivan for her ongoing support and patience throughout the completion of the book. I would like to thank all the authors for contributing to this volume, and my colleagues in the School of Media, Art and Design at Canterbury Christ Church University for their continued encouragement and support. In particular, I am grateful to my fellow conference organisers: Julia Bennett, Andrew Butler, Agnes Gulyas, Sarah O'Hara and Tim Long, for making such a fantastic conference team. Stuart Price provided valuable academic advice and encouragement. I am deeply indebted to Carmen Barragán and Jill Mason, whose friendships have been particularly important in the last few months and have taken me through the final stages of putting this book together. To Donald I owe his unconditional support, and to my mother, Pepa, and my brother Enrique, their endless love and dedication.

Contents

Editor and Contributors

About the Editor

Ruth Sanz Sabido is Senior Lecturer in Media and Communication at Canterbury Christ Church University, UK. She is the author of *Memories of the Spanish Civil War: Conflict and Community in Rural Spain* (2016), and co-editor of *Sites of Protest* (2016) and *Contemporary Protest and the Legacy of Dissent* (2015). Her research interests include memory studies and media discourses about conflict, social movements and violence against women. Ruth is Chair of the MeCCSA Social Movements Network.

Contributors

Anita Biressi is Professor of Media and Society. Her publications include *Reality Television* (2005), *The Tabloid Culture Reader* (2008) and *Class and Contemporary British Culture* (2013). Her research interests include the popular articulation of neoliberalism, representations of social class and the relationship between the media sphere and social self.

Rosalind Brunt is a Visiting Research Fellow at Sheffield Hallam University. In the 1970s she researched the cablevision community project and Granada Television's access experiments. She was an active member of the Free Communications Group and ComCom (the national association for community communications). She has continued to research the media and popular culture and was the founding chair of the MeCCSA Women's Media Studies Network, and is currently Vice-Chair of its Social Movements Network.

Rinella Cere is Reader in Media and Cultural Studies at Sheffield Hallam University. Her publications include books, chapters and articles on news media and popular culture in Italy and Britain. Recent publications include a chapter for an edited collection on the EU Referendum and the media (Palgrave Macmillan 2017), and a chapter for *Postcolonial Studies Meets Media Studies. A Critical Encounter* (Transcript Verlag, 2016).

Anna Khlusova is a Ph.D. candidate in the Department of Culture, Media and Creative Industries at King's College London. Her research interest lies at the intersection of gender studies, diaspora studies, identity and feminist media studies, with a particular focus on post-Soviet contexts. Anna holds a M.A. in Culture and Creative Industries (King's College London) and a B.A. (Hons) in History of Art/Film Studies (Oxford Brookes University).

Mikko O. Koivisto is a doctoral candidate at the Aalto University School of Arts, Design and Architecture in Helsinki. His research is located in the intersection of art education, public pedagogy and disability studies, and focuses on the interplay of the themes of disability, madness and horror in rap music and hip-hop culture. In 2016–2017 he was a visiting scholar at the Department of Disability and Human Development in the University of Illinois at Chicago under the ASLA-Fulbright Pre-Doctoral Research Fellows Program.

Elizabeth Lakey recently completed her Ph.D. at RMIT University, Melbourne, in the school of Global, Urban and Social Studies. Her Ph.D. examined the contested identities of young Somalis living in Melbourne. She currently works in the Faculty of Arts at the University of Melbourne.

Heather Nunn is Professor Emeritus at the University of Roehampton. She is the author of *Thatcher, Politics and Fantasy* (2002), *Reality Television* (2005) and *Class and Contemporary British Culture* (2013). Her research interests include Thatcherism and popular Conservatism, media and social class, and discourses of gender, authority and experience.

Richard Pendry is a Lecturer at the University of Kent Centre for Journalism. He researches how journalists and sources use each other in areas of conflict, and has written about contemporary reporting practices in Iraq and Syria. Richard is a former member of Frontline News Television, a news agency that specialised in reporting conflict.

Stuart Price is Professor of Media and Political Discourse at De Montfort University, Leicester, and Chair of the Media Discourse Group. He is the author of *Worst-case Scenario?* (2011), *Brute Reality* (2010), *Discourse Power Address* (2007 and 2016) and co-editor with Ruth Sanz Sabido of *Sites of Protest* (2016) and *Contemporary Protest and the Legacy of Dissent* (2015). He is currently editing a book called *Investigative Journalism* and writing a monograph called *Corbyn and the Media* (both 2018).

Robin Roberts is Professor of English at the University of Arkansas. She is the author of several books and numerous articles on gender and popular culture. Her latest book is *Subversive Spirits: The Female Ghost in British and American Popular Culture* (University Press of Mississippi 2018). She is currently working on a book about the representation of New Orleans on television.

Corinna Schäfer is a doctoral researcher in Media and Cultural Studies at the University of Sussex. Her interdisciplinary research project is funded by the Consortium for the Humanities and the Arts in South-East England (CHASE) and Funds for Women Graduates (FfWG).

LIST OF FIGURES

CHAPTER 1

Introduction: Communities, Discourse and Contexts

Ruth Sanz Sabido

INTRODUCTION

The variety of social groupings to which the term 'community' refers has grown exponentially over the years. Sociologists have spent a great deal of effort attempting to define and disentangle the wide range of characteristics and factors that constitute a community. Whether it denotes a city 'standing together' against terrorism, or migrants setting up a new life away from their home countries, or protest groups attempting to effect some social change, 'community' seems to have become a fitting notion to describe these and many other (literal or symbolic) gatherings of people. It is not surprising that, even back in 1955, Hillery's only definitive conclusion to his analysis of a sample of definitions of the term community was that there is only one common element to all of them: "they all deal with people. Beyond this common basis, there is no agreement" (Hillery 1955).

Traditionally, communities were bound to specific places or localities in which social relations developed amongst people within their

R. Sanz Sabido (✉)
Canterbury Christ Church University, Canterbury, UK
e-mail: ruth.sanz-sabido@canterbury.ac.uk

© The Author(s) 2017
R. Sanz Sabido (ed.), *Representing Communities*,
DOI 10.1007/978-3-319-65030-2_1

1

immediate contexts. Such was, and still is, the case with tribes and villages that, set apart from other similar configurations, consist of well-defined groupings with relatively complex fabrics of interpersonal connections (Mackenzie and Dalby 2003). These communities are defined on the basis of their geographical locations, with their own sets of traditions, local norms and social histories. Indeed, this traditional type of rural community forms the basis for the original definitions of the term, to the extent that the development of urban societies and the characteristics of these emerging industrialised communities were assessed negatively against the nets of tightly knit social relations that had been known up to that point. The close associations and social cohesion that are typically associated with rural environments were at the heart of the discipline, which held a romantic view of pre-industrial times (Tönnies 1974 [1887]; see also Elias 1974).

Since those early days, the term has been applied to a wider range of settings and social relationships. For one, it is no longer limited to geographically circumscribed areas, but has come to reflect the fact that social groups come together for a variety of reasons, beyond the traditional possibilities and limitations of the immediate local sphere. So, for example, the term has come to describe—to varying degrees of accuracy—communities of migrants who try to negotiate their identities in their host cities or countries (Sanz Sabido 2017), and grassroots groups and communities that fight for social rights and improvements in the provision of social services (Staples 2012). What these types of communities have in common is that the individuals who compose them share a sense of belonging through their identities, or through the need to cope with a collective problem or to achieve a joint interest. They consist of networks of solidarity that are not necessarily defined by their location (although both factors are not mutually exclusive), for what matters is to accomplish a goal that is both personal to each member of the community and collective for the entire group.

More recently, applications of the term community have continued to expand and the notion has increasingly been used in media studies and social research to describe groups that have emerged on online platforms, thereby eliminating the question of distance and geographical location. So, for instance, some authors have spoken about gaming communities (Jacobs 2008), and about online communities around specific networks, themes and contexts (Kim and Ahmad 2013). This extension has been mirrored in the parallel development of ethnographic approaches, which have traditionally been applied to geographically bound communities, to include online ethnographic methods that examine the culture and social relations that evolve on specific online sites (Schrooten 2012). Here, too, members are drawn together by common interests, by taking part in joint activities, or by a shared sense of purpose or belonging. Oftentimes, the interests and purposes that bind online communities together are direct manifestations of the more physical types of social groups described earlier, as is the case, for example, with protest groups that conduct some of their awareness-raising and organisational work in the online realm.

Despite the wide range of configurations that may merit the community label, depending on the criteria that one might follow, they seem to share certain characteristics. Scholars have previously attempted to study and classify communities according to a variety of features (Delanty 2003), identifying key elements such as empowerment, cohesion, integration or resilience (Gilchrist 2009; Karner and Parker 2011). Some of the interdependencies that develop amongst individuals are voluntary, while others are structurally fixed, adding further layers to the complex web of factors that underpin different communities. The question of what brings and keeps communities together remains outstanding, and so many realities exist that it would arguably be counterproductive to formulate one framework that attempts to explain all possibilities. There is no room here to provide a detailed analysis of what constitutes a community, but for the purposes of this book, I would like to highlight three of the elements that define them: context, purpose and identity.

Communities, regardless of the medium through which they operate, are defined by the context that surrounds them. It is necessary to understand the history of a community, the circumstances through which it emerged, the challenges that it has and may still be facing, and the ways in which it relates to other (types of) communities. Understanding their context also involves acquiring an awareness of the members' common interests or purposes that give meaning to that community, keeping it together and making it evolve over time. Whether their aim is to maintain an immediate safe environment to survive and in which their daily social and economic relations can continue to develop, or to share their passion for a leisure activity, or to pose some resistance to what they may perceive as a threat to their wellbeing and social rights, communities hold a shared interest that also defines their identity. It is who they are, not only as individuals but also as collectives that, permanent or transient, provide them with some structure, direction, sense of belonging and validation. These points are by no means exhaustive, but help to elucidate some of the key characteristics that determine the ways in which each community is spoken about in the public sphere.

These and other elements of communities are underpinned by yet another element that defines them all, the community's relations to power, including: those relations that exist within the community itself; with other communities; with the state; and with supra-national entities and structures. It is here that we need to acknowledge that, despite its common context, purpose and identity, community is not a synonym for harmonious relationships, consistent and efficient teamwork, solidarity, or a guaranteed sense of belonging, even in its most traditional and romanticised format. In rural (and other) environments, for instance, gossip can sometimes act as an efficient control mechanism to enforce conformity to community norms (Gilmore 1978: 89; see also Gluckman 1963). Tensions and disputes arise in communities, both amongst their members and in their relationships with other communities. Despite the common purpose that may keep a community together, individualism and self-interest remain a reality. So are violence, poverty, fear, suffering and mistrust, to name a few of the many disruptive elements that can affect social groups.

This is due to the fact that, wherever there are social relations and interdependencies, there are also power imbalances. This happens both between members of the same community, and between members of different communities, becoming more acute within states, where different communities may be empowered or disempowered to varying degrees. In any given community, there are social groups made up of men and women, natives and others, rich and poor, young and old. There are members of the ruling class and there are workers, and there are different professional and trade sectors. There are citizens and non-citizens, and there are those who fit into the heteronormative culture and those who do not. Some groups want to maintain existing rules and activities for the sake of preserving cultural traditions, while others would rather see some progress. There are a wide variety of factors, such as social status, economic interests, educational background, disabilities, religion, political beliefs and more, all of which contribute to the emergence of divisions within the social fabric. As Elias (1974: xxiv) points out, "almost invariably the threatened loss of function and power of social units on the verge of becoming a lower level of integration leads to struggles of dominance, to balance of power struggles of a specific kind". He further argues that

> as societies become more differentiated and the hierarchy of levels of integration grows in size and complexity, communities develop into one of the lower levels of integration. The range of decisions which can and must be taken at the community level decreases with the upward development of societies towards greater differentiation and complexity [...] if [communities of less differentiated societies] have to rely largely on self-help, on the mobilization of their own communal resources in the case of outside attacks, of internal conflicts and acts of violence or of natural catastrophes, [communities of more differentiated societies] are in these, as in many other cases, dependent on state authorities and their local agents to a much greater extent. (Elias 1974: xxv–xxvi)

In contexts of power imbalances and a diversity of needs, members of different communities may develop connections or interdependencies amongst one another on the basis of a common purpose that joins them together, perhaps to counteract the effects of injustice, exclusion and inequality.

Representing Communities

The connections between discourse, power, dominance and social inequality have been examined in depth from a variety of perspectives, including media theory (Hall 1997), Critical Discourse Analysis (van Dijk 1993; Fairclough 1995), and through frameworks that benefit from a combination with other critical traditions, such as class, postcolonial and feminist approaches (Lazar 2007; Prakash 1995; Said 1978). For instance, in the 1970s, critical linguistics focused on the analysis of media texts and the ways in which linguistic choices (re)produce preferred ideological perspectives and a social order founded on inequality and oppression. It has long been argued that discourse not only depicts pervading structures of power but also contributes to the perpetuation of systemic inequality. One of the processes involved in the promotion of certain discourses (and the obscuration of others) is the naturalisation of linguistic categories, a process though which power imbalances are presented as 'natural' and 'inevitable'. Other approaches to the analysis of media texts also helped to identify the connections between, for example, representations of women and patriarchal relations of power, and the ways in which the media favour privileged ethnicities to the detriment of Other (non-white) social groups.

It is therefore important to remember that it is not language as such that obscures the reality of socio-political structures, but the processes that surround the production of discourse. Much literature has focused on the connections between the use of language and the socio-political practices and contexts that surrounded it (Wodak 2014), by placing discourse analysis within critical social theory and understanding that media discourse both constitutes, and is constituted by, social formation (Fairclough 1995). According to Fairclough's (1992) three-dimensional model of discourse, any discursive 'event' is simultaneously a piece of text, an instance of discursive practice, and an instance of social practice. While the 'discursive practice' dimension is concerned with the processes of text production and interpretation, 'social practice' refers to the "institutional and organisational circumstances of the discursive event" (Fairclough 1992: 4). The sum of both dimensions contributes to the development of the constitutive effects of discourse. For this reason, it is essential to examine discourse in relation to the social conditions that surround its production.

One of the social resources on which power is based is the privileged access to discourse and communication, which, according to van Dijk (1993: 256), refers to the varying degrees of "freedom in the use of special discourse genres or styles, or in the participation in specific communicative events and contexts", which include control over the discourse conditions and consequences. In other words, there is a direct connection between social power and access to discourse, as the media tend to reflect the interests of those in power by reproducing the categories and representations that they promote. This is seen, for example, in journalism practices, and more specifically in the use of news sources (Bell 1991; Manning 2001). The newsgathering process ensures that the powerful maintain their access to the media, perpetuating the imbalance of access to discourse and, subsequently, the power imbalance in the existing social order. Similar processes also remain in place in other areas of media production and representation.

The power that social groups, institutions or elites hold is directly proportional to the number of discourse genres, contexts, participants, audiences, scope and text characteristics that they (may) actively control or influence (van Dijk 1993: 256). The reverse is also true, lack of power can be measured based on the lack of active access to discourse. There are, therefore, "hierarchies of definitional power" (Allan 1995: 131). For 'ordinary' people, active conversations only happen with relatives or friends, presenting varying degrees of passivity in bureaucratic or institutional situations. Of course, these hierarchies are challenged, to some extent, by "modest forms of counter-power" (van Dijk 1993: 256), which include, for example, Letters to the Editor sections in newspapers, carrying slogans in demonstrations and, more recently, through the use of tools provided by social media.

However, the limited productivity of these counter-power techniques within the wider scope of mainstream discourse is indicative of the fact that power and substantial access to discourse are linked. Indeed, the availability of certain tools—particularly, those enabled by social media—has served to empower citizens and to support their participation and mobilisation to achieve social change (Curran et al. 2012). This has been particularly useful, for example, in the development and maintenance of social movements, which have benefitted from the ability to organise and to acquire a stronger presence in the public sphere (Shirky 2008). While some successes have been achieved thanks to these social media, it is necessary to take stock of these achievements and assess their relative impact on the larger picture. An event such as the engineers' occupation of the centric Telefónica headquarters in Barcelona in 2015 (Sanz Sabido and Price 2016), was hardly covered in the national media due to the powerful influence that the national telephone company exerted through its advertising contracts. Evidently, economic and political structures, which are inextricably linked to large media organisations, continue to hold the key to large-scale visibility and the potential for social change.

Therefore, despite the more optimistic assessments of social media tools and their impact on inclusion and participation, it remains necessary to be cautious about such overly positive analyses. The structures and resources of mainstream media, and the continued perception of their legitimacy amongst the audience, mean that their power to set the agenda and influence public debates remains strong. While mainstream media continue to select and frame stories, choose some sources over others, amplify and distort the world view that audiences tend to see, they will also continue to decide what is visible and what remains invisible, which voices are heard and which marginalised, and which causes are legitimate and which are not.

Despite the burgeoning literature that has examined the possibilities that social media provide for communities to challenge the trends imposed by mainstream media, the state and other social, economic and political structures, the analysis of media representations remains a crucial step towards uncovering the complex and often subtle ways in which hegemonic power relations are discursively produced, exposing the causes and consequences of specific discourses, and denouncing the social, cultural or political wrongs that they sustain, insofar as the media continue to represent and perpetuate unequal relations of power.

Of course, systems of meanings cannot be fixed, and media representations evolve with them. Even though the essential processes of selection and structuring of meaning have persisted in the capitalist-patriarchal society, it is worth noting that representations have become increasingly fractured, producing a host of often contradictory images. These fragmented media representations are explained by the convergence of a variety of macro-forces that are, to varying degrees, contingent upon the specificities of micro-contexts that are defined in time and space. Crucially, the broader context is characterised by an increasingly fragmented media production landscape, and by the realisation that media audiences are similarly fragmented in their backgrounds and identities. More thorough understandings of the heterogeneity of media audiences have therefore questioned previous monolithic notions of the public, leading to a plurality of representations.

However, resulting representations are not usually explained by a principled and firm commitment to fair and equal representations of all social groups. Instead, it must be understood in terms of their value as saleable goods and their potential to become objects for the purpose of producing spectacle, in a context where the capitalist market and related processes of commodification determine the communicative needs that must be served, dictating the rules of production, representation practices and, consequently, of what is ultimately consumed. These communicative needs are therefore served by institutional and media structures which work in the interest of the 'powerful', thereby leaving minority and unprivileged social groups on the margins, both in terms of the quantity and the quality of their media representations.

At a time of communicative abundance and technological transformation (Keane 1999), the critical analysis of media discourse is more pertinent than ever. Despite the recent 'fragmentation' of media as a system, there still remains a sense that there is much left to change and improve. Systemic social and ideological conditioning continues to take place through the representation of the capitalist-patriarchal-postcolonial order as 'normal', and through the creation of normative conceptions about the roles and positions held by individuals as conventional and characteristic of the entire social group to which they are seen to belong. Representational *choices* are still determined by the ideological systems that underpin them, defining events and social relations through their own lenses (Croteau and Hoynes 1997), while "preferred meanings" are defined by hierarchical relations of power that remain protected (Hall 1980). Truly alternative versions of the real can only occur if the media are committed to transforming the existing social order, which is an option that is not typically pursued. The practices involved in media representations, and the commercial, ethical and cultural structures that underpin it, must be subjected to a continuous (re)assessment within their contexts.

OVERVIEW OF CHAPTERS

This book presents a critical analysis of the pervading reproduction of hegemonic discourses and the ways in which the description and evaluation of different social groups affects their ability to exercise cultural and political autonomy. It is based on an analysis of the representations of a number of communities and social groups, both within their micro-contexts, and with reference to the economic, political, social, cultural and technological macro-contexts in which they are embedded. This requires an understanding of both the immediate circumstances and challenges that are faced by those communities within their particular milieus, and the broader systemic structures in a capitalist, patriarchal and postcolonial context. To introduce these themes, Part 1, titled 'Challenging the System', includes four chapters that contribute to the development of critical perspectives on the role of discourse in reproducing deeply rooted inequalities as a first step towards challenging the system in which those imbalances are fostered and embedded. In Chap. 2, Rinella Cere offers a more in-depth discussion of the concept of communities, reviewing sociological and philosophical approaches to this notion. She focuses particularly on the relational aspects of community, and provides an overview of some of the ways in which this notion has developed from traditional settings to industrial contexts, and how social relations have evolved accordingly in different economic climates.

The following three chapters focus more specifically on questions of gender, class and postcolonial legacies. Chapter 3, authored by Anita

Biressi and Heather Nunn, examines some of the ways in which women are silenced in the public sphere and explores some of the mechanisms that women develop to counteract the attempts to render them invisible. The authors focus on two women who were the targets of sexist criticism: Mary Beard was the recipient of insults and threats for refusing to remain quiet in a normative context that expected her to do so; and Ghazala Khan, whose quiet appearance next to her husband while he criticised Donald Trump's politics attracted sexist and racist comments. After reviewing the historical legacy of women's disenfranchisement, Biressi and Nunn argue that enfranchisement is not a guarantee of fair representation, visibility and access to equal opportunities, and discuss some of the challenges that continue to stop women from being taken seriously in the public sphere.

In Chap. 4 Stuart Price turns our attention to some of the discursive strategies developed in the capitalist context, examining in particular the responses of the elites to the rise of populism. The author points out that leading establishment figures only oppose populist approaches because they threaten the conditions that are needed for capitalist accumulation. In fact, as Price shows, populist discourse is a device frequently used by the elites themselves to garner support amongst their electoral base and to protect their own interests. With the notion of community at the centre of the analysis, the chapter examines the rhetoric used during the UK's 2017 General Election and makes connections with Tony Blair's political discourse, while also considering other recent developments, such as Brexit and the election of Trump.

In Chap. 5 Corinna Schäfer focuses on the press German settler's set up during their colonial occupation in Africa. Through her analysis, Schäfer points out some of the ways in which the settlers managed to achieve their economic objectives by reframing their activities discursively as being part of a 'cultural mission'. In reality, of course, they tried to stop Africans from engaging in intellectual endeavours that might jeopardise their enterprise. The author pays attention to the development of the infrastructure that enabled the German colonists to achieve their goals, although they remained dependent on African labour to build and operate it. This meant, Schäfer points out, that the native population had a certain degree of power to destroy that very infrastructure. Yet, stories of any acts of resistance remained largely invisible, as it was against their interests to promote alternative voices that questioned their supposedly beneficial effects on the local community.

The themes and contexts covered in Part 1 continue to emerge throughout Parts 2 and 3. Part 2, 'Representing Communities, Perpetuating Inequality', examines the ways in which the representations of certain communities and social groups continue to perpetuate inequality. Bearing in mind the intersections between class, gender, sexuality, race, nationality, legal status and disability, this part of the book offers an assessment of the complexities of media representations from a firm commitment to the perspective that the critical analysis of media representations continues to matter, perhaps more than ever.

In this section, Anna Khlusova provides us with an analysis of homophobic discourse in Russia. Contextualised in relation to the Kremlin's enactment of 'anti-homopropaganda' legislations, Chap. 6 examines two Russian news broadcasts, Channel One's *Vremya* and Rossiya's *Vesti*, and explores the connections between representations of homosexuality and growing prejudice against the LGBTQ community. Khlusova argues that Russian news broadcasts constitute clear examples of homophobic propaganda that achieves two goals: first, it delegitimises the LGBTQ community by perpetuating the heteronormative culture; and second, it promotes queer sexuality as a direct effect of Western influence, which is presented as alien to Russia, thereby defining Russian national identity and setting it apart from its Western Other. Furthermore, the author shows the affinities that exist between the homophobic representations seen in the news broadcasts and the political rhetoric of the Russian government, confirming that the state holds the key to the ideological messages that are mobilised.

In Chap. 7 Elizabeth Lakey takes us to Melbourne, Australia, and focuses on the community of Generation 1.5 Somalis who are caught in the middle of two cultures. The chapter takes into account both the negative representations of Somali Australians in the media, and their own reflections of those portrayals. The author sheds light on the various types of violence that this community endures on a daily basis, including legal, cultural and economic disadvantages, and the identity struggles that they face as a consequence of the public judgements to which they are constantly exposed. Their legal status has serious implications for the difficulties that they encounter and the access that they have to most facilities. Lakey argues that the representations of Generation 1.5 as being prone to violence is in conflict with their actual expression of identity, even though this community seems no more likely to engage in violent behaviour than the average Australian.

The state is also central to the discussion presented in Chap. 8. Here, Ruth Sanz Sabido examines the news coverage of a women's hunger strike at Puerta del Sol, in Madrid, against the current Spanish legislation on chauvinist violence. Starting from the perspective that this is a public health matter and a consequence of the patriarchal order, the author analyses the coverage of the hunger strike by six national newspapers. The chapter provides an insight into the newsworthiness of the strike throughout its duration, and considers the extent to which the women's objectives were reflected in the discourse. Sanz Sabido concludes that, even though the news media have come a long way in the representation of chauvinist violence, there is still much room for developing a more committed and socially responsible forum for discussion and action in the public sphere.

This hunger strike, conducted in a popular square in the centre of Madrid, was a protest event that sought to resist and to address, through material action, a problem that, directly or indirectly, affects a sector of the community. It was for the national news media to represent their struggle fairly in the news discourse. In Chap. 9 Mikko O. Koivisto focuses on resistance from a discursive perspective, paying attention to two distinct forms of hip hop culture, horrorcore and Krip Hop, to explore how they resist ableist and racist narratives of mental disability. Introducing the concept of egress, that is, the strategies that help to resist the stereotypes that are often circulated about mental disability, this chapter identifies several examples of counter discourses that emerge in the work of Bushwick Bill and Kounterclockwise. The author points out that the conventions of horrorcore and Krip Hop are challenged, for example, by the themes that are covered by some of the songs that he analysed, and by the refusal to use discriminating language to describe minority groups. The role of the nation is also discussed by Koivisto, who argues that, by using the concept of nation to refer to a group of people who do not share the same cultural identity, language or ethnicity, but do share the experience of living as or in disabled bodies, Krip Hop Nation abandons the normative notion and challenges some of its related practices, such as police brutality and ethnic profiling.

Finally, Part 3, 'Communities and their Contexts', builds on the discussions presented in previous chapters and offers an overview of the representation of some communities within their own contexts. In Chap. 10 Robin Roberts examines the TV series *Frank's Place* and *Treme* to analyse the representation of New Orleans food, considering the changes in cultural and televisual sensibilities in the twenty-five-year span that separates the shows. Roberts analyses the particular characteristics of traditional foodways in New Orleans, and shows the importance of race and gender in the representation of the chefs in the episodes that she explores. The characters face issues related to their race and gender, while authenticity and creative expression clash with profit-seeking capitalism. Yet the chefs survive thanks to the support of their communities. The author argues that these representations have implications for the African American community and for the city, encouraging it to value its foodways, and giving outsiders an opportunity to appreciate the city's unique cultural features.

In Chap. 11 we move away from discursive representations to consider the process of discourse production, particularly in relation to the use of news sources in Ukraine. Richard Pendry examines the activities of reporters and news sources in the Ukrainian conflict, considering the group of citizen journalists *Bellingcat* as an example of 'parajournalists' or news sources that act as reporters. The author considers the contemporary relevance of concepts such as objectivity, and suggests that transparency, the process of working through the evidence, may be a more important practical consideration in Ukraine. Pendry also questions the role of the journalist in relation to other participants in the newsgathering process. He highlights the increasing dependency of journalists who keep themselves away from conflict areas and rely on local sources that speak the language, know the local customs and are close to the action.

To conclude, Rosalind Brunt offers, in Chap. 12, an overview of the representation of class and community in Britain, by examining two 1970s BBC television outputs: an episode of *Late Night Line-up* that features London factory workers who question the ways in which 'ordinary people' are represented on television; and the 'documentary serial' *The Family*, as an early example of reality television and the representation of a supposedly 'typical' British family. Through her discussion, Brunt raises questions about the notions of representation and representativeness, and applies her insights to two contemporary programmes that also consist of 'ordinary' people, *The Jeremy Kyle Show* (ITV) and *Gogglebox* (C4), to conclude that the dynamics of power between those who represent and those who are represented are at the heart of the politics of representation, and that it is necessary to gain a deeper understanding of the notions of community and diversity in order to provide more nuanced and less stereotypical representations.

Based on a combination of theoretical and empirical analyses, this collection offers an array of macro-social critiques based on the analysis and critical understanding of contemporary contexts and representations, and how they contribute to political, social, economic and cultural practices. In doing so, the book attempts to answer a number of critical questions: To what extent have media representations changed? What is the connection between recent developments in media representations and social power today? Have recent trends and transformations (social, technological and so on) become a tool of commerce for a fragmented public, or is it a true demonstration of a more democratic media? Have political, economic, social, cultural and technological changes reconfigured representations and the practices involved in their production? Are traditional perspectives still helpful to explain these processes and to uncover contemporary dynamics of power through the analysis of media discourse, and to what extent?

This book turns the reader's attention back to core structural issues through new research into the latest media representations, in the context of present-day social, economic and political developments. In doing so, the book builds upon traditional discourse studies to argue that, despite the latest technological and industry developments, the essential issues are still very much unaltered and alternative voices are still only heard marginally. To conduct a comprehensive analysis of discourses about communities, it is necessary to address a number of questions about the intersection of discourse and capitalist, patriarchal and postcolonial infrastructures. Through this critical analysis, we can gain an up-to-date understanding of how and why social relations continue to operate in the way that they do.

REFERENCES

Allan, S. (1995). "News, truth and postmodernity: Unravelling the will to facticity". In: Adam, B. and Allan, S. (eds.) *Theorizing Culture: An Interdisciplinary Critique after Postmodernism*, 129–144. London: UCL Press.

Bell, A. (1991). *The Language of News Media*. Oxford: Basil Blackwell.

Croteau, D. and Hoynes, W. (1997). *Media/Society: Industries, Images, and Audiences*. London: Pine Forge Press.

Curran, J., Fenton, N. and Freedman, D. (2012). *Misunderstanding the Internet*. London: Routledge.

Delanty, G. (2003). community. London: Routledge.

Elias, N. (1974). "Foreword—Towards a theory of Communities". In: Bell, C. and Newby, H. (eds.) *The Sociology of* community: *A Selection of Readings*, ix–xlii. Abingdon: Frank Cass and Co. Ltd.

Fairclough, N. (1992). *Discourse and Social Change*. Cambridge: Polity Press.

Fairclough, N. (1995). *Media Discourse*. London: Edward Arnold.

Gilchrist, A. (2009). *The Well-connected* community: *A Networking Approach to* community *Development*. Bristol: The Policy Press.

Gilmore, D. (1978). "Varieties of Gossip in a Spanish Rural community". *Ethnology*, 17(1): 89–99.

Gluckman, M. (1963). "Gossip and scandal". *Current Anthropology*, 4: 307–316.

Hall, S. (1980). "Encoding/Decoding". In: Hall, S. et al (eds.) *Culture Media Language*, 128–138. London: Hutchinson.

Hall, S. (ed.) (1997). *Representations: Cultural Representations and Signifying Practices*. London: Sage.

Hillery, G.A. (1955). "Definitions of community: Areas of agreement". *Rural Sociology*, 20(2): 111–123.

Jacobs, M. (2008). "Multiculturalism and Cultural Issues in Online Gaming Communities". *Journal for Cultural Research*, 12(4): 317–334.

Karner, C. and Parker, D. (2011). "Conviviality and conflict: Pluralism, resilience and hope in inner-city Birmingham". *Journal of Ethnic and Migration Studies*, 37(3): 355–372.

Keane, J. (1999). "On communicative abundance". *Centre for the Study of Democracy*. London: University of Westminster Press. Accessed on 15 June 2017. Available at http://www.johnkeane.net/wp-content/uploads/1999/01/on_communicative_abundance.pdf.

Kim, Y.A. and Ahmad, M.A. (2013). "Trust, distrust and lack of confidence of users in online social media-sharing communities". *Knowledge-Based Systems*, 37: 438–450.

Lazar, M.M. (ed.) (2007). *Feminist Critical Discourse Analysis*. Basingstoke: Palgrave Macmillan.

Mackenzie, A. and Dalby, S. (2003). "Moving mountains: community and resistance in the Isle of Harris, Scotland, and Cape Breton, Canada". *Antipode*, 35: 309–333.

Manning, P. (2001). *News and News Sources: A Critical Introduction*. London: Sage.

Prakash, G. (1995). "After Colonialism". In: Prakash, G. (ed.) *After Colonialism: Imperial Histories and Postcolonial Displacements*. Princeton: Princeton University Press.

Said, E.W. (1978). *Orientalism*. London: Routledge and Kegan Paul.

Sanz Sabido, R. (2017). "Online communities of Spanish migrants in times of austerity". *JOMEC Journal*, 11: 83–95.

Sanz Sabido, R. and Price, S. (2016). " 'The Ladders Revolution': Material struggle, social media and news coverage". *Critical Discourse Studies*, 13(3): 247–260.

Schrooten, M. (2012). "Moving ethnography online: researching Brazilian migrants' online togetherness". *Ethnic and Racial Studies*, 35(10): 1794–1809.

Shirky, C. (2008) *Here Comes Everybody*. London: Allen Lane.

Staples, L. (2012) "community organizing for social justice: Grassroots groups for power". *Social Work with Groups*, 35(3): 287–296.

Tönnies, F. (1974 [1887]) "Gemeinschaft and Gesellschaft". In: Bell, C. and Newby, H. (eds.) *The Sociology of* community: *A Selection of Readings*, 7–12. Abingdon: Frank Cass and Co. Ltd.

van Dijk, T.A. (1993). "Principles of Critical Discourse Analysis". *Discourse & Society*, 4(2): 249–283.

Wodak, R. (2014). "Discourse and politics". In: Flowerdew, J. (ed.) *Discourse in* context. *Contemporary Applied Linguistics, Vol. 3*, 321–346. London: Bloomsbury.

PART I

Challenging the System

CHAPTER 2

Constructing Community: Notes on a Slippery Concept

Rinella Cere

> If there is a 'work in progress' in contemporary philosophy, it is undoubtedly in work on community – on the common, communism, communitarianism, being-in common, being-with, being-together (Nancy 2016: 7)

The concept of community has been at the centre of much discussion about its definition. The persistent questions 'what *is* community?', or 'how might *a* community differ from *the* community?', have prompted many different answers and have assumed that there are obvious explanations and clear paradigms out there. The concept of community has been of particular importance to the sociological field, where it originated. However, many other writings, especially in philosophy and political theory have sought to answer this question. This chapter has two aims: one, to enquire into the discussion of the nature and possibility of community; and two, to outline expressly political interpretations of those concepts of community that have been at the heart of political action and solidarity.

R. Cere (✉)
Sheffield Hallam University, Sheffield, UK
e-mail: R.Cere@shu.ac.uk

© The Author(s) 2017
R. Sanz Sabido (ed.), *Representing Communities*,
DOI 10.1007/978-3-319-65030-2_2

The two main bodies of writings discussed come from the philosophical and sociological fields. The first part of this chapter looks at writings from the philosophical field, in particular at the debate between Jean-Luc Nancy and Maurice Blanchot and their respective concepts of 'inoperative' and 'disavowed' and 'unavowable' community. This is followed by a consideration of Giorgio Agamben's idea of 'the coming community' espoused in his eponymous book. The chapter concludes by suggesting that his reading of community could be adopted to understand the 'impossibility' of mediated community. The second discussion looks at how key sociological texts that followed Marx's writings, namely work by Tönnies, Weber and Durkheim, set the distinction between community and society (*Gemeinschaft* and *Gesellschaft*) and whether their interpretations are still useful models for the understanding of community today.

The choice of writings on community for this discussion is dictated by a perceived link between them on the utopian potential of community and their undoubted connection, sometimes explicit and sometimes less so, with Karl Marx's critique of capitalism. Many others have been interlocutors in the debate about community, but this chapter can only make a passing reference to them, without implying their lesser relevance in the sociological and philosophical discussion of the concept of community.[1] In recent years, the term has been adopted to accompany many different social and cultural phenomena, and it has gained a pride of place in the politics of identity and, more recently, in network politics. In this process it has often been hollowed out of its utopian potential and separated from its twin etymology of communalism and communism.

THE IMPOSSIBILITY OF COMMUNITY? BLANCHOT, NANCY AND AGAMBEN

The starting point for Blanchot's and Nancy's reflections on community posits a different question: *Why community?* The terms of this question were initially set by the French surrealist philosopher, Georges Bataille. While his own answers to this question were often aphoristically obscure, the way he posed it has proved productive for later commentators on community. For Bataille's method of labyrinthine thought requires an open-ended, open-minded commitment to challenging any taken-for-granted, naturalistic approaches to community. Instead, it proposes a kind of 'disorientation', a way of looking anew—by looking askew—at the whole multifarious notion of community. In sum, it asks how is the notion used to define people's values, beliefs and aspirations? How does it relate to people's experience of simply 'being' in the world?

All these questions have been taken up by Maurice Blanchot, a French philosopher and literary theorist, and close friend of Bataille, in his short book *The Unavowable Community* (1988), which is composed of two parts: 'The Negative Community' and 'The Community of Lovers'. The answer Blanchot gives is deceptively simple, because of "the principle of incompleteness" and, continuing to draw on Bataille's work, he argues about the "insufficiency at the root of each being" and the need for the other and plurality in short communion. These "existential exigencies", he argues, are also community/communist exigencies that cannot be ignored:

> Communism, by saying that equality is its foundation and that there can be no community until the needs of all men are *equally* fulfilled (this is in itself but a minimal requirement), presupposes not a perfect society but the principle of a transparent humanity essentially produced by itself alone, an "immanent" humanity (says Jean-Luc Nancy). (Blanchot 1988: 2)

Blanchot, explicitly refers to the "flaw in language", which the words community and communism contain, that refers to the preoccupation of how we get to communism (and hence community) when the "ability to understand community seems to have been lost" (ibid.: 1). In an opaque form of phrasing, resembling Bataille's mode of thought, he argues at the same time that this is not about the necessity for completion or recognition, but about a necessity for contestation that we could read as the possibility of community: "A being does not want to be recognized, it wants to be contested; in order to exist it goes towards the other" (ibid.: 6). Blanchot uses the word 'summon' to address both singularity and community, as ultimately one and the same:

> The existence of every being thus summons the other or a plurality of others...It therefore summons a community: a finite community, for it in turn has its principle in the *finitude* of the beings which form it and which would not tolerate that it (the community) forget to carry the *finitude* constituting those beings to a higher degree of tension. (ibid.: 6, italics in the original).

In the second part of the book, on "The Community of Lovers", Blanchot's model is decisively that which is generated in a voluntary association, such as lovers of two or more, again inspired by Bataille's writings on eroticism, and that this also distinguishes it from traditional communities, which are normally involuntary and imposed. This interpretation of community also resonates with earlier writings by Hannah Arendt and her conception of community as friendship (Arendt 1998 [1958]; Nixon 2015).

Like Blanchot, the text by Jean-Luc Nancy, *The Inoperative Community* (1991), continues the discussion by exploring the idea of community in relation to its past history, its mythical element and what we are to do with it today. In the first lines he states that, "the gravest and most painful testimony of the modern world, the one that possibly involves all other testimonies to which this epoch must answer…is the testimony of the dissolution, the dislocation, or the conflagration of community" (Nancy 1991: 1).

The 'loss' of community is traced in the Christian tradition right up to the modern idea of the "desired or pined for" community, which he sees in many thinkers from Rousseau to Marx (ibid.: 9). In particular he considers Jean Jacques Rousseau one of the first sources of thinking about community, in the sense of something to return to, after modern society (and the loss of the divine) has wrought havoc on human experience: "Until this day history has been thought on the basis of a lost community—one to be regained or reconstituted" (ibid.: 9).

The idea of the loss of community, or at least of an original community, is a theme that accompanies much of contemporary philosophical writings, and in some philosophical quarters, especially in communitarian thought, it has been reintroduced as a necessity for returning to small and traditional communities of shared culture and values. Nancy demolishes the nostalgic element of community in the chapter "Myth Interrupted" by tracing its mythic element embedded in the stories we tell ourselves: "We know this scene well. More than one storyteller has told it to us, having gathered us together in learned fraternities intent on knowing what our origins were" (ibid.: 44).

On another level, although research generated from a sociological examination of community is not often explicitly mentioned in philosophical writings, we find that Nancy takes up the *Gemeinschaft/Gesellschaft*'s dichotomy and sees it as unrelated, he comments that the first has not been replaced by the second, as it is a mere "projection" on our part of something that has never taken place, he feels that there was no "communitarian minimum" in traditional social ties: "*Society* was not built on the ruins of *community*. It emerged from the disappearance or the conservation of something—tribes or empires—perhaps just as unrelated to what we call 'community' as what we call 'society'" (ibid.: 11, italics in the original).

For both Nancy and Blanchot community transcends the historical, it is about the here and now and it carries no normative ideal. In fact, even experientially it can only ever be impossible and/or absent. In a recent attempt to tackle the idea of community, and in response to Blanchot's "avowed community" of thirty years earlier, he offers a renewed reading of the political in our time and its ongoing insecurity when attached to community. The discussion in this latest effort to tackle the idea of the community, departs entirely from the received notion that it is a phase or a final stage in a historical continuum or a concrete form of belonging, political or otherwise (Nancy 2016).

Agamben, similarly to Nancy and Blanchot, in his *The Coming Community* (1993), takes the idea of community further along the idea of possibility or impossibility and along the non-ontological continuum of 'being' or what he calls "the coming being is whatever being" (*qualunque* in Italian) in the very first line of his text. This is written in short 'thought-bursts' with insights that allude to hundreds of years of human communication and spans from early philosophical thought, to the society of the spectacle, to the commodification of society, which he describes as "the alienation of language itself, of the very linguistic and communicative nature of humans" (Agamben 1993: 79).

So, what is the community to come and where, if anywhere, do we need to look for it? Not in common property or identity or belonging, but in the first instance in 'being-in-language' and only subsequently in singular community. It is the idea of the singularity of community that Agamben shares with Nancy and to a lesser extent with Blanchot. Like them, he contemplates that there is no return to nostalgic or mythical ideas of community but he is more obviously concerned with the idea of communion in language.

Elliott argues that Agamben shares with Nancy the tendency "to reduce the political theory of Marx to a merely residual sense of potential future change" (Elliott 2009: 901) leaving it open to the criticism of indeterminacy and relinquishing the pursuit of social justice. Yet, Agamben's text reads as Marx's does on the fate of the petty bourgeoisie, what he calls "planetary petty bourgeoisie" and the "form in which humanity is moving towards its own destruction" (Agamben 1993: 64).

At the end of the pages "Without Classes", he envisions a prospect for change: "Selecting in the new planetary humanity those characteristics that allow for its survival, removing the thin diaphragm that separates bad mediated advertising from the perfect exteriority that communicates only itself—this is the political task of our generation" (ibid.: 64). Agamben's musings on the coming community are actually invaluable for understanding how the media, and what we improperly call media and/ or online communities, expropriates us of our sociality:

> The extreme form of this expropriation of the Common is the spectacle, that is, the politics we live in. But this also means that in the spectacle our own linguistic nature comes back inverted. This is why (precisely because what is being expropriated is the very possibility of a common good) the violence of the spectacle is so destructive; but for the same reason the spectacle retains something like a positive possibility that can be used against it. (ibid.: 79)

The positive possibility mentioned here is somewhat prophetic but perhaps it is about openness, about language and human beings' ability to overcome the violent being-in-the world that comes from borders and camps. Where do we go from here in relation to community? We may want to return to Nancy's more recent work previously mentioned, *The Disavowed Community,* in which he is prospecting the need to save for ourselves, if not the idea of community, at least the idea of the common (Nancy 2016), as the only way to ensure that it is not about belonging as that would be a betrayal of the "community of all human beings" (ten Bos 2005: 27).

MARX AND COMMUNITY

Marx's idea of community is scattered across many of his writings, and is a recurrent theme in what Carol Gould termed Marx's social ontology or the ontology of individuals-in-relations; in other words, the idea of individuality in Marx is not just based on the liberal construct of individualism but is conjoined with the idea of community, "individuals cannot be understood apart from their relations" (Gould 1980: 3). In her fourth thesis on Marx's social ontology, Gould claims that "for Marx a just community is required for the full development of free individuality. Further, the value of free individuality and the value of community are consistent with each other" (ibid.: xiv). In addition these individuals-in-relations are themselves formed and embedded in the different stages of historical development, of which capitalism is one, albeit a fundamental one, in the transition to communism.

Marx wrote about three historical stages of development (especially in the *Grundrisse*). Stage one, the primitive community, is not only "self-enclosed" and "stable" (Megill 1970: 385), but also formed by dependent individuals characterised as relations of domination, as master–slave relations and as belonging to a greater whole; usually (there are exceptions) based on an economic order tied to "the soil and tools": "The aim of production in these pre-capitalist forms is the reproduction of the individual in his or her specific relation to the community" (Gould 1980: 10–12).

In fact, it is the community itself, both in terms of place and relational entity that determines their unfolding as driven by the force of tradition and which makes it appear as natural and capable of internal unity. This unity can only be forced apart by external relations, that is through exchange with other communities and subsequently through the rise of the worker in industrial capitalism, whose only property is his/her labour, which brings about the dissolution of the traditional community. Marx's stage two replaces dependency with freedom of exchange but at a price, human beings' communal nature is denied.

Again Gould argues that "the objective dependence that emerges in capitalism takes three forms: the objectivity of money/exchange; of capital; of the machine" (ibid.: 16). These are also three moments that move individuals away from their personal relations (as we have seen in pre-capitalist forms) and into entities of value in the marketplace. Specifically with the first, the symbolic form of money changes the concrete form of use value into an abstract and universal medium. Labour power then becomes capital power (the domination of labour by capital) in two distinct ways: one where the commodity of labour power produces surplus value and hence increases (only) the value of capital; and two, the worker's labour is objectified as a result, which brings about the confrontation with 'alien power' and individuals' exploitation.

Gould aligned the three stages (pre-capitalist formations, capitalism and communal society) with various forms of social relations in turn, community, individual and external sociality, and communal individuality (ibid.: 5). She also posited that "the third moment of objective dependence" (ibid.: 19), that is, the dependence on the machinery, is central to workers' recognition of the alienation and objectification and is a necessary passage to the third social stage, which for Marx will be realised in a community of the future: "in the third stage Marx anticipates the reestablishment of a community of social individual, but now as concretely free" (ibid.: 22).

The better known *Thesis on Feuerbach* goes some way in giving answers to the abstract-concrete dialectic on the third stage. Thesis six in particular states that "the human essence is no abstraction inherent in each single individual. In reality, it is the ensemble of the social relations". Thesis eight declares that "Social life is essentially *practical*. All mysteries which lead theory astray into mysticism find their rational solution in human practice and in the comprehension of this practice" (Marx 1998: 64–65).

Others have characterised Marx's philosophy of community in similar ways by looking at the ontological status of community. For example, Megill also argued that the third stage is "the community as a way of being. Man as a communal animal who can only achieve his complete existence through community" (Megill 1970: 384). At the same time, a nexus is introduced between democracy and community, where the latter is understood as "a democratic form of association which replaces the state" (ibid.: 384). He also goes on to say that Marx's democratic community "would be universal, historical, classless and scientific" (ibid.: 393). Marx's writings were certainly behind the sociological research on community that followed, whether explicitly acknowledged or not, which I am going to discuss next.

TÖNNIES, DURKHEIM AND WEBER ON COMMUNITY VS. SOCIETY

Community turned into a central concept with the rise of a new field of study of sociology and as the nineteenth century came to a close. This section discusses the pioneering work of classical sociologists who investigated the origins and nature of community; and in their separate but linked trajectories theorised on the enormous changes brought about by industrialisation and modernity and the impact these had on the fabric of social relations.

The earliest sociological study that specifically concerned itself with the social and cultural dimension of community was by German sociologist Ferdinand Tönnies. When Tönnies first wrote about community in 1887 it was very much in the context of a new horizon emerging in social relations which went beyond the immediate proximity, whether familial, geographical or in class terms. The title of the book translated into English more than a half a century later as *Community and Society* cannot do justice to the nuance of the German title *Gemeinschaft und*

Gesellschaft, which has been retained in many of the following discussions of community and society.

Tönnies' argument posited various antinomies between the two types, organic and mechanical, rural and urban, natural and rational (will). In particular *Gemeinschaft* is described as composed of many different categories, which are all interrelated and linked by human will, whether it is the "*Gemeinschaft* by blood, of Place, of Mind, Kinship, Neighborhood, Friendship". According to Tönnies the first three imply the latter three: "It is... possible to deal with (1) kinship, (2) neighborhood, and (3) friendship as definite and meaningful derivations of those original categories" (Tönnies 1963: 42). These foundational categories of community have been revisited, as well as contested, at many points of crisis in twentieth-century history.

In the discussion that followed from his definitions, illustrations of concrete examples are given. Peasant life is recognisable in the detailed description of the home, the fields, the village and even in relation to the town, what are titled in the English translation as the "complementary poles" of town and country and the ensuing "exchange mechanism" outside monetary value which it instigated between farmer, artisan and trader. In the *Gemeinschaft* model, "a brotherly spirit of give and take will remain alive in the relationship of town and country" (ibid.: 56).

This was not so dissimilar from Marx's own formulations and definitions of community as a primitive form of association but, as we will see below, for Marx this is only the first stage of human development and what is crucial is that this early historical condition is followed by two further stages in which the primitive community undergoes a transformation as a result of the development of the capitalist economic system to become a true community once it reaches its final stages of development, that is to say the community as a way of life. For Tönnies there is no dialectical process, no concrete human essence, once community is abandoned and the utopian ideal is precisely encapsulated in *Gemeinschaft* only.

In an examination of *Gesellschaft*, the opposite is true, there is no such thing as brotherly spirit and the human will is isolated and even renders any individual action socially ineffective and against a spirit of unity: a separation has taken place; common values no longer exist, although they can be brought back by an act of "fiction on the part of the individuals, which means that they have to invent a common personality and

[his] will, to whom this common value has to bear reference" (Tönnies 1963: 65).The description of *Gesellschaft* moves away from Marx's idea of a communal human nature, which remains recognisable even when subjected to the transformation from human-centred ontology to a value-centred one with its objective quality.

Even at the time of Tönnies' writings there was considerable criticism of his distinction, in particular from Durkheim, who turned Tönnies' argument on its head. Durkeim was a contemporary of Tönnies (and Weber) and, like them, was a central figure in the development of the field of sociology, in fact more consciously so than either of them, who in their work never openly talked about sociological method, although it was often implied. Durkheim also took up the challenge of providing an explanation for the changes that were taking place with industrialisation and modernity and, for our purpose here, his particular interpretation of the relationship between community and society.

In his book *The Division of Labor*, he argued, amongst other things, that modern society was developing forms of "civic" responsibility that were far more "organic" than the "collective consciousness" of traditional small rural communities in pre-modern society, as argued by Tönnies. He arrived at this conclusion by undertaking a similar analysis to Karl Marx's, at least in the sense that he was also concerned with the relations of the individual to society, as well as with the transition of pre-modern to modern society. The fundamental difference, however, was that he did this not explicitly in reference to the workings of capitalism but rather adopting a "theory of social evolution", in which he argued that the increase in population, towns and transport increased contacts and communication, and therefore caused a competition for resources; the division of labour is the social instrument by which individuals need not fight for their survival. According to Royce, "the striking originality of Durkheim's contribution" is that "he shifts the focus from the economic significance of the division of labor to its moral significance" (Royce 2015: 76).

Durkheim's introduction and interpretation of the concepts of mechanical versus organic solidarity is an exact opposite to Tönnies'. For Durkheim, in pre-modern society the common system of beliefs and values produces a mechanical solidarity, in other words the individual is subordinate to the system to which he or she belongs, a kind of "mechanical" community (in a fixed social order). On the other hand in modern society, which at the time of Durkheim's writing was still in the early stages, the idea of "organic" solidarity is precisely generated by the unique configuration of the division of labour.

The postulate of organic solidarity remains, however, abstract and somewhat marginal (and perhaps even in contradiction) to his overall analysis of modernity's condition evident in anomie, egoism and injustice; in particular he links the idea of egoism to his study of suicide, a first of its kind, and points towards the evaporation of the collective ties that sustained individuals in the past. He specifically mentions that the absence of communal ideals and the moral void this engenders reduces society to a "pile of sand". Egoism is but one of the developments of modernity, anomie is another, again with its implicit question of disrupted moral order, but this time linked to economic development. And, following on from that, is injustice, which is again described as a pathological phenomenon dictated by an abnormal "forced" division of labour, class conflict and unequal conditions of exchange and opportunity.

Durkheim is not as concerned as Marx to dissect the capitalist economic system in order to unravel its contradictions, but is rather more concerned with the necessity of instituting moral and legal regulations in the process of industrialisation and market exchange. Paradoxically, in spite of the perceived similarity with Marx's formulations about class conflict, alienation and inequality, Durkheim does not consider it an intrinsic problem of capitalism, or of the process of industrialisation, or of the rise of a market economy: "the problem is not the economic system per se, but a *disorganized* modern economic system" (Royce 2015: 142).

In terms of our theme of community it is important to note Durkheim's introduction of relations in terms of occupational and professional bodies, organisations which stimulate the collective spirit of people in the same work but which are separate from the state and private interests, or rather, that they stand at the crossroads of state and individual to safeguard self-interested developments. Traditional institutions (family, church, the state) are no longer adequate collective formations for an industrial society and Durkheim sees in occupational groups, which are traceable in history—for example in the form of medieval guilds—as solutions to injustice.

There is a sense, however, that by introducing this new categorisation of community, the community of the modern industrial age, the mechanical/organic solidarity dichotomy is undermined by these organisations, which "reincorporates mechanical elements in his notion of organic solidarity" (Thijssen 2012: 467). Nonetheless, Durkheim's occupational associations are undoubtedly behind the idea that tradition is no longer a central factor in the formation of community and communal identity. Royce goes as far as to say that he "defends modernity against the backward-looking proponents of traditionalism" (Royce 2015: 69).

Durkheim's modern community with its moral purpose has been behind much of communitarian thought that has looked at the normative ideal encapsulated in Durkheim's moral force and his emphasis on the survival of the spirit of community within, and in spite of, the divisive modern economic system. As already stated, it is the connection of the latter to a moral framework that also distinguish his analysis fundamentally from that of Karl Marx.

Weber, like Tönnies, adopted the community versus society dichotomy in his description of social relationships. However, Weber's distinction between communal and associative is more akin to Durkheim's formulations; he also introduced the idea that community need not necessarily be exclusively defined in terms of locality (the rural) and/or close-knit relationships (neighbourhood/friendship). In an unfinished essay on the theory of community in one of his volumes on *Economy and Society* he offered an exhaustive discussion of many different types of community, ranging from the private to the public sphere but all tied to capitalist economic development, thus moving away from the idea of community as involuntary and bringing about an analysis of the rational basis of a community intimately tied to the rise of capitalism. Capitalism undoubtedly transformed relationships previously rooted in tradition and affective closeness, but at the same time it provided the basis for a different type of community, which he termed as associative, based on "rational agreement by mutual consent" and associational ties that are just as likely to generate exclusion and conflict as inclusion and solidarity.

In a passage about community formation, Neuwirth states that

> In order to achieve this objective [limit the number of contenders] one segment of the competitors may seize upon an easily ascertainable and differentiating characteristic of any potential and actual contenders – such as local or social descent, racial or ethnic origins, lack of property or educational qualifications – and use it as a pretext for excluding them from competition. (Neuwirth 1969: 149)

Community formation read in this light takes on a very different meaning; an increase in solidarity is not about sharing outside the delimited community but about monopolisation, resource limitation and exclusion. Community formation as a result is followed by community closure at both economic and political levels: "Successful monopolization of economic and/or political advantages is accompanied by claims of corresponding social esteem" (ibid.: 150).

Within these categories of formation and closure of community Weber introduces a further concept of 'status communities', which is discussed in the better-known text 'Class, Status, Party', and "it constitutes one of Weber's three dimensions of stratification" (ibid.: 151). The dominance of status communities determines in turn the "negatively privileged status groups" that Neuwirth applies in her study of the 'Dark Ghetto' and ethnic minority community formation in the United States. Weber's analysis of closed and open relationships is very useful for a critique of online mediated communities that are closed communities in spite of claims to the contrary.[2] In particular, the way he looked at the process in the light of economic and political analysis brought about the realisation that members of community could be separated by interests other than those explicitly attached to their regular interactions. Similar studies applied to online communities would unearth similar results as to the nature of contemporary media communities.

CONCLUSION

This chapter has hoped to offer some insights into the complex thinking that has accompanied the concept of community, in its very many binary readings of possible/impossible, past/future, singular/relational. Community remains a much contested concept although paradoxically it has been adopted in many different settings and situations, as if the term which may more accurately describe our times (i.e. society) was exhausted.

Identifying traits and types of communities has become "a major undertaking", certainly in ethnographic media research and the word has even been "tagged" to the Internet generational numbers (Brabazon 2012). The communication and media sphere has often turned to the notion of community in search of a perceived collective imaginary or unity, especially since Marshal McLuhan launched his idea of a global village whose model was based on community; discourses and representations of community have not sought necessarily to look beyond the surface when looking at, for example, network and online communities, television communities, cinematic, and so on; or what are more generically referred to as digital communities. That is to say, the positivist idea of community has come to pass.

The question '*why* community?', rather than '*what is* community?', has a bearing on present-day discourses, along with an exploration that involves bringing in the related spatio-temporal considerations of '*where* community?' and '*when* community?'. This is necessary, because so much of the thinking around community has always contained the utopian elements of past golden ages, which have been lost, or of looking forward to future fully 'communitarian' societies still to be realised. All this may well be about "melancholic" cravings for community (ten Bos 2005: 22).

It is worth noting, by way of a conclusion, that not all writings on digital culture have adopted the concept of community 'no questions asked'. For example, Gere (2012) has suggested that a digital community is "a community without community" as its very essence is about "separation, gap and distance", which makes the idea of coupling digital with community problematic, at least in the sense of beings-in-relation. The questions of possibility/impossibility of such relations and collective identity in the digital and non-digital world would have to be at least asked, if not given a final answer. Definitional issues are central to the study of media communities and of their discourses and representations.

Finally, what I hope has surfaced in this chapter, is the ongoing preoccupation with the task of defining community, the sense that it is unlikely to reach a final destination any time soon or even an agreed working construct. Problematising it is a necessity because its adoption in many different walks of life has often signified its departure from radical politics and the kind of 'coming together' we want to see in the future. As Nancy's citation at the beginning of this chapter states, this semantic family is still very much a work in progress.

NOTES

1. For a comprehensive account of all the different writings about community (see Delanty 2003).
2. "A social relationship is called 'open' to outsiders if and insofar as participation in it is not denied to anyone who wishes and is able to participate. A relationship is 'closed' if and insofar as the participation is subjected to limiting conditions. Both communal and associative relationships can be characterized as open or closed" (Neuwirth 1969: 161).

BIBLIOGRAPHY

Agamben, G. (1993). *The Coming Community*. Minneapolis: University of Minnesota Press.

Arendt, H. (1998 [1958]). *The Human Condition*. Chicago: The University of Chicago.

Blanchot, M. (1988). *The Unavowable Community*. Barrytown: Station Hill Press.

Brabazon, T. (2012). *Digital Dialogues and Community 2.0. After Avatars, Trolls and Puppets*. Burlington: Elsevier.

Delanty, G. (2003). *Community*. London: Routledge.

Durkheim, E. (1964). *The Division of Labor*. New York: Free Press of Glencoe.

Elliott, B. (2009). "Theories of Community in Habermas, Nancy and Agamben: A Critical Evaluation". *Philosophy Compass*, 4(6): 893–903.

Freund, J. (1968). *The Sociology of Max Weber*. London: Allen Lane, Penguin.

Gane, N. (2005). "Max Weber as Social Theorist. 'Class, Status, Party'". *European Journal of Social Theory*, 8(2): 211–226.

Gere, C. (2012). *Community without Community in Digital Culture*. Houndmills, Basingstoke: Palgrave Macmillan.

Goe, R.W. and Noonan, S. (2006). "The Sociology of Community". In: Bryant, C.D. and Peck, L.D. (eds.) *21st Century Sociology: A Reference Handbook*, 455–464. London: Sage.

Gould, C. (1980). *Marx's Social Ontology. Individuality and Community in Marx's Theory of Social Reality*. Cambridge, MA: MIT Press.

Marx, K. (1973). *Grundrisse*. Harmondsworth: Penguin Books and New Left Review.

Marx, K. (1998). *The German Ideology: Including Theses on Feuerbach and Introduction to the Critique of Political Economy*. Amherst, NY: Prometheus Books.

Megill, K.A. (1970). "The Community in Marx's Philosophy". *Philosophy and Phenomenological Research*, 30(3): 382–393.

Nancy, J. (1991). *The Inoperative Community*. Minneapolis: University of Minnesota Press.

Nancy, J. (2016). *The Disavowed Community*. New York: Fordham University Press.

Neuwirth, G. (1969). "A Weberian Outline of a Theory of Community: Its Application to the 'Dark Ghetto'". *The British Journal of Sociology*, 20(2): 148–163.

Nixon, J. (2015). *Hannah Arendt and the Politics of Friendship*. London: Bloomsbury.

Royce, E. (2015). *Classical Social Theory and Modern Society. Marx, Durkheim, Weber*. Lanham: Rowman and Littlefield.

ten Bos, R. (2005). "Giorgio Agamben and the Community Without Identity". *The Sociological Review*, 53(1): 16–29.

Thijssen, P. (2012). "From Mechanical to Organic Solidarity, and Back: With Honneth Beyond Durkheim". *European Journal of Social Theory*, 15(4): 454–470.

Tönnies, F. (1963). *Community and Society*. New York: Harper and Row.

Weber, M. (2005). *Economia e Società. Comunità*. Roma: Donzelli.

Whyte, J. (2010). "'A New Use of the Self': Giorgio Agamben on the Coming Community". *Theory and Event*, 13(1): 1–19.

CHAPTER 3

Transforming the Politics of Gender and Voice: Strategies of Expertise and Experience

Anita Biressi and Heather Nunn

INTRODUCTION

This chapter critically reflects on the ways in which women's voices have been silenced in the public sphere, and explores some of the counter-tactics deployed by women in reply. We begin by outlining four important mechanisms through which women's voices have been silenced and managed in the public realm: through political disenfranchisement; through political under-representation; through media under-representation/misrepresentation and public denigration; and lastly, through the internalisation of social disadvantage and inequality. The purpose here is to remind ourselves of the historical legacy of women's disenfranchisement and to establish the precarious footing upon which women's participation now stands. Bearing this in mind, the chapter moves on to consider the politics of gender and voice in the contemporary moment. Here we focus on two specific cases in which

A. Biressi (✉) · H. Nunn
University of Roehampton, London, UK
e-mail: A.Biressi@roehampton.ac.uk

H. Nunn
e-mail: h.nunn@roehampton.ac.uk

© The Author(s) 2017
R. Sanz Sabido (ed.), *Representing Communities,*
DOI 10.1007/978-3-319-65030-2_3

women have been caught up in the sexist dynamics of the public sphere. Firstly, we turn to the British academic Mary Beard, whose refusal to 'shut up' and to capitulate to a normative politics of voice attracted misogynistic abuse. Secondly, we examine the Ghazala Khan/Donald Trump dispute, in which Khan's appearance in the media was condemned, not for her speech, but for her silence. In this chapter we take the cases of Beard and Khan as prompts to reflect on the historical lessons learnt in cultural and communication studies about the politics of the gendered voice, and to show how expertise (Beard), experience (Khan), and combinations of the two, can be deployed strategically to reply to insult and dismissal in the public sphere.

The Gendered Distribution of Voice

The burden of history acts as a drag on progress. As women move forward, unevenly, both slowly and quickly, in leaps and bounds and in incremental steps, managing this impediment demands constant energy, negotiation, management and attention. Energy and confidence are needed in equal measure to take part, and to thrive, in public debate. These characteristics are difficult to develop and to nurture when history and the common practice of both politics and the media are against you. The relative silence and disparagement of female voices in the public sphere is historically embedded in political and public culture in four important ways. First, in many nation states men were politically enfranchised far earlier than women and, for this reason alone, it is inevitable that men's voices have accrued an enduring political authority. Now it is mostly taken for granted that female enfranchisement is an essential component of national citizenship, and that women are both persons and citizens. Ramirez et al. (1997) argue that the allocation or extension of the vote to women has become an increasingly ordinary feature of democratic enhancement. They observe, for example, that:

> Between 1890 and 1994, women in 96 percent of all nation-states acquired the right to vote and seek public office. What in 1906 appeared to be a 'great victory' for women in Finland went virtually unnoticed in South Africa in 1993. Contemporary South Africa witnessed no distinct struggle for women's suffrage, no debate questioning a women's right to vote, and no celebrations of the simultaneous acquisition of the franchise by women and men of color. (Ramirez et al. 1997: 735)

Early battles for (and against) female suffrage were rooted in robustly national contexts, and securing voting rights for women was considered a national victory (or loss) and a national cause for celebration (or regret) (ibid.: 736). Ramirez et al.'s research goes on to argue that, more recently, women's enfranchisement has increasingly hinged on the contradictions experienced between national conditions that impeded women's right to political participation, and more universalistic principles of citizenship. The argument is that, over time, there has been a cumulative effect, which is reinforced by factors such as the growing numbers of nations with full franchise, the geographical proximity of these nations, and the political dominance of the West, whereby women's right to vote became an obvious requirement for any country seeking independence and international recognition as a nation state.

From this perspective, it seems to be a given that the voices, interests and opinions of women must be, and are, afforded equal weight to those of men, if only because of the pressures nation states experience to conform in the context of geo-politics. The question for women today is whether the accrued historical authority of men's speech continues to be sustained under these conditions of growing or long-standing female participation, and we suggest that it does. Enfranchisement is not, per se, a guarantee of representation, opportunity and access, audibility and influence. "Although men and women vote at similar rates today, women still trail men in important participatory attitudes and activities such as political interest and discussion" (Kittilson 2016: 1). Just because a woman is given the vote, it does not mean that she feels her vote will count for something.

The second exclusion of women from the public sphere is through the unequal numbers of men and women working in the arena of mainstream politics (Norris and Lovenduski 1995; Lovenduski 2005). For example, Dahlerup and Leyenaar (2013: 1–2) explain that, after more than a hundred years of women's suffrage, established democracies struggle to maintain even a 30 to 40% presence of women in national parliaments and assemblies. Based on extensive research they make the case that despite the "engendering" of political life, representation in terms of numbers is unequal, stagnant or even experiencing a "backlash". These conditions suggest that the time lag theory of political participation (in which women should eventually catch up with their male peers) may yet be proven wrong. Moreover, even when women join political bodies, it is far more difficult for them to occupy executive roles such as ministerial posts (Annesley and Gains 2010). Their relative absence is, again, significant, because the visibility of women in these posts is fundamental to any optimistic reading of current political representation. This is in part because executive roles are iconic in themselves (e.g. the Chancellor of the Exchequer as the figurehead of the economy) and it is important for women to be *seen* to hold power. These executive roles also allow politicians access to resources and furnish them with the capacity to make things happen or, in current parlance, to "make a difference" (Annesley and Franceschet 2015). Finally, we need to understand that while certain kinds of power reside in the ability to frame, refine, support or oppose policy and legislation (to make things happen), women are also excluded from what are sometimes referred to as 'soft' power domains. These are the less quantifiable access points to the networks and flow of power inside male-dominated institutions; the credentials required to enter these are oftentimes obscure or intangible. In sum, there is a hidden life in institutions, often taking place, quite literally, behind closed doors, from which outsiders (by gender, race or class) are excluded.

A third historical factor women need to take on board is the problem of finding a media platform from which to speak across all domains, including politics, the arts, sports, economics and so on. The fact is that, historically, women have featured far less often than men in the news media. This has led to the argument, formulated by Tuchman (1979), that their under-representation in the media, their symbolical annihilation, may be indicative of their disempowerment in the social realm. She also warns (1979: 532) that "ever alert and energetic, they [the media] transform and absorb dissent". Matters have not improved enough since Tuchman's time. For example, scholars scrutinising the post-Tuchman decades have expressed concern about the ongoing exclusion of women's voices from politics, with specific reference to political journalism. Adcock's (2010) study of the electoral news narratives of the late 1990s showed, for example, how both ordinary women and female politicians were either marginalised, confined to image rather than the spoken word, or else figured as "condensing symbols" for the worth of male counterpart politicians and their parties (or combinations thereof) (see Chapell and Waylen 2013). A classic example of women deployed as condensing symbols is recounted by British Labour MP Jess Phillips (2017) in her memoir *Everywoman*, which lamented the conventional publicity shot featuring a male Party leader surrounded by women. She cites a 2016 appearance by Labour Leader Jeremy Corbyn accompanied by eight female colleagues, which was designed, as she put it, to make men and the Party look good. Phillips advice to women commandeered for publicity shots in all walks of life is to demand something in return for cooperation: "Let's stop turning up dutifully...and start saying, 'no... my sisters and I will not walk around with you, making you look all woman-friendly, not unless you bloody well publish an equal pay audit of your office staff'" (Phillips 2017: 74).

Alongside this ongoing sexist representation of female politicians during the recent 2000s (e.g. Ross and Comrie 2012; Ross et al. 2013), research on this period continues to identify the problem of the under-representation of women in the news across the board. This under-representation is evidenced by the paucity of women as both news sources (de Swert and Hooghe 2010) and as the subjects of news in print, broadcasting and, now, even social media news (e.g. Yun et al. 2007; Armstrong and Gao 2011; Ross 2010). Ross and Carter's (2011) investigation, made as a contribution to a series of Global Media Monitoring Project reports (GMMP—a series of impressively large longitudinal studies), suggested that while the relative visibility of women compared to men has improved over time (as both the producers and the subjects of news), it has now stuck at a ratio of 1:3. Other GMMP studies have observed that women comprise only about 21% of all news subjects, and feature more often in stories addressing leisure, consumerism and celebrity than in hard news and current affairs (Minic 2008: 301; see also Djerf-Pierre 2011; Montiel 2014).

These findings continue to be confirmed in major studies. In their study of the coverage of female subjects across English language printed news between 1880 and 2008, Shor et al. (2014) examined 13 newspapers to test the long-held assumption that women are substantially and/or increasingly represented. Their longitudinal evaluation, spanning nearly 130 years, audited press coverage via a software system that identified and logged male and female names. This survey confirmed that female subjects' representation has remained low "throughout modern history", with a peak reaching about 27% in 2008 (Shor et al. 2014: 764). The study revealed that, despite several spikes or "modest uptakes" in some decades, "no newspaper section comes even close to equality between male and female names" (ibid.: 759).

One of the consequences of this under-representation is the problematic ideological message that women's activities and social concerns lie largely in the private/domestic sphere (Burns et al. 2001). As Ross and Carter (2011: 1148) note:

issues and topics traditionally seen to be particularly relevant to women tend to be pushed to the margins of the news where the implicit assumption is that they are less important to those which interest men. In so doing, men's views and voices are privileged over women's, thereby contributing to the ongoing secondary status of women's participation as citizens.

Our fourth and final historical constraint on the voices of women is the less measurable mechanism of the ways in which women and girls have often struggled to break through the social and psychological disadvantages that can limit the ambition and confidence required to speak in public. Much of this struggle is rooted in historical experience (personal, collective or learnt from earlier generations), which warns women that their voices are less valued in public domains, including classrooms, newsrooms, courtrooms and government. Women may recall and internalise the message that breaking through exclusion risks mockery and derision (e.g. Brown 1998; Gilligan 1982; Spender 1980). Consequently, women may also battle with the symptoms of "imposter syndrome" (Clance and Imes 1978). This pressure on women has prompted some to ask, in Carol Gilligan's words, "is it selfish to speak about what I know or what I want? Or should I do what other people know and say or what other people want me to do?" (in Hamer 1999: 175).

In post-feminist, neoliberal times the imperative to speak when silence feels safer becomes a particularly individualised challenge, and this brings with it a different set of pressures. Now life coaches, celebrity role models and business leaders advise ambitious women who wish to make themselves heard to "lean in" to the discussion (Sandberg and Scovell 2013), to put themselves forward and take personal responsibility for breaking through institutional barriers (Gill and Orgad 2015). The platforms from which to speak have expanded massively since the 1980s and 1990s, when much of the scholarship was undertaken on sex role stereotyping and the damage it wrought to girls and women. But so too have the opportunities for hecklers and trolls to heap abuse on users of social media sites like YouTube and Twitter, to the extent that we can argue that a new formation of online popular misogyny has emerged (García-Favaro and Gill 2016).

These four historical mechanisms of exclusion and dismissal continue to make their mark today in the proscribed opportunities to speak, the scope of the political field of discourse available, and the ways in which women's incursions, conversations and interventions are relayed, reported and commented upon. In other words, as Nick Couldry (2010: 120) explains, the "wider social distribution of ...voice" remains "highly gendered", and the media, as a map of social reality, inevitably reflects and even reinforces this in various, deleterious, ways.

It's not Misogyny Professor-Beard, It's You

The above mapping describes the complexity of the historical and current terrain that must be negotiated by women who 'choose' to step into the public sphere.[1] It usefully establishes some of the grounds upon which gender inequality arises and develops. But it tells us little or nothing about the specific tactics of disparagement and dismissal levelled against women and the strategies of reply and resistance that women reach for in return. We move on then to a consideration of the British classicist scholar Professor Mary Beard, who has become a notable national figure in British cultural life. Beard, a Cambridge scholar and a Professor at the Royal Academy of Arts, has been a media don for some years, although it is only in the past five years or so that she has become a prominent media figure. A long-term editor of the Classics section of *The Times Literary Supplement*, she has also written journalism on contemporary topics and presented several television series based on her academic specialisms. In addition to these, she has addressed far more personal subjects, for example, authoring a piece for the *Guardian* recalling her experience of rape (Beard 2000) and fronting a BBC Radio 4 documentary called *Glad to be Grey* (2016), about the cultural expectation that women tint their hair (she is conspicuous in the media sphere for her undyed hair).[2] As a prolific tweeter, she takes every opportunity to comment on current affairs and has been the subject of many newspaper interviews.

Beard is a woman of late middle age, who speaks with confidence. She is well known as someone who has refused to compromise her values around her personal appearance for the benefit of the media. It seems that these combined features rendered her especially liable to vitriolic abuse. An example, which has attracted much commentary, followed her participation in the BBC political panel programme *Question Time* (17 January 2013).[3] During the days that followed, she was subject to threats of sexual assault ("I'm going to cut off your head and rape it"), 'cunt talk', personal insults regarding her appearance, and a picture of her face superimposed onto a vagina (see Dowell 2013; Mead 2014); all of this played out on social media. The *Spectator* magazine journalist Rod Liddle (2013), concerned that she might misconstrue this reaction as woman-hating and woman-baiting, observed "it's not misogyny Professor Beard, it's you", before going on to explain that producers invite her onto shows precisely because she "looks like a loony". He also observed that she was a front-runner to win his 'light-hearted' annual competition for the most stupid woman to have appeared on *Question Time* in the past 12 months.[4]

It is important to note that criticism levelled at women such as Beard extends on two fronts: the undermining of intellect; and the disparagement of the female body as it is seen on television and in media profile pages. As Liz Lane (2015) has noted in her discussion of feminist rhetoric, "digital representations of the body (profile pictures, usernames, biographies) cannot be divorced from the speaker's voice, and even when a speaker's presence is seemingly neutral, gendered attacks are hurled at an assumed body". It was Beard's body upon which insult was inscribed, and the *Question Time* incident was not the first occasion she had encountered this. For instance, Beard's earlier 2010 and 2012 appearances hosting TV history series had already attracted insults from critic A.A. Gill, who had mocked her "corpse's teeth" and disastrous hair and suggested she should appear on the Channel 4 show for "undateable" people living with disfigurements and disabilities. Gill's supporter, former TV Executive, Samantha Brick (2012) also observed: "While there is no denying that Ms Beard is a supremely intelligent and fiercely ambitious woman, there is absolutely no chance of her becoming a successful broadcaster in prime-time slots on flagship TV channels. The plain truth is that Ms Beard is too ugly for TV".

Such responses split the intellect from the female body and disparage the former by resorting to clichéd insults about the latter, as though Beard's appearance and so-called lack of attractiveness could be deployed to discredit her voice. This practice highlights the all-too-familiar way in which women are measured as purely body in public space. Men, in contrast, are accorded the metaphysics of presence associated with the intellectual, philosophical, reasoning and *reasonable* public voice. Beard, a scholar possessed of a wide and cultured vocabulary, and from a prestigious academic background, arguably unsettles critics by her willingness to convey complex historical and contemporary ideas in approachable, media-friendly ways. Moreover, she often does so through the prism of gender and her own experiences. She herself maintains that critics who cannot do justice to her arguments resort to judging her via crude standards of beauty and female anatomy. Beard then, in her insistence on being physically seen and heard in the media, offends on two counts. Firstly, she refuses the reduction of women to a narrow version of acceptable femininity and, secondly, she insists upon educating the public about the politics of female silence and invisibility in the public realm. Her own experience is testament to how women's participation is perceived as an interruption of the status quo of civic society and public life, which is why it is obstructed and proscribed. Her authority, however, rooted in her undoubted expertise, provides her with the ammunition to reply. Hence Beard (2012) countered A.A. Gill by arguing that he was obviously afraid of smart women:

> even the greenest of my students would not present me with an essay as ill-argued and off the point as Gill's critique. Possibly this is where we reach the heart of AA Gills's [sic] problem: maybe it's precisely because he did not go to university that he never quite learned the rigour of intellectual argument and he thinks that he can pass off insults as wit. It may well be the reason why he feels the need to sneer at intelligent, educated women.

Despite the best efforts of Liddle and Gill, and of many others who cloaked themselves in anonymity, Beard refused to 'shut up' and to capitulate to the normative politics of voice that commonly denigrates women's expressions in the public sphere. Indeed, Beard's (2014) subsequent, well-received and widely circulated lecture titled "The Public Voice of Women" outlined the historical roots of men's entitlement to speak and how this has been depicted in culture. She took the opportunity to demonstrate that she was the recipient of a historically embedded misogynistic practice by recalling how effective rhetoric has been figured as a masculine attribute. She also stressed the ways in which women's voices have been condemned for being discordant and irritating, their views dismissed as amateurish and ill-informed, and that they have only been permitted to contribute to public conversations under constraint.

Beard's intervention was one of many challenges recently launched by feminist intellectuals and activists to the current gendered configuration of the public sphere with regards to "voice" (see Hooks and Harris-Perry 2013; Mendes 2015). Interventions such as these act as critical reflections on the work still to be done in ensuring that media citizenship is fully inclusive and respectful of women's contributions. As an historian, Beard (2014) reminds us that "right where written evidence for Western culture starts, women's voices are not being heard in the public sphere", and that the long view shows us the "culturally awkward" relationship between women's voices and the political sphere in its broadest sense. Here, she highlights the broader issue of the landscape from which women speak and the pre-established network of material and social resources from which women have been excluded. As other feminist critics of the rational public sphere have argued, deliberative democracy requires not only "an equality of resources" to speak but also the "guarantee of equal opportunity to speak" to convey what is viewed as a persuasive argument (Norval 2007: 25). Underlying this, women must equally possess the "epistemological authority" to "evoke acknowledgment of one's arguments" (ibid.: 26). We suggest that Beard's essay operated as an elegant reply to all challengers, and a reply grounded in an expertise that was built on resources of education, cultural capital and her professional authority. As a scholar and a public intellectual, Beard's strategic response was to deploy, with confidence, her knowledge and long-honed academic skills of argument, evidence and critical reflection. At the same time, she contends with the fact that women are not afforded the markers of respect and openness merited by their expertise. She knowingly addressed women's long-term deprivation of the competencies, platforms and respect needed to fully engage with public cultural and political life.

WITHOUT SAYING A THING, ALL THE WORLD, ALL AMERICA, FELT MY PAIN

In our case above, Beard was condemned for speaking. We now turn to a case in which a woman was publicly disparaged for her silence and thus incited to speak. During the 2016 American presidential race, Ghazala Khan and her husband Khizr Khan, a Muslim American couple, appeared in the national media spotlight. The Khans' loss of their son Humayun Khan, an army captain who died in Iraq while protecting his unit from a suicide bomber, rendered them noteworthy supporters of Hillary Clinton in the lead-up to the election. The couple stood together at the rostrum at the 30 July 2016 Democratic National Convention in Philadelphia. In a six-minute speech, Mr Khan strongly criticised then Republican nominee Donald Trump for his divisive politics, stating that he "consistently smears the character of Muslims. He disrespects other minorities, women, judges, even his own party leadership". He stated that Trump vowed "to build walls and ban us from this country". He then brandished a pocket-sized US Constitution and asked Trump if he had ever read it (Wall Street Journal 2016). Throughout the speech, Ghazala Khan stood by her husband at the rostrum, sometimes turning to him as he spoke and sometimes looking out at the audience. She appeared calm, composed, attentive and, from time to time, visibly moved. The Khans' entry into the pre-constituted set of political performances and narratives of electioneering was covered quite positively in the media. News interviewers and commentators demanded a reply from Trump.

On 31 July 2016 Trump was being interviewed for *This Week* by ABC's George Stephanopoulos. He was invited to turn his attention to Khan and his wife Ghazala:

> I saw him. He was, you know, very emotional. And probably–looked like a nice guy to me. His wife, if you look at his wife, she was standing there, she had nothing to say. She probably, maybe she wasn't allowed to have anything to say. You tell me. But plenty of people have written that. She was extremely quiet. And it looked like she had nothing to say. A lot of people have said that (Turnham 2016).

Elsewhere we have discussed how the invitation for ordinary people to speak in the public realm can render the speaking subject a hostage to fortune, "as views expressed become circulated, amplified, co-opted and/or elaborated by others" (Biressi and Nunn 2013: 143ff). In this case, Trump attempted to elaborate on the Khans' appearance, to neutralise both Khans by turning the topic towards Islamic family relations. Trump suggested that Khizr was well meaning but "emotional", and thereby implied he was probably unqualified to take part in rational political communication. And, through the kind of ventriloquism adopted by politicians who seek to deploy implicitly racist or sexist criticism, Trump mobilised populist hearsay ("people have written", "people have said") to convey criticism of Ghazala. He deflected any direct discussion of his policies and his own knowledge of the Constitution by relaying the suggestion (made by unnamed others) that Ghazala was unable to speak because she was a Muslim wife. He then doubly denigrated her by stating that, in any case, she appeared to have "nothing to say".

In response, *The Washington Post* published a piece, written by Ghazala Khan (2016) herself, in which she explains her reasons for not speaking at the convention:

> Donald Trump has asked why I did not speak at the Democratic convention. He said he would like to hear from me. Here is my answer to Donald Trump: Because without saying a thing, all the world, all America, felt my pain. I am a Gold Star mother. Whoever saw me felt me in their heart... Walking onto the convention stage, with a huge picture of my son behind me, I could hardly control myself. What mother could? Donald Trump has children whom he loves. Does he really need to wonder why I did not speak? ... Donald Trump said that maybe I wasn't allowed to say anything. That is not true. My husband asked me if I wanted to speak, but I told him I could not.

The couple also featured in an exclusive interview on MSNBC in which Khizr emphasised his wife's contribution to his speech and its delivery: "She was my coach. I was strengthened by her presence" (MSNBC 2016). Here is another case, we suggest, of a woman disrupting the political order: firstly, merely by her silent presence as a bereaved mother and a supportive wife: and then, as a woman who disrupts public space by making a claim for recognition and for authority on the back of a felt injury inflicted by Trump. She adopted the position of the politicised mother to stake her claim for her's and her family's status as patriotic citizens who are equally also Muslims. In doing so, she drew upon a form of embodied experience—that of loss and of maternity—which is grounded in faith and gender and provides a biographically informed authority that refuses political exclusion. She thereby asserts herself as a mother, as a wife, as a Muslim and as a political subject who upholds the equality and deliberative democracy that the Khans had argued is central to the constitutional rights of all American citizens.

This deployment of motherhood is a tricky strategy. Women, in particular, already find themselves positioned and defined in relation to motherhood by the media and politicians. When women are invited to speak, it is often in their capacity as 'working' mothers or 'stay-at-home' mothers of young children, as 'lone mothers', as the mother of a crime victim or of a soldier fighting overseas (Slattery and Garner 2007, 2012). The emphasis on the maternal as the basis of a more nuanced and ethical polity has been criticised by many feminists, and it can be a positioning which is limiting and open to co-option by political forces. However, we also want to acknowledge that, in the case of Ghazala Khan and other women, oftentimes this maternal experience affords the lay person a degree of respect and recognition that allows her voice to be more fully heard. Indeed, historically, political activists have used their gender and their maternal experience tactically to marshal opposition to war and conflict, and to promote "women-driven" solutions to war and militarism (Rosen 2013). In addition, individuals such as Doreen Lawrence, Diana Lamplugh and Sara Payne (all mothers of murder victims) in Britain, Rosie Batty in Australia (who campaigned against domestic violence after her son's murder by his father) and Cindy Sheehan (the mother of a soldier killed in Iraq) in the USA have made significant inroads into the public political arena, garnering some criticism but also huge respect. We suggest they have achieved this not only through their organisational skills, determination and intelligence, but also via an affective politics of experience that confers authority and value to their contributions (Dawney 2013). In sum, we consider their deployment of 'political motherhood' (Yuval-Davis 1999) to be an effective strategy of incursion.[5]

Conclusion: Refusing to Change the Subject

The concept of experience has been interrogated at length by feminist scholars. Here we signal the importance of applying context and the historicisation of experience, and the need to hold together the affective, symbolic, economic and political domains women inhabit. As we outlined above, women's experience of sexism and the historical burden of gendered expectations can be an impediment to action. On the other hand, women's strength as activists and their insistence on speaking out may be motivated and sanctioned by their experiences as women in general, and as mothers, carers, educators and so on. The problem for women who choose to deploy personal experience in the public realm, however, is that this invites gendered criticism: that men debate and argue from an objective position; while women speak subjectively and from an information base originating from the personal and the private realm. But, as historian Joan W. Scott argues, experience has been one of the ways in which women have understood and articulated the specificity of their place in the world, and to jettison this is to abandon the commonplace interpretations of a speaker's place: a position "neither self-evident nor straightforward" and "always contested, therefore always political" (Scott 1992: 37). As Scott notes, experience is also a word and framing structure which is "so much a part of everyday language, so imbricated in narratives, that it serves as a strategy for women to talk (sometimes with reluctance or hesitation) about what has spurred them to act in the public field" (ibid.). The rhetorical recourse to experience made by women can be a way to mark "difference and similarity" and to claim knowledge that is "unassailable" (ibid.). Hence, we chose above to highlight historical experience as the fourth dimension of women's oppression but, importantly, we argue that we should also understand it as a resource for action, for progress and for the public articulation of voice.

The strategic value of experience, in the form of testimony for example, is that it allows women to justify public activism and to advocate for change, for compensation for injury, or to reply to an accusation. Women who find themselves in the media spotlight are often under duress; cornered by the heavyweight world of institutional structures and legal frameworks. In response, a woman's experience and her testimony can be a resource deployed to credit oneself as a subject with rights, to maintain confidence and to insist on recognition or redress.

Nancy Fraser has argued that the "struggle for recognition" was one of the key paradigmatic forms of conflict in the late twentieth century (Fraser 1998: 430). This struggle extends into the early decades of the twenty-first century, and one of the central patterns of injustice she outlines is that of cultural or symbolic injustice, which is "rooted in social patterns of representation, interpretation, and communication" (ibid.: 433). Mary Beard's and Ghazala Khan's participation was traduced through "non-recognition" and "disrespect" (ibid.). But, in both cases, the women chose to reply and to counter discriminatory practices, to struggle for recognition, albeit from very different power bases and for different reasons.

In Beard's case, hostility was levelled at her political interventions, her expertise and her physical appearance, arguably aimed at detracting from her authority as a public intellectual. We argue that these sexist derogatory tactics are all attempts to literally *change the subject*, that is, to re-direct the public conversation back to those who have been historically entitled to speak. To achieve this switchover, Beard must also be changed from an expert subject into a foolish object of derision and abuse. So too Trump's tactic was to derail the Khans' political criticism by changing the subject to that of Islamic attitudes towards women, reproducing a stereotypical disparagement of Ghazala as a Muslim wife. Again, an attempt is made here to render a political subject into a gendered, ethnically different object. In cases such as these, criticism is mobilised from a position of rationality and mastery against women who have been deemed too stupid, too oppressed, too silent, too voluble, too opinionated or too ill-informed to qualify for a platform in the media. But, in response, we find that Beard, Khan and many others, some cited above, refuse to change the subject and refuse to change their subject positions.

NOTES

1. For some, this 'choice' to take part in media debate may, in fact, be non-negotiable or, at the very least, an unspoken professional expectation. The complexity around women's media self-exposure manifests the postfeminist discourse of choice and arguably places another gendered burden of responsibility on women in the public eye; one that is tied to the success of one's work. We are indebted to Caroline Bainbridge for this insight and for her generous feedback on an earlier draft of this chapter.
2. Available at: http://www.bbc.co.uk/programmes/b071x87c. Accessed 11 April 2017.
3. Available at: https://www.youtube.com/watch?v=CTDByiSRerk. Accessed 11 April 2017.
4. Disparagement of women on *Question Time* is not confined to panel speakers. See, for example, the mockery of 'Mrs Flowery Woman' (York 2017) and 'the woman wearing orange' (Tolhurst 2017).
5. This is not to say that maternity and discourses of motherhood always work in favour of the speaker. See, for example, Bainbridge's (2010) discussion of the media coverage of the Madeleine McCann case.

REFERENCES

Adcock, C. (2010). "The politician, the wife, the citizen, and her newspaper: Rethinking women, democracy, and media (ted) representation". *Feminist Media Studies*, 10(2), 135–159.

Annesley, C. and Franceschet, S. (2015). "Gender and the executive branch". *Politics & Gender*, 11(04): 613–617.

Annesley, C. and Gains, F. (2010). "The core executive: gender, power and change". *Political Studies*, 58(5): 909–929.

Armstrong, C. and Gao, F. (2011). "Gender, Twitter and news content: An examination across platforms and coverage areas". *Journalism Studies*, 12(4): 490–505.

Bainbridge, C. (2010). "'They've taken her!' Psychoanalytic perspectives on mediating maternity, feeling and loss". *Studies in the Maternal*, 2(1). Available at www.mamsie.bbk.ac.uk.

Beard, M. (2000). "The story of my rape". *Guardian*, 8 September. Available at: https://www.theguardian.com/world/2000/sep/08/gender.uk.

Beard, M. (2012). "Too ugly for TV? No, I'm too brainy for men who fear clever women". *Mail Online*, 23 April. Available at: http://www.dailymail.co.uk/femail/article-2134146/Too-ugly-TV-No-Im-brainy-men-fear-clever-women.html.

Beard, M. (2014). "The Public Voice of Women". *London Review of Books*, 36(6): 11–14. Available at: http://www.lrb.co.uk/v36/n06/mary-beard/the-public-voice-of-women.

Biressi, A. and Nunn, H. (2013). *Class and Contemporary British Culture*. London: Palgrave Macmillan.

Brick, S. (2012). "'Sorry, some women ARE too ugly for TV': So says that self-proclaimed beauty, and former TV executive, Samantha Brick". *Mail Online*, 2 May. Available at: http://www.dailymail.co.uk/femail/article-2138177/Samantha-Brick-Sorry-women-ARE-ugly-TV.html.

Brown, L.M. (1998). *Raising their Voices: The Politics of Girl's Anger*. Massachusetts: Harvard University Press.

Burns, N., Lehman Schlozman, K. and Verba, S. (2001). *The Private Roots of Public Action: Gender, Equality, and Political Participation*. Harvard: Harvard University Press.

Chappell, L. and Waylen, G. (2013). "Gender and the hidden life of institutions". *Public Administration*, 91(3): 599–615.

Clance, P.R. and Imes, S. (1978). "The imposter phenomenon in high achieving women: dynamics and therapeutic intervention". *Psychotherapy Theory, Research and Practice*, 15(3), Fall. Available at: http://www.paulinerose-clance.com/pdf/ip_high_achieving_women.pdf.

Couldry, N. (2010). *Why Voice Matters: Culture And Politics After Neoliberalism*. London: Sage.

Dahlerup, D. and Leyenaar, M. (Eds.) (2013). *Breaking Male Dominance in Old Democracies*. Oxford: Oxford University Press.

Dawney, L. (2013). "The figure of authority: the affective biopolitics of the mother and the dying man". *Journal of Political Power*, 6(1): 29–47.

de Swert, K. and Hooghe, M. (2010). "When do women get a voice? Explaining the presence of female news sources in Belgian news broadcasts (2003–5)". *European Journal of Communication*, 25(1): 69–84.

Djerf-Pierre, M. (2011). "The Difference Engine: Gender equality, journalism and the good society". *Feminist Media Studies*, 11(01): 43–51.

Dowell, B. (2013). "Mary Beard suffers 'truly vile' online abuse after Question Time". *Guardian*, 21 January. Available at: https://www.theguardian.com/media/2013/jan/21/mary-beard-suffers-twitter-abuse.

Fraser, N. (1998). "From Redistribution to Recognition? Dilemmas of Justice in a 'Post-Socialist' Age". In: Phillips, A. (Ed.) *Feminism and Politics*, 430–460. Oxford: Oxford University Press.

García-Favaro, L. and Gill, R. (2016). "'Emasculation nation has arrived': sexism rearticulated in online responses to Lose the Lads' Mags campaign". *Feminist Media Studies*, 16(3): 379–397.

Gill, R. and Orgad, S. (2015). "The confidence cult(ure)". *Australian Feminist Studies*, 30(86): 324–344.

Gilligan, C. (1982). *In a Different Voice: Psychological Theory and Women's Development*. Massachusetts: Harvard University Press.

Hamer, M. (1999). "Listen to the voice: An interview with Carol Gilligan". *Women: A Cultural Review*, 10(2): 173–184.

Hooks, B. and Harris-Perry, M. (2013). "Black female voices: who is listening?" [video]. Available at: https://www.youtube.com/watch?v=5OmgqXao1ng.

Khan, G. (2016). "Trump criticized my silence. He knows nothing about true sacrifice". *Washington Post*, 31 July. Available at: https://www.washingtonpost.com/opinions/ghazala-khan-donald-trump-criticized-my-silence-he-knows-nothing-about-true-sacrifice/2016/07/31/c46e52ec-571c-11e6-831d-0324760ca856_story.html?utm_term=.0269bbdb17f0.

Kittilson, M.C. (2016). "Gender and political behaviour". *Oxford Research Encyclopaedia of Politics*. Available at http://politics.oxfordre.com/view/10.1093/acrefore/9780190228637.001.0001/acrefore-9780190228637-e-71?rskey=wsKL38&result=10.

Lane, L. (2015). "Feminist rhetoric in the digital sphere: digital interventions & the subversion of gendered cultural scripts". *Ada: A Journal of Gender, New Media, and Technology*, 8. Available at: http://adanewmedia.org/2015/11/issue8-lane/.

Liddle, R. (2013). "It's not misogyny, Professor Beard. It's you". *The Spectator*, 26 January. Available at: http://www.spectator.co.uk/2013/01/its-not-misogyny-professor-beard-its-you/.

Lovenduski, J. (2005). *Feminizing Politics*. Cambridge: Polity.

Mead, R. (2014). "The Troll Slayer". *The New Yorker*, 1 September. Available at: http://www.newyorker.com/magazine/2014/09/01/troll-slayer.

Mendes, K. (2015). *Slutwalk: Feminism, Activism and Media*. Basingstoke: Palgrave Macmillan.

Minic, D. (2008). "What makes an issue a Woman's Hour issue? The politics of recognition and media coverage of women's issues and perspectives". *Feminist Media Studies*, 8(3): 302–15.

Montiel, A.V. (Ed.) (2014). *Media and Gender: A Scholarly Agenda for the Global Alliance on Media and Gender*. Paris: UNESCO.

MSNBC (2016). "Slain soldier's dad: GOP should call out Trump". *MSNBC*, 29 July. Available at: http://www.msnbc.com/the-last-word/watch/slain-soldier-s-dad-gop-should-call-out-trump-735109699658.

Norris, P. and Lovenduski, J. (1995). *Political Recruitment: Gender, Race and Class in the British Parliament*. Cambridge: Cambridge University Press.

Norval, A. (2007). *Aversive Democracy*. Cambridge: Cambridge University Press.

Phillips, J. (2017). *Everywoman: One Woman's Truth About Speaking the Truth*. London: Hutchinson.

Ramirez, F.O., Soysal, Y., and Shanahan, S. (1997). "The changing logic of political citizenship: Cross-national acquisition of women's suffrage rights, 1890 to 1990". *American Sociological Review*, 62(5): 735–745.

Rosen, R. (2013). "Women and the language of peace protest". *50.50 Inclusive Democracy*, 24 May. Available at: http://www.opendemocracy.net/5050/ruth-rosen/women-and-language-of-peace-protest.

Ross, K. (2010). *Gendered Media: Women, Men and Identity Politics*. Plymouth: Rowman and Littlefield.

Ross, K. and Carter, C. (2011). "Women and news: A long and winding road". *Media, Culture and Society*, 33(8): 1148–1165.

Ross, K. and Comrie, M. (2012). "The rules of the (leadership) game: Gender, politics and news" *Journalism*, 13(8): 969–984.

Ross, K., Evans, E., Harrison, L., Shears, M. and Wadia, K. (2013). "The gender of news and news of gender: a study of sex, politics, and press coverage of the 2010 British General Election". *The International Journal of Press/Politics*, 18(1): 3–20.

Sandberg, S. and Scovell, N. (2013) *Lean In: Women, Work, and the Will to Lead*. London: W.H. Allen.

Scott, J.W. (1992). "Experience". In: Butler, J. and Scott, J.W. (Eds.) *Feminists Theorize the Political*. New York and London: Routledge.

Shor, E., van de Rijt, A., Ward, C., Blank-Gomel, A., and Skiena, S. (2014). "Time trends in printed news coverage of female subjects, 1880–2008". *Journalism Studies*, 15(6), 759–773.

Slattery, K. and Garner, A.C. (2007). "Mothers of soldiers in wartime: A national news narrative". *Critical Studies in Media Communication*, 24(5): 429–445.

Slattery, K. and Garner, A.C. (2012). "Mobilizing mother: from good mother to patriotic mother in World War I". *Journalism & Communication Monographs*, 14(1): 5–77.

Spender, D. (1980) *Man Made Language*. London: Routledge and Kegan Paul.

Tolhurst, A. (2017). "Question Time woman mocked after asking if EU citizens have to leave after Brexit then 'who will serve us coffee in Pret?'". *Sun*, 3 March. Available at: https://www.thesun.co.uk/news/3000556/question-time-woman-mocked-after-asking-if-eu-citizens-have-to-leave-after-brexit-then-who-will-serve-us-coffee-in-pret/.

Tuchman, G. (1979). "Women's Depiction by the Mass Media". *Signs*, 4(3) (Spring): 528–542.

Turnham, S. (2016). "Donald Trump to Father of Fallen Soldier: 'I've Made a Lot of Sacrifices'". *ABC News*, 30 July. Available at: http://abcnews.go.com/Politics/donald-trump-father-fallen-soldier-ive-made-lot/story?id=41015051.

Wall Street Journal (2016). "Muslim Soldier's Father Delivers Message to Trump" [video]. *Wall Street Journal*, 28 July. Available at: http://www.wsj.com/video/muslim-soldier-father-delivers-message-to-trump/E04FBC58-649E-4388-927D-0239B285D0A5.html.

York, C. (2017). "BBC Question Time Audience Member Says Britain Ruled Like A 'Light To The World'". *Huffington Post*, 10 February. Available at: http://www.huffingtonpost.co.uk/entry/bbc-question-time-audience-member_uk_589d6e1be4b094a129e9ca2b?.

Yun, H.J., Ancu, M., Ramoutar, N. and Kaid, L.L. (2007). "Where is she?: Coverage of women in online magazines". *Journalism Studies* 8(6): 930–947.

Yuval-Davis, N. (1999). "Institutional racism, cultural diversity and citizenship: Some reflections on reading the Stephen Lawrence Inquiry Report". *Sociological Research Online*, 4(1). Available at: http://www.socresonline.org.uk/4/lawrence/yuval-davis.html.

CHAPTER 4

Populism, "Community" and Political Culture: The Revenge of the Liberal Elite

Stuart Price

"The next Labour government will rebuild communities ripped apart by globalisation and neglected for years by government".
(Labour Party, General Election 2017)

"Without a strong economy, we cannot guarantee our security, our personal prosperity, our public services, or contented and sustainable communities".
(Conservative Party, General Election 2017)

"We're not against anybody, based on religion or ethnicity ... we're for ourselves, we're for our country, we're for our communities".
Nigel Farage (2017) (Westwood, 24 February 2017)

Introduction: The Political Context

The year 2016 was widely regarded as one in which unforeseen events disturbed the routine management of the liberal social order.[1] Basic assumptions—about the ability of electorates to act in the 'rational self-interest'[2] ascribed to them by political analysts—were called into question.

S. Price (✉)
De Montfort University, Leicester, UK
e-mail: sprice@dmu.ac.uk

© The Author(s) 2017
R. Sanz Sabido (ed.), *Representing Communities*,
DOI 10.1007/978-3-319-65030-2_4

Two developments in particular seemed to epitomise the affront offered to that coalition of forces known variously as the 'Establishment' or the 'liberal elite': the British decision to leave the European Union; and the election of Donald Trump as President of the United States. Regarded in some quarters as a catastrophe, the 'Brexit' vote cast doubt on the future of Europe as a cohesive entity[3]; while Trump's unforeseen victory seemed to reinforce the disquiet felt by those who identified with more 'enlightened' social and cultural values. These groups were unsettled by Trump's emphasis on exclusion, reinforced through seemingly endless references to rigid gender roles, national security, borders and walls.

The two major electoral upsets described above (supposedly the fault of a neglected lumpen proletariat on both sides of the Atlantic[4]) caused consternation among the cheerleaders of the transnational capitalist elite, but were received as a *moral shock* by liberal voters who found Trump's scurrilous remarks distasteful, or who were offended by the anti-immigrant stance adopted by some elements of the UK's Leave campaign.[5] Many on the losing side of the argument ('Remainers' in the UK and Democrats in the USA) mounted a sustained critique of the intolerance they detected in the ranks of their victorious opponents. British protestors held pro-Europe marches in London (Johnston 2017), while American activists staged events like the Women's March against Trump, which gained support from almost two million people across the globe (Khomami 2017).

One of the most notable responses to the more obviously reactionary positions adopted by Trump and Farage—on, for instance, gender, ethnic identity and the environment—was to reassert the socially 'progressive' values that are thought to underpin the advanced political systems of the Western hemisphere. Yet, even before this reaction against bigotry had appeared (in the form of the protests and marches noted above), a number of politicians and influential commentators had begun to revive the notion that liberal democracy was threatened, not only by far-right nationalism, 'Islamist' terrorism or the dangers of excessive military adventurism, but by the revival of an avowedly more insidious and generalised challenge, that of populism.

The "Populism" of Left and Right: An Equal Threat to Democracy?

Populism, at least in its electoral manifestation, is generally understood as the use by demagogues or political outsiders of strategic appeals or actions designed to resonate with those (usually 'ordinary') citizens who resent the dominance of a group designated as both privileged and remote. Populists are meant therefore to exploit this distrust and suspicion, taking advantage of the "hopes, fears, and concerns" of disillusioned individuals by subsuming all issues into a simple binary opposition—"the people versus an intransigent elite" (Judis 2016: 17). As Judis notes "the exact referents of the people and the elite don't define populism; what defines it is the conflictual relationship between the two" (15). The conceptual elasticity of this process meant that predatory members of the upper classes, like Trump, could disguise themselves as self-made outsiders in touch with the 'real' concerns of the subaltern.

My focus here is not, however, the mercurial character of one individual. It is rather the recent experience of British, American and French citizens, and the way in which their leaders have been so obsessed with the populist phenomenon. Why is it that major political figures in the West have decided to identify populism as a particularly dangerous malaise? Have they aligned themselves with the liberal/leftist movements that oppose (on broadly moral grounds) a resurgent British, European and American Right? Or have sections of the dominant political class (represented by patricians like Blair, Macron, Merkel and Osborne) identified a threat to the continuous rule of a centrist, economically neo-liberal, yet supposedly 'culturally progressive' social order? The populist threat was used by the 'elite' to attack a *variety* of targets, some of which were designed to resonate with the perceptions of socially liberal citizens; the offenders were meant to include far-right demagogues, left-wing leaders who revived the fear of proletarian democracy, the weakness of Establishment politicians, and the gullibility of sections of the voting public.

Whatever the exact formula employed, senior politicians and mandarins in Europe and beyond were fully aware of the electoral flashpoints that might threaten their position. Throughout 2016 a variety of patriarchs warmed to the populist theme. Manuel Valls, the French Prime Minister, declared that "Europe could die" because of "attacks from populists" (Goulard 2016), while Wolfgang Schäuble, the German Federal Minister of Finance, warned that "demagogic populism is not only a problem in America" (Chambers and Nienaber 2016). Schäuble believed that, in the West as a whole, the standard of political deliberation had declined and was now "in an alarming state". Meanwhile, the former head of the British Secret Intelligence Service, Sir Richard Dearlove, argued that "if Europe cannot act together to ... gain control of its migratory crisis, then the EU will find itself at the mercy of a populist uprising" (BBC 2016).

The CEO of the anti-radicalisation group, the Quilliam Foundation, was more specific about the political colouring of the populist enemy. He complained in a letter to *The Times* that "conversations about identity, immigration and integration have been ceded to populists both left and right" (Rafiq 2016). The suggestion that populist appeals could be mobilised by extremists—drawn from both a Left and a Right that are either deemed irrelevant or (despite their mutual antagonism) a threat to democracy—became a standard theme in the repertoire of the neo-liberal faction of the transnational elite. This is not to deny that there are some superficial similarities between the populism of Left and Right, particularly where an attempt is made to appeal to a mass audience. However, as Judis (2016: 15) pointed out, one of the basic differences between the two poles of populism is the fact that "leftwing populists champion the people against an elite or establishment", whereas "rightwing populists champion the people against an elite that they accuse of coddling a third group". This third group, in his opinion, can include immigrants, Islamist militants and minority ethnic groups.

Post-Brexit and post-Trump the broad discursive framework created by the populist debate has generated a number of similar narratives, in the sense that the relentless theme of insecurity and threat, so common to the daily governance of liberal capitalist societies (Mulholland 2012), has been reanimated to meet a new contingency. One of the most commonly cited political hazards is, of course, terrorism, particularly that associated with the violent actions of jihadist groups and their sympathisers.[6] A common theme (widely repeated, for example, in the wake of the May 2017 Manchester bombing and the June 2017 London Bridge attack) is that terrorists 'hate our way of life', and by extension the democratic order itself.[7] This discourse has a material/ideological base, in the sense that it is produced not only by repeated utterance, but also by the fact that physical attacks are carried out, both against visible symbolic targets that evoke the democratic process (like Parliament), and against civilians engaged in leisure and other everyday pursuits.[8]

The questions, however, remain the same: what do we mean when we speak of democracy; and which social forces represent a serious threat to its survival? In the case of the populist turn, the deep, visceral desire to preserve the hierarchical order seems to have revived those currents of thought that question the wisdom of allowing the 'ignorant' masses to vote (see Clark 2017). Yet, besides this impulse (and the comic suggestion that a subdivision of the working class has helped to ruin liberal culture), another more persuasive critique appeared, already suggested above, that irresponsible or negative appeals to the prejudices of fractured or disillusioned communities—in other words, the use of populism as a political tactic—signalled a dangerous retreat from *liberal democratic norms.*[9]

TECHNOCRATIC RULE: A "SUPPLEMENT" OR AN AFFRONT TO DEMOCRACY?

If, however, the edifice of democratic society had been placed under duress by the disreputable tactics associated with populism, then it is also the case that autocratic modes of transnational corporate rule (those types of governance that do not require elections and thus avoid an 'ordeal by public approval'), are more common than imagined; for instance, clear departures from routine practices occurred after the fiscal meltdown of 2007/2008. In this case, the rise of 'anti-democratic' forces had their origin not in an upsurge of populism, but in the top-down imposition of technocrats on supposedly peripheral European countries like Greece and Italy.

In November 2011, for example, the 'troika'—consisting of the European Union, the European Central Bank (ECB), and the International Monetary Fund (IMF)—had replaced the Greek Prime Minister George Papandreou with the unelected former ECB member Lucas Papademos. At the same time, in Italy, the scandal-prone Silvio Berlusconi had been exchanged for one-time European Commissioner Mario Monti (Biondi and Moody 2011). It would be easy to dismiss objections to this process, on the basis that the leaders concerned were superannuated, corrupt, or both, but this does not diminish the urgency of the argument that normal democratic processes were being further undermined. In this respect it is worth noting that Berlusconi had indicated his desire to call an election, while Papandreou had wanted to hold a referendum on membership of the European Union. In other words, when placed under duress, both politicians sought to renew some kind of democratic mandate.

At the time, well-known news organisations were quite open about the reasons why the nominees of an unelected elite had been used to depose leading politicians. In Greece, according to the BBC (2011), the appearance of Papademos signalled "another round of austerity measures, which have already proved hugely unpopular with the Greek public", while a Reuters article noted that, in Italy, Monti had been pushed "*by markets* for weeks as the most suitable figure to lead a national unity government that will urgently push through painful austerity measures" (Biondi and Moody 2011, my emphasis). An analysis published in the *New Statesman* declared that "if democratically elected leaders do not satisfy the markets, the IMF and the European Commission, they are now, in effect, summarily dismissed, without any reference to *the wishes of the people*" (Skelton 2011, my emphasis). A theme that has emerged among the more serious sections of the commentariat has been the declaration that the real struggle is not between Left and Right (endlessly described as outdated), but between "globalists" and "nationalists" (Williams 2017; Forsyth 2017; Bremmer 2017).

None of these references to a clash between political creeds, or to the autocratic behaviour of international organisations, is intended to deny the existence of a reprehensible, nationalistic populism. The point is rather to separate the latter (a right-wing phenomenon, often containing fascistic undertones) from a number of other tendencies: those leftist social movements that rely on visible public mobilisation (Price and Sanz Sabido 2015, 2016; Gerbaudo 2017); the more private machinations of economic coalitions like the troika; and the public strategies of mainstream politicians that have advanced 'centrist' goals using the populist tactics they affect to despise. Before this form of complicity is discussed, the basis of populist assumptions must be examined, centred on one pivotal concept, that of 'community'.

POPULISM AND "COMMUNITY" AS A POLITICAL CODE

Populist discourses are an established feature of liberal cultures because all political groups must face the challenge of describing the social collective upon which they base their claim to democratic legitimacy. In electoral systems, the safest approach is to create the impression that an entire national population constitutes a 'virtuous public', to which entreaties can be made, and which can be defended from the supposed slights or insults directed at it from each party's political rivals. If there is a righteous group, however, there must also be a villainous force determined to undermine it. In the case of populist appeals, opponents can be identified (as we have seen) with a negligent elite, while the advantage of referring to a community derives in part from the sense it creates of a close-knit, voluntary association, one that can be devolved from the national to the local, or conversely expanded from the local to the national, without losing its imprecise inclusivity (evidenced by its regular appearance in election literature, as analysed below).

As a flexible category, community has another advantage; it may resonate with the listener more readily than specific references to class, creed, gender or race. It is also useful because it suggests both "community as a complex of social relations" and "community as a complex of ideas and sentiments" (Calhoun 1980: 110). If, therefore, successful political address depends on the use of smooth transitions between ambiguous categories, the assignation of positive values to large, vaguely drawn social groups (such as the oft-repeated mantra that the British are known for their tolerance[10]) may help maintain the base upon which electoral victory depends. Two more points should be mentioned: first, that differences between particular uses of community reveal the political attitudes underlying the mobilisation of the term; and second, that the designation of a collective as a community also functions as a way of maintaining the distinction between leaders and the worthy, but subservient, base from which they claim to draw strength.

One of the plural uses of the term (communities), reproduced at the head of this chapter, was made by Nigel Farage, once leader of Britain's right-wing anti-European party UKIP, a substantial proportion of which, post-Referendum, was absorbed into the ranks of the Conservatives. In this case, the notion of community can be read within both its political and linguistic context. Intended as a defence against the accusation that his wing of the Brexit campaign was racist, Farage deployed an argument (exemplifying the rhetorical techniques identified by Atkinson in 1984) that could only reinforce the critique he intended to counter. Instead of the explicit racism associated with the 'old' Right, he used a coded reference to community, declaring that, "we're not against anybody, based on religion or ethnicity … we're for ourselves, we're for our country, we're for our communities" (Westwood 2017).

Here, references to inclusive forms of identity are reminiscent of the typical right-wing riposte to the advocates of ethnic minority justice, misreading their position as a plea for entitlement, so that its own defence of (predominantly white) communities simply 'mirrors' the privileges supposedly sought by other racial groups. This notion of an exclusive, yet mythical ethnic/national group that deserves special treatment or requires robust defence in the face of some insidious threat, is one of the hallmarks of far right politics (Wodak et al. 2013). Farage, who became the target of liberal opprobrium, argued that the populist explosion in the UK and America was actually a "return to nation-state democracy and proper values" (Farage 2017).

COMMUNITY AND THE 2017 UK ELECTION

An awareness of the need to appeal to communities that identify themselves as working class, especially when these groups have been neglected by their traditional representatives, motivated the Conservatives' turn, in 2017, to the 'working poor'. In a newspaper article, the journalist Tim Shipman (2017: 18) cited the opinion of a former Tory minister, who described the party's Election manifesto as evidence that "modernisation [of the Party] will never be complete until we address the central question of class". This refocused effort included, according to one insider, the realisation that "the communities we've got to connect with want to see [immigration] reduced".

The basic change in attitude, however, was evident before the manifesto appeared, and was present in Theresa May's declaration after the Copeland by-election victory that "the Conservative party is going to deliver for everyone across the whole country—a country that works for everyone, not just the privileged few" (Mason 2017). The simple contrast between the many and the few was, of course, no more than the standard appeal of any politician who wished to win more (rather than fewer) votes. A mere twenty days before the Conservative leader uttered this remark, Jeremy Corbyn had called for "an economy based on fairness for all, strategic investment and a government working for the many not just the few" (Labour List 2017). Tony Blair, whose rhetorical tactics are analysed below, had also used this ploy over twenty years before, when he insisted that Britain should be "working in the interests of the many and not the few" (Blair 1996: 298). The force of my argument, therefore, remains the same: that populism is not so much an ideology that is peculiar to demagogues or insurgents, as much as a tool that is available to all organised political groups, including mainstream parties.

Rawnsley (2017: 37, my emphasis), in an analysis of the Conservative General Election campaign of 2017, noted that "community and *social cohesion*" had been a consistent theme of Tory rhetoric. In this instance, cohesion calls to mind both the internal harmony of a homogenous collective and, when uttered by politicians of the Right, the disciplinary impulse that expects citizens to conform to normative standards. The contrast between the various ways in which community was deployed in the manifestos of the main political parties in (2017), offers an insight into the divergent values that underpin particular expressions.

References to community or communities occur no less than forty-seven times in the Conservative party manifesto, and on forty-four occasions in Labour's document (including, in both publications, major headings, but excluding section indices at the bottom of pages). Although there is no scope in this chapter to analyse every contextual variant, echoes of the populist agenda are apparent in Labour's promise that "the next Labour government will rebuild communities ripped apart by globalisation and neglected for years by government" (Labour Party 2017: 11). Here, communities are portrayed as the victims of transnational forces over which they have no control, while Labour offers to reconstruct these undefined collectives. Identifying government as the culprit, however, is a curious notion for a Party that hopes to win an Election and assume power. Again, it seems to chime with the 'populist' stance adopted by the Party.

In comparison, the Tory excerpt (see the beginning of this chapter) places its emphasis on "a strong economy", in *the absence of which* the Party "cannot guarantee our security, our personal prosperity, our public services, or contented and sustainable communities" (Conservative Party 2017: 8). There is a clear distinction between the positions of the two political camps. The Conservative approach refers to a "strong economy" without describing its essential features, but is explicit about the complete dependence of social goods on the existence of economic strength. In other words, there seems to be no absolute *right* to security, the NHS, or a supportive communal life. The notion of sustainability, so often used as a positive reference to a balanced (natural or ecological) way of life, is applied here to communities themselves, suggesting that they are subject to market forces and might in fact become unsustainable and thus no longer viable.

In other passages within the Tory manifesto, some collectives are represented as a potential threat. Where 'divisions' within communities are highlighted, this is not necessarily because they are divided by inequality, but because in some cases they are split "along racial or religious lines" (ibid.: 55). The Conservative's solution to this problem is to "bring forward a new integration strategy" rather than make a direct financial investment. The goal here is to teach people, particularly the young, "about pluralistic, British values and help them to get to know people with [sic] different ways of life" (ibid.). The concept inequality (or inequalities) appears just five times in the Tory document, on one occasion as "inequality of opportunity" (ibid.: 8), on another as part of a list of evils that the Party claims to "abhor" ("social division, injustice, unfairness and inequality") (ibid.: 9), and finally, in two separate places, in a reference to the need to "reduce inequalities between communities across our four nations" by using a "dividend" that will be returned to Britain by the European Union. In Labour's case, again on the few occasions when this term appears, it is embedded within an economic context.

The widespread notion of "left behind" communities, another coded expression that avoids identifying a supposedly discontented 'white working class' as the source of social ills, is employed in the Labour Party Manifesto (2017: 13). The document also refers to the devolution of power to local communities (ibid.: 27), while in addition there is an attempt to present Labour's retreat from a purely *anti-racist* stance, to the more ambiguous defence that communities are 'undercut' by the unscrupulous use by employers of foreign workers. The relevant passage reads, "the current arrangements for housing … are not fair to refugees *or to our communities*" (ibid.: 29, my emphasis). The elastic use of the term community is therefore evident in both manifestos, and in many cases relates directly to attempts not only to echo, but also to soften, some of the populist terminology produced by the right of the political spectrum. This task was made easier because the roots of populism are not only located in the practices of far-right demagogues, but in the standard discourses produced by major political figures who still dominate the outlook of their respective parties. In the Tory case, this is the late Margaret Thatcher. In the Labour camp, much is owed to the still highly vocal Tony Blair.

The Blairite Roots of Populism?

In order to understand the centrist version of populism, it would be useful to look back twenty years, to one of the founding moments of this political tendency. In the run up to the 1997 General Election Tony Blair fashioned a political critique that went beyond specific criticisms of Conservative government policy. He identified a *general social malaise* as the main barrier to national renewal, attacking not just Tory incompetence, but the existence of a retrogressive and debilitating attitude that threatened to stifle the "enormous untapped potential" that he claimed to have witnessed on his travels around the UK (Blair 1996: ix). In one sense, it is hardly surprising that this particular strategy was adopted; insisting on a radical overhaul of public life is an attractive option for 'insurgent' candidates (a notable example is the call for change issued by Obama during his 2008 bid for the White House). The question, however, is which social and political forces Blair saw as an obstacle to his goal of 'modernisation', when he first began to orchestrate New Labour's election campaign.

An essential source for Blair's early outlook is his (1996) book, *New Britain: My Vision of a Young Country*, an uneven compendium of speeches, media statements, and excerpts from interviews, given context by a general Introduction, in which several assertions are sewn together without necessarily observing any logical development. It also contains some peculiar photographs of Blair in various situations—meeting voters and constituents, waiting for a train, conversing with colleagues, eating a suitably ordinary meal like fish and chips, and so on. The volume itself opens by declaring that "this is a book about Britain: its past, its future, and above all its people" (1996: ix). Blair's leading contention is that "we have the potential to create a much better future for ourselves and our children", but only if we "work together with new purpose, new direction and *new leadership*" (1996: ix, my emphasis).

A little further into the book, Blair repeats his reference to this temporal theme, arguing that "we are a country with a great past but too often we seem to live in it rather than learn from it" (1996: x). Students of rhetoric will already have identified the use of two basic techniques known as: the collective we, where the speaker seeks to draw the listener into a shared assumption about some aspect of reality; and contrast and juxtaposition, in which a positive goal is set alongside its undesirable opposite (Atkinson 1984). In the first case an idea is promoted (the greatness of Britain) which no reasonably patriotic citizen is meant to refuse. In the second instance the attractive alternative to nostalgic inertia is supposed to be a willingness to learn from the past.

Once again there is nothing particularly original in the proposition that old ways of thinking should be displaced by fresh ideas, but one particular aspect of this vision is notable. The list of problems assembled by Blair includes references designed to attract attention and mobilise support from more than one political constituency. Topics usually animated by the right of the political spectrum, particularly those related to criminal behaviour, are combined with other material, such as allusions to education, designed to appeal to those on the left. Yet it is the combined effect of the items within this broad litany, which reveals Blair's conception of his mission:

> Children in classes too big for them to learn properly; young people in their twenties who have never had a job; trains vandalised, city centres clogged up, the countryside spoiled; elderly people unable to enjoy their retirement because they live in fear; political institutions so remote that they no longer seem to serve the people but to serve only themselves. (1996: ix)

The concern expressed over education and employment sounds like a standard socialist trope, while the reference to vandalism and old people living in fear draws upon the discourse of law and order. The notion that organisations created to represent the citizen are, in fact, self-serving, is again unremarkable, and there is a fleeting recognition of environmental degradation in the almost petulant remark about "city centres clogged up, the countryside spoiled" (ibid.). One obvious feature of this paragraph is *the absence of any specific social actors* responsible for the production of these unwelcome effects. Just who or what is creating fear, damaging trains, ruining the countryside, forcing children into oversized classes and so on, is unclear. Desire for change, meanwhile, is *attributed* to "people" in general, who "want to be proud of Britain" but "sense that we are losing an old identity without finding a new one", and therefore wish "to keep the best of the past as we move forward" (ibid.).

At some point, however, these ambiguous notions about the relationship between an attractive but vaguely drawn past, a dystopian present and a hopeful future, would have to be turned into concrete policies, and New Labour would be expected to identify those political forces that it was designed to oppose. As Blair moves on from the initial depiction of periodicity, he revisits the economic allusion first touched upon when he mentioned "young people in their twenties who have never had a job" (x). As this crucial theme is revived the concern with youth disappears, and is superseded by a more clearly party-political plea, to the effect that "we cannot afford the costs of mass unemployment and poverty" (ibid.). Although the nature of these costs—monetary losses and/or some form of moral deficit—is unspecified, Blair begins to warm to his subject, and the dim outline of his position begins to emerge from the pink mists of post-socialist rhetoric.

Identifying "social justice" as a theme, Blair defines this as the "extension to all of a stake in a fair society" before contending that it is the natural partner of "economic efficiency" rather than "its enemy" (ibid.). Social justice, in other words, does not appear as a dominant value, within which other aspects of national life must be accommodated, but rather as a way of attacking what Blair *contends* are established attitudes to the economic system. When Blair argues that there is no need to choose between "a less divided society and a more productive economy", but that we must strive to establish the unity of both conditions (ibid.), we find an early clue to New Labour's adoption of a tactic that became a distinctive feature of its political practice—the occupation of a position that would seem contradictory, if only its authors were more explicit about the meaning of the terms employed.[11]

The glaring absence in Blair's testament may seem to be any critique, or even description, of 'capitalist' enterprise as a system of exploitation. There is indeed only one reference in the index of Blair's book to capitalism, but the page in question contains no mention of the term. Instead, there is more neutral talk of capital, in the sense of capital markets. Meanwhile, the wide-ranging but imprecise nature of Blair's agenda is easily explained; although he was engaged in an attack on the Tory administration he wished to displace, an equally urgent task was to counter the more radical social vision offered by the Left within his own Party. To achieve this goal, he needed to establish his credentials as a national leader, energising the electorate without creating a permanent base that might eventually become an autonomous political force.

A "Socially Liberal" Elite?

As noted in detail above, ex-UK Prime Minister Tony Blair was (and is) particularly notable for his attempts to align his brand of political leadership with progressive modernity, offering an apparently compassionate form of centrism as the antidote to "the new populism of left and right which exploits the anger and drives the world apart" (Office of Tony Blair 2016). His version of the left/right problem mentioned above, was that the left was "anti-business", and the right "anti-immigrant", while his real concern was "the convergence between" these creeds, "especially around isolationism and protectionism", which amounted in his opinion to "an essentially closed-minded approach to globalisation and its benefits".

If, however, populism is identified not only by its hostility to free-market economics, but because it cuts across the fault lines of traditional political allegiance, then Blair's own practices could be cited as an example. As Mair (2013: 4) noted, in an analysis of the New Labour era, "Blair [talked of] combining 'dynamic markets' with 'strong communities'", which was "at one level, a simple populist strategy". Philip Gould (1998: 209), once one of Blair's leading advisers, praised him for making "the essential populist point" about the huge distance that was meant to exist between left-wing thought and the beliefs of "ordinary people". It was, Gould wrote, "a point I had been waiting twenty years for a Labour leader to make" (ibid.).

Perhaps more telling was the comparison offered by an academic who, at the very beginning of the twenty-first century, greeted Blair's 'new' politics with enthusiasm. At that time, Melanie Sully (2000) believed that "Europe is unsure whether it is drifting to the left or lurching to the right", but found comfort in the fact that "the smart populism of a Blair or Austria's Jorg Haider cuts across these political fault lines". Haider, of course, was the far-right leader of the fascistic Freedom Party (and later head of another, less successful political initiative). His prominence as a political operator, already in decline after the split in the organisation he founded, was brought to an abrupt end in 2008 by a fatal car crash.

The overt racism associated with fascistic demagogues is obviously anathema to those who (often literally) trade on notions of progressive, 'globalised' modernity. I would argue however that many of the objections voiced against the rise of populism (noted above) were not overly concerned with the moral backwardness of particular communities, but were more troubled by how 'nationalist' discourses might reinforce popular hostility to an economic and social project that represented itself as both egalitarian and cosmopolitan, but which depended, as Lorey (2015: 20) notes, on the imposition of precarity as a mode of governance.

While an attachment to globalisation as an economic principle may require the exploitation of increasingly precarious labour, elements of the transnational capitalist elite may find the cruder forms of (for example) racial prejudice embarrassing and repugnant, since it offends against a quite widespread sense that cultural sophistication should include, at the very least, a basic tolerance of people from diverse backgrounds. This impulse was present, I would argue, in Angela Merkel's 'congratulatory' speech, delivered after Donald Trump's victory in the US elections, in which she drew attention to the notion that "Germany and America are bound by common values—democracy, freedom, as well as respect for the rule of law", adding the pointed reminder that these nations were supposed to value "the dignity of each and every person, regardless of their origin, skin colour, creed, gender, sexual orientation, or political views" (Faiola 2016).

Such utterances also, however, focus on the practical requirements of the Western economy—a multi-national workforce that can provide the highly skilled or highly flexible labour required by capital. A variant of the same discourse was mobilised by George Osborne, former UK Chancellor of the Exchequer, against Theresa May. Osborne, now editor of the *London Evening Standard*, gave an interview in which he claimed that both May and Corbyn were "offering, in very different ways, a retreat from international liberalism and globalisation", before going on to defend "socially liberal, pro-business and pro-free market" policies (Press Association 2017).

If the state has indeed become neo-liberal in this respect, maintaining what I would call transnational economic insecurity as the "basis for capitalist accumulation" (Lorey 2015: 20), while at the same time its centrist adherents call for increased national security as a bulwark against existential threats, then even the most sophisticated political operatives are bound to be caught in a contradictory position and, at those points at which the electorate is called upon to ratify the next period of consensual rule, might suffer the consequences (these visible representatives are meant, however, to act as a lightening rod for discontent, while the management of the system is left to the permanent bureaucracies that ensure continuity between political administrations).[12]

Conclusion: A Populist Elite

Although some authors attribute popular disengagement with politics to systemic deficiencies that could, with effort, be overcome, others argue that it is "the *reality of representative democracy*" that "creates frustration" among certain segments of society (Pelinka, in Wodak et al. 2013: 3, my emphasis). If this is the case, then contemporary democratic cultures may reinforce, rather than alleviate, economic and social inequality. As noted above, in pursuing 'genuine' forms of participation and democracy, some social collectives are able to articulate their opposition to the powers that be through an independent, extra-electoral mechanism, without needing the guidance of 'rogue' politicians—the anti-austerity movements that developed in Arab countries and in Europe, are a case in point.

Meanwhile, the conviction that the mainstream political parties that usually protect the interests of the 'bourgeois elite', have suffered at the hands of populist insurgents, supplies a very practical reason for privileged groups to mount a sustained opposition to the wave of xenophobia that was meant to be sweeping civilised nations. This force seemed to have expended its energy in 2017, albeit temporarily, with the defeat in France of Marine Le Pen at the hands of the cultured yet essentially opportunistic neo-liberal Emmanuel Macron.[13] One of Macron's earliest acts as French President received little publicity, in comparison to the reams of paper and online commentary devoted to his decisive victory over the far right. Macron's intention was to carry out a labour reform, in this case a plan to allow company executives to bypass long-standing agreements with the trade unions, in preparation for a further assault on pension rights and redundancy pay (Sage 2017).

In the face of working-class dissent, and especially in the periods between elections, the rhetorical maintenance of liberal-democratic values is the task of those "public intellectuals" and politicians who support an "assertive free-market society" (Mulholland 2012: 307), and whose role it is to "becalm and mollify ... a restive public" (Mirowski 2013: 336). This 'public' may wish, in Mirowski's opinion, to ameliorate the negative effects of market forces, but are seldom presented with a set of policies that guarantees this outcome, quite beside the fact that electoral contests seem to disempower voters. The consequence of giving a political party a mandate, especially under the first past the post method, is exactly that it cannot be revoked, if and when promises are discarded by an incoming government.

This chapter contends, as noted above, that the use of populist entreaties does not always mark a departure from standard electoral practices, but is often an established procedure found within the repertoire used by bourgeois politicians (see below).[14] Of course, one simple reason for the strength of the antipathy to populist rhetoric is that these individuals identified with, and in some respects were indeed members of, the nebulous elite that had come under attack. My argument is therefore that some of the more powerful groups and individuals responsible for circulating the notion that the populism of both Right and Left were comparable, or even interchangeable, were never really interested in defending the civil liberties of citizens and/or beleaguered migrants, but were actually intervening on behalf of the 'Western' state project and its neo-liberal principles. If this perception is correct, it would mean that certain elements of the transnational European elite were more concerned with Trump's early remarks about the inadequacy of the NATO alliance, his relationship with Putin, his poor judgement in dealing with North Korea, and his withdrawal from the Paris accords, than it was about human rights, the social and economic welfare of women, the fate of ethnic minorities, or the opinions of a disoriented but potentially still dangerous working class.

NOTES

1. See, for example, Gray's "The Iron Law of Oligarchy", *New Statesman*, 18–24 November 2016, 25–28.
2. The concept of rational self-interest is associated with those (mainly psychological) theories that identify personal gain or advantage as the prime factor in motivating social actors, although it is not often that this model of behaviour is presented as the sole explanation for human conduct, since cooperation and mutual support is also beneficial to individuals: see the discussion in De Dreu (2006) written in response to Meglino and Korsgaard (2004).
3. See, for example, Hutton's review of books on Britain's political referendum, published in the *Guardian* on 21 November 2016.
4. Mulholland (2012) argues that, as a result of the "economic restructuring" that took place in the "advanced economies", the lower echelons of the working-class became demoralised, one effect of which is that "this so-called 'underclass' is demonized and even criminalized by respectable society" (307). The automatic attribution of reactionary beliefs to those whose communities had suffered from globalisation, was a notable feature of the coverage dedicated to both the UK referendum and the Trump campaign. For an insight into this phenomenon as it relates to America, see the critical assessment written by Smarsh in the *Guardian* online, published on 13 October 2016, at https://www.theguardian.com/media/2016/oct/13/liberal-media-bias-working-class-americans [accessed 13 May 2017].
5. The designation of transnational capitalist elite refers to the shifting alliance of groups dedicated to perpetuating the dominance of capitalist social relations.
6. For a recent discussion of the perspectives on terrorism aired in the media, see Freedman, 'The Terror News Cycle', in the *London Review of Books Blog*, 24 May 2017.

7. This meme recurred throughout the utterances of leading politicians: in the case of the far right, it was still being used as a headline argument after the Manchester bombing by figures like Paul Nuttall of UKIP, as late as the televised Leaders' Debate of 31 May 2017. The Mayor of London, Sadiq Khan, used the same terms after the London Bridge attack of 3 June 2017.

8. The actions of the murderers, therefore, associate the mechanisms of liberal democratic power with the 'ordinary' life of citizens, reinforcing the belief that the two are coterminous.

9. See, for instance, the remark in the *New Statesman's* editorial of 21–27 April 2017, which described one of the policies of French Presidential candidate Jean-Luc Mélenchon as a "hard Euroscepticism appeal to the *disenchanted*" (my emphasis).

10. The UKIP General Election Broadcast of 1 June 2017 celebrated British tolerance but warned against 'tolerating the intolerance' of Islamist beliefs.

11. Blair's s ruling cabal was later analysed in depth by (among others) Fairclough (2000) in *New Labour, New Language?*, and Steinberg and Johnson (2004) in *Blairism and the War of Persuasion: Labour's Passive Revolution*.

12. One of the problems caused by the Tories' 'U-turn' over social care was the confusion it caused the permanent civil service, which drafts the detailed plans for any incoming government based upon the positions adopted in Party manifestos.

13. See Hussey, in the *New Statesman*, 23 April 2017, 28.

14. I use 'bourgeois' here in the sense employed in Mulholland (2012: 4), where the bourgeoisie is not regarded solely as an industrial class, but as a professional cabal.

References

Atkinson, M. (1984). *Our Masters' Voices: the Language and Body Language of Politics*. London: Psychology Press.

BBC. (2011). "Lucas Papademos named as new Greek prime minister". *BBC News*, 10 November. Available at: http://www.bbc.co.uk/news/world-europe-15671354.

BBC. (2016). "Europe migrant crisis: EU faces 'populist uprising'". *BBC News*, 16 May. Available at: http://www.bbc.co.uk/news/world-europe-36304721.

Biondi, P., and Moody, B. (2011). "New Italian government seen within days". *Reuters*, 10 November. Available at http://www.reuters.com/article/us-italy-idUSTRE7A72NG20111110.

Blair, T. (1996). *New Britain: My Vision of a Young Country.* London: Fourth Estate.

Bremmer, I. (2017). "The wave to come: the forces that made nationalism a crisis in the West will go global". *Time,* 22 May, 19–21.

Calhoun, C.J. (1980). "Community: towards a viable conceptualization for comparative research". *Social History,* 5: 105–129.

Chambers, M., and Nienaber, M. (2016). "Merkel allies warn of Trump effect, poll shows Germans dismayed". *Reuters,* 10 November. Available at: http://uk.reuters.com/article/uk-usa-election-germany-idUKKBN1352GI.

Clark, T. (2017). "Voting out". *Prospect,* February 2017, 18–23.

Conservative Party. (2017). *Forward, Together: our plan for a stronger Britain and a prosperous future.* London: Conservative Party. Available at: https://s3.eu-west-2.amazonaws.com/manifesto2017/Manifesto2017.pdf.

De Dreu, C. (2006). "Rational self-interest and other orientation in organizational behavior: a critical appraisal and extension of Meglino and Korsgaard". *Journal of Applied Psychology,* 91(6): 1245–1252.

Faiola, A. (2016). "Angela Merkel congratulates Donald Trump—kind of". *Washington Post,* 9 November. Available at: https://www.washingtonpost.com/news/worldviews/wp/2016/11/09/angela-merkel-congratulates-donald-trump-kind-of/?utm_term=.5e00c1e72da6.

Fairclough, N. (2000). *New Labour, New Language?* London and New York: Routledge.

Farage, N. (2017). "Donald Trump's Inauguration shows our revolution is in full flow—I can't wait to see where it goes next". *Daily Telegraph,* 20 January. Available at: http://www.telegraph.co.uk/news/2017/01/20/donald-trumps-inauguration-proves-revolution-full-flow-cant/.

Forsyth, J. (2017). "The New Third Way". *The Spectator,* 25 February, 10–12.

Freedman, D. (2017). "The Terror News Cycle". *London Review of Books Blog,* 24 May. Available at: https://www.lrb.co.uk/blog/2017/05/24/des-freedman/the-terror-news-cycle/?utm_source=LRB+blog+email&utm_medium=email&utm_campaign=20170530+blog&utm_content=ukrw_nonsubs.

Gerbaudo, P. (2017). *The Mask and the Flag: populism, citizenism and global protest.* London: Hurst.

Goulard, H. (2016). "Manuel Valls: 'Europe could die'". *Politico,* 17 November. Available at: www.politico.eu/article/manuel-valls-europe-could-die/.

Gould, P. (1998). *The Unfinished Revolution: How the Modernisers Saved the Labour Party.* London: Little, Brown and Co.

Gray, J. (2016). "The Iron Law of Oligarchy". *New Statesman,* 18–24 November, 25–28.

Hussey, A. (2017) "The Decline of the Fifth Republic". *New Statesman,* 23 April. Available at: http://www.newstatesman.com/world/europe/2017/04/decline-fifth-republic.

Hutton, W. (2016). "All Out War; The Brexit Club; The Bad Boys of Brexit review—rollicking referendum recollections". *Guardian*, 21 November. Available at: https://www.theguardian.com/books/2016/nov/21/all-out-war-tim-shipman-the-brexit-club-owen-bennett-bad-boys-of-brexit-arron-banks-review.

Johnston, C. (2017). "Brexit protest: thousands march in London to 'unite for Europe'—as it happened". *Guardian*, 25 March. Available at: https://www.theguardian.com/politics/live/2017/mar/25/brexit-protest-thousands-march-in-london-to-unite-for-europe-live.

Judis, J.B. (2016). *The Populist Explosion: How the Great Recession Transformed American and European Politics*. New York: Columbia Global Reports.

Khomami, N. (2017). "Protests around world show solidarity with Women's March on Washington". *Guardian*, 21 January. Available at: https://www.theguardian.com/us-news/2017/jan/21/protests-around-world-show-solidarity-with-womens-march-on-washington.

Labour List. (2017). "Jeremy Corbyn: This is not North versus South—it is the people versus the establishment". *Labour List*, 4 February. Available at: http://labourlist.org/2017/02/jeremy-corbyn-this-isnt-north-versus-south-its-the-people-versus-the-establishment/.

Labour Party. (2017). *For the Many, Not the Few*. London: Labour Party. Available at: http://www.labour.org.uk/page/-/Images/manifesto-2017/Labour%20Manifesto%202017.pdf.

Lorey, I. (2015). *State of Insecurity: Government of the Precarious*. London and New York: Verso.

Mair, P. (2013). *Ruling The Void: The Hollowing of Western Democracy*. London and New York: Verso.

Mason, R. (2017). "Theresa May: Copeland victory shows Tories are governing for everyone". *Guardian*, 24 February. Available at: https://www.theguardian.com/politics/2017/feb/24/theresa-may-copeland-victory-shows-tories-governing-everyone.

Meglino, B.M., and Korsgaard, A. (2004). "Considering rational self-interest as a disposition: organizational implications of other orientation". *Journal of Applied Psychology*, 89(6): 946–959.

Mirowski, P. (2013). *Never Let a Serious Crisis Go to Waste: How Neoliberalism Survived the Financial Meltdown*. London: Verso.

Mulholland, M. (2012). *Bourgeois Liberty and the Politics of Fear: From Absolutism to Neo-Conservatism*. Oxford: Oxford University Press.

New Statesman. (2017). "Leader: The French National Crisis". *The New Statesman*, 21–27 April, 3.

Office of Tony Blair. (2016). "Tony Blair announcement on new organisation". *The Office of Tony Blair*, 1 December. Available at: http://www.tonyblairoffice.org/news/entry/tony-blair-announcement-on-new-organisation/.

Press Association. (2017). "May and Corbyn offer 'retreat from international liberalism' says Osborne". *Guardian*, 27 May. Available at: https://www.theguardian.com/politics/2017/may/27/theresa-may-jeremy-corbyn-liberalism-george-osborne-evening-standard.

Price, S., and Sanz Sabido, R. (2015). *Contemporary Protest and the Legacy of Dissent*. London: Rowman and Littlefield International.

Price, S., and Sanz Sabido, R. (2016). *Sites of Protest*. London: Rowman and Littlefield International.

Rafiq, H. (2016). "Segregation and social integration in Britain". *The Times*, 7 December. Available at: https://www.thetimes.co.uk/article/segregation-and-social-integration-in-britain-07fzqmgkv.

Rawnsley, A. (2017). "Something old, something new, something stolen, but still blue". *Observer*, 21 May, 37.

Sage, A. (2017). "Macron strikes while unions are on holiday". *The Times*, 27 May, 49.

Shipman, T. (2017). "The class warrior turning May red". *Sunday Times*, 21 May, 18.

Skelton, D. (2011). "Government of the technocrats, by the technocrats, for the technocrats". *New Statesman*, 16 November. Available at: http://www.newstatesman.com/blogs/the-staggers/2011/11/european-greece-technocrats.

Smarsh, S. (2016). "Dangerous idiots: how the liberal media elite failed working-class Americans". *Guardian*, 13 October. Available at: https://www.theguardian.com/media/2016/oct/13/liberal-media-bias-working-class-americans.

Steinberg, D.L., and Johnson, R. (2004). *Blairism and the War of Persuasion: Labour's Passive Revolution*. London: Lawrence and Wishart.

Sully, M.A. (2000). *The New Politics of Tony Blair*. Columbia, New York: Social Science Monographs.

Westwood, S. (2017). "Farage fights racism allegation: 'We're not against anybody'". *Washington Examiner*, 24 February. Available at: www.washingtonexaminer.com/farage-fights-racism-allegationwere-not-against-anybody/article/2615699.

Williams, R. (2017). "The politics of mass democracy has failed. It's time to wake up and work for a humane alternative". *The New Statesman*, 18–24 November, 23.

Wodak, R., KhosraviNik, M., and Mral, B. (eds.). (2013). *Right-wing Populism in Europe*. London and New York: Bloomsbury.

CHAPTER 5

Discursive Colonialism: German Settler Communities, Their Media and Infrastructure in Africa, 1898–1914

Corinna Schäfer

All our obedience and patience with the Germans is of little avail, for each day they shoot someone dead for no reason at all. Hence I appeal to you, my Brother, not to hold aloof from the uprising, but to make your voice heard so that all Africa may take up arms against the Germans. Let us die fighting rather than die as a result of maltreatment, imprisonment or some other form of calamity.[1]

German rule in its African colonies was precarious. Settlers not only felt threatened by local leaders, like the writer of the above letter, Samuel Maharero of the Herero, and its addressee, Hendrik Witbooi of the Nama, both of whom fought a war against the colonists in German Southwest Africa. Settlers often also felt forsaken by their own political leaders. Local newspapers founded by the settlers became an important medium for them to build supportive networks, make their voices heard and bring their colonial projects forward. Settler newspapers depended on infrastructures that enabled their initial establishment, the supply of necessary materials, a sustained inflow of information and

C. Schäfer (✉)
University of Sussex, Brighton, UK
e-mail: c.schafer@sussex.ac.uk

© The Author(s) 2017
R. Sanz Sabido (ed.), *Representing Communities*,
DOI 10.1007/978-3-319-65030-2_5

the distribution of the finished print product. This chapter explores the settler press, both as a site that depended on technologies like printing presses, railways and telegraphs, and as a site of construction and circulation of discourses on infrastructure. It argues that infrastructures also communicated a message on their own, one that could be contested by African communities who were otherwise largely excluded from an active contribution to the discourse of the settlers.

GERMAN COLONIAL IMAGINATION AND AFRICAN REALITIES

Colonial fantasies (Zantop 1997) existed in German culture before the high period of German colonialism (1884–1914). The emerging colonial culture was increasingly imbued with notions of a European supremacy of "culture" and "race" (Zantop 1997; Schubert 2003). When the German *Reich* (Empire) became unified in 1871, colonial enthusiasts argued that Germany needed overseas possessions in order to become equal with other imperial powers (Conrad 2012: 16–17). The many emigrants who left their homes to seek their fortunes abroad were supposed to maintain their Germanness and to found a new *Heimat* (homeland) where German nationalism could thrive (Manz 2014: 11). After its initial reluctance, the German government gave into the pressure from colonial activists and transnational merchant houses, successively declaring, from 1884, various territories in Africa and Asia as German "protectorates" (Zimmerer 2015). The former German colonies in Africa are today largely covered by the states of Namibia, Tanzania, Ruanda, Burundi, Cameroon and Togo.

The belief in a "cultural mission" was, according to Schubert (2003: 368), central to German colonial culture and important for its legitimisation. But when prospective settlers arrived in the new colonies, their supremacist ideas were often challenged by local populations, who defended their land and way of life. Settlers who moved to Africa found themselves outnumbered by Africans who were skilled in trade and warfare, sometimes literate and often aware of the workings of the colonial legal system (see examples in Lau 1995; Beez 2005; Sebald 2013).[2] The two major wars against German colonists, the Herero and Nama War in German Southwest Africa 1904–1907, and the Maji Maji War in German East Africa in 1905, contributed to the settlers' feeling of permanent precariousness, although not many of the victims were actually German. However, many Africans lost their lives at the hands of the Germans, whose short colonial endeavour was characterised by significant brutality. In German Southwest Africa, a genocide was committed by order of General von Trotha, resulting in the death of 80,000 Herero and 20,000 Nama. During the initial attack of the Herero, 123 Germans were killed (Zimmerer 2003: 45; Gründer 2012: 131). Iliffe (1979: 165) estimates that, as a result of the Maji Maji War in German East Africa, up to 200,000 Africans died.

In this context the settlers attempted to do what they called *Kulturarbeit*, meaning 'cultural' as well as 'cultivating' work. While in the wider German colonial discourse *Kulturarbeit* was mostly associated with a so-called cultural or civilising mission, for the settlers in the colonies it predominantly meant the transformation of the land and the people for economic exploitation (see also Zimmermann 2006: 429–436). Conducting this cultural or cultivating work while maintaining their Germanness was a task that depended strongly on the connection of the settlers to other colonists, and with the German homeland. Building networks was therefore essential for carrying out colonial projects.

INTRODUCING SETTLER NEWSPAPERS

These networks rested upon technologies that the colonists introduced into the places they appropriated, which in turn assisted further appropriations. Marvin (1988: 5) has highlighted how the introduction of technologies into a space impacts on the negotiations between its social groups and potentially challenges existing power relations. Following Massey (2005: 9), space is understood here not as given but as constituted through interactions between individuals and the physical space. Space is just as dynamic as time (Massey 2013). German colonists did not merely encounter or conquer the colonial space, but they played their role in creating it. Discourse, as disseminated through settler newspapers, contributed to this. Discourse is constitutive for the social world, as Jäger (2011: 96), drawing on Foucault, has emphasised. Constitutive for the colonial space was also the introduction of technologies like railways and the telegraph as materialisations of discursively created knowledge. Such objectified knowledge is structured by discourse and, at the same time, impacts further on discursive processes (Bührmann and Schneider 2013: 24). Within this dynamic space, the newspapers provided a platform for an exchange about successful methods of appropriation, maintained a connection to the homeland that financed colonial projects, represented the settlers' needs to their governments, defended the exploitation of Africans and fought for the expansion of railway and telegraph networks.

Settler newspapers, a genre distinct from the official gazettes of the colonial governments and from missionary papers that sought to proselytise, did not develop in all the German colonies. The most diverse press landscape existed between 1898 and 1916, with five publications in German Southwest Africa (*Deutsch-Südwestafrikanische Zeitung, Windhuker Nachrichten, Lüderitzbuchter Zeitung, Südwest* and *Keetmanshooper Zeitung*) and three publications in German East Africa (*Deutsch-Ostafrikanische Zeitung, Usambara-Post* and *Deutsch-Ostafrikanische Rundschau*), although the titles of these publications changed several times throughout their lifespans. In their early years, the newspapers focused on providing local news and establishing a platform for the settlers to exchange knowledge. They encouraged their readers to send in reports about their farming experiences and recommended techniques for an environment that was alien to many of them in terms of climate, soils, vegetation and diseases (Schröder 1903). In the advertisement section settlers could learn where to find the necessary equipment, seeds and livestock from local suppliers in the colonies and from larger companies located in Germany (*Windhoeker Anzeiger* 1898; 1899). Through this mechanism, the newspapers supported the appropriation of the colonial space in a very practical sense.

Early on, contributors to settler newspapers discursively linked their cultivating efforts to their 'civilising' ambitions. The *Deutsch-Ostafrikanische Zeitung* proclaimed that settlers needed to "pull the natives out of their natural state of apathy and laziness so they can become hard-working peasants who strive for gains" (1902).[3] In one breath the newspaper constructed the Africans as lazy, and themselves, in contrast, as diligent, while disguising their own for-profit motivation as a humanitarian act. Africans were supposed to cultivate the soil for the Europeans, under conditions that the Europeans dictated. This basic discursive principle regarding the colonial Other, which would fit the settlers' economic needs, persisted in most of the settler newspapers throughout their existence. The representation of Africans only became more derogatory during and after the big colonial wars.

Furthermore, the newspapers supported the building of—to use Anderson's ([1983] 2006) term—an "imagined community" as German language and nationalism were practised through the newspapers. Their circulation ensured that the scattered settlers were aware of the existence of fellow countrymen in the colonies. In this spirit settler newspapers also emphasised the connection to the German homeland. The *Deutsch-Ostafrikanische Zeitung* describes the *Kaisergeburtstag* (Emperor's birthday) on 27 January, for example, as "an important holiday for all in the *Heimat* and abroad who have a true German heart beating in their chest" (*Deutsch-Ostafrikanische Zeitung* 1903). By reporting extensively about the celebrations in the colonies and printing various laudations on the *Kaiser*, the newspapers affirmed the Germanness of the settlers and reinforced their shared national identity with the *Kaiser* and his supporters. Settler newspapers were available in Germany too, so the strong national spirit was also demonstrated to a readership back home (Dresler 1942: 17).

Settler newspapers not only helped to create and practise a collective German identity, they also served as a site to develop a particular settler identity that maintained a difference to the homeland. Lester's observation, regarding the British Empire, that settler newspapers "helped to create new colonial identities within each site of colonization" (Lester 2002: 31), also holds true for the German context. Settlers saw themselves as colonial experts (discussed later) and often contested decisions made by the government. They believed they knew how to develop the colonies much better than the policymakers. In the absence of established political parties, the newspapers represented the demands of the settlers to both the colonial governments and the imperial government in Germany, earning themselves the title of the settlers' "lawyers" (*Windhuker Nachrichten* 1909). The *Deutsch-Ostafrikanische Zeitung* permanently challenged the government of German East Africa. The government did not, according to the newspaper, do enough to support the settlers in their quest to "cultivate" the colony and to subjugate the African population sufficiently (Redeker 1937: 20–21). Settler newspapers put much effort into legitimising the subjugation and exploitation of local populations. The unfolding discourse rested as much on the settlers' economic needs and notions of race as on their anxieties.

THE FEAR OF THE COLONIAL OTHER

Settler newspapers occupied radical supremacist positions that differed, on the one hand, from the more moderate positions represented by the government, and on the other hand, from the approach of missionaries who were active in the colonies. The settler press largely spoke in favour of coercing Africans into employment with Europeans, and defended the use of corporal punishment if they refused to play by the settlers' rules (*Deutsch-Ostafrikanische Zeitung* 1905a; *Deutsch-Südwestafrikanische Zeitung* 1907). They demanded—against the objectives of missionaries and their schools—that Africans should not be educated intellectually, but only trained to become docile labourers. In the newspaper discourse Africans who could read, write and had some command of the German language were constructed as a danger to the settlers because of their enhanced ability to connect with each other and form anti-colonial initiatives. The *Deutsch-Ostafrikanische Zeitung* argued in retrospect of the Maji Maji War:

> In our opinion the Black is culturally in such a low position that he should not be introduced to the blessings of school education yet. ... The black disciple is occupied with studying, singing, gymnastics, drumming and playing the trumpet but does not find the time to do work. But primarily, he does need to be trained to do physical labour. ... When people say that disciples ... have written letters to the people of the interior: Come now, the right moment is here! We take this as proof how easily school education can have disastrous consequences. (*Deutsch-Ostafrikanische Zeitung* 1905b)

On the other side of the continent, the *Windhuker Nachrichten* explained that Christian education would make Africans useless as labourers:

> From experience we know that the native Christians with their undigested and confused ideas of equality and human dignity pose a constant threat to the security of the white population who lives in their midst and they cannot be considered for the economy because they are unwilling to work, thievish and false. (*Windhuker Nachrichten* 1905: 11)

The settler newspapers repeated these arguments frequently. Especially after the major colonial wars Africans were represented as naturally malicious. This representation helped to legitimise their further subjugation, exploitation and—in the case of the Herero and Nama—attempted annihilation. The fear of African intellectual activities that the discourse generated also grasped the colonial governors, even though they tended to promote more moderate policies. But when the governors were

consulted in the process of drafting a specific press law for the colonies—
an initiative that originated from the wish to have better legal protection against the attacks of the settler newspapers—they suggested that
a clause should be added to prevent Africans from publishing anything
that could incite anti-colonial activities (Bundesarchiv Berlin-Lichterfelde
R1001/4696, 1907, 1909). Discursive battles between settler newspapers and colonial governments consequently led to the introduction of
legal measures to prevent Africans from developing their own discursive
strategies. The Colonial Press Law only became fully effective in 1912,
but other measures—like the confiscation of letters between Africans
in Southwest Africa—had been in place since 1904 (Mantei 2007: 36).
Although conversing in writing played an important role, at least for the
leaders of some African nations and societies, none of them used settler
newspapers as a medium to publish their messages. However, Africans
from German colonies did publish in newspapers outside their own colony. Togolese writers, for example, published in the African-led *Gold
Coast Leader* of the adjacent British colony (Sebald 2013: 171), while
Marengo, a guerrilla fighter from the late German Southwest Africa,
gave an interview to a newspaper in South Africa (Hillebrecht 2003:
128). Some also read settler newspapers, the same ones that debated
how best to subjugate Africans (Hillebrecht 2003: 125; Redeker 1937:
114). They also found other ways to interact with newspapers, as an
example from German East Africa demonstrates. One day, the African
typesetters and printers of the *Deutsch-Ostafrikanische Zeitung* abandoned their workplace when a particularly voluminous issue was due to
be printed (Redeker 1937: 44–45). This spontaneous industrial action
reminded the editors of their dependence on their African employees.
In most colonies, it was mainly Africans who kept infrastructure like the
printing presses running. The telegraph and railways also depended on
their labour. At the same time, those technologies were seen as a panacea
by many colonists and, above all, by settler newspapers. Infrastructures
were central to the functioning of the settler press as well as a central
theme in their discourse.

Railways as Colonial Weapon, Buffer and Message

A demand for the construction of railways was present in all the settler newspapers across German colonies in Africa. The *Deutsch-
Ostafrikanische Zeitung* lobbied for this persistently, presenting itself as

an 'expert' on colonial railway issues, and stated that, in its many reports, it had proven the profitability of a new railway for the centre of the colony (1901: 1). Calculations and figures in the articles were supposed to support this claim. At the same time the paper tried to appeal to the heart of their readership back in Germany and was hoping it could convince the reluctant *Reichstag* (German Parliament) to grant money for railway projects. The newspapers even put the expansion of railways at the top of their figurative Christmas wish list, and reminded the "dear motherland" and the "strict stepfather *Reichstag*" of their responsibility towards their "child", German East Africa (ibid., 1900). This was explained, in the first instance, by the practical reason that railways provided access to resources that could be exploited. In times of conflict the survival of settlers and colonial troops depended on those "lines of communication" for their fast deployment of information and soldiers (Brode [1911] 1977: 65, 84, 94). Newspapers could be distributed, along with the mail, faster and more securely in the colonies than prior to the introduction of railway lines. Prior to the construction of the railways from the East African coast to the interior, the mail travelled for 13 weeks, a period that was later reduced to a few days (ibid.: 47). In German Southwest Africa, delivery times of two to six weeks between Windhoek and Swakopmund were reduced to two days (Mantei 2007: 35). However, to fully grasp the meaning of the railways, it is important to understand their status in German and, more generally, in European and American culture at the time.

In the nineteenth century technology was perceived in European cultures as a characteristic of advanced societies and a necessary tool to undertake "civilising missions" (Müller 2016: 118). In Germany the *Kaiser*, an important figure of identification for the settlers, staged himself as an expert on technology and promoted its advancement as a means of expanding German influence into new territories (König 2007: 18–19, 202, 274; Manz 2014: 262). Schivelbusch (1977: 58) observed that by the mid-nineteenth century contemporary literature was comparing railways with projectiles and missiles, associating their availability with the possibility of aggressive conquest. These representations, which persisted until the end of the century, are illustrated in excerpts such as the following quote, which was assigned to Cecil Rhodes and used to introduce an 'expert' book on German colonial railways. The quote described the railways as the ultimate colonial weapon: "in the colonies the railway is cheaper than the cannon and reaches further" (Baltzer 1916: 15).

Railways not only served the fantasy of conquest, but also altered the perception of the landscape. Schivelbusch (1977: 27, 30) pointed out that passengers perceived the railway and the landscape through which it ran as two separate worlds. The outside world was mediated both through the machine itself and through alterations of its immediate environment, by cutting through it or towering over it on a bridge. In the colonial situation, where Europeans often perceived the land as hostile, railways could therefore function as a buffer between the passenger and the environment. Railways transformed the land and, at the same time, allowed the passengers to keep a safe distance when travelling through it.

This double notion of railways as a tool to conquer and to act as a buffer was also present in the settler newspaper discourse. The *Windhuker Nachrichten* printed the report of a railway surveyor who could not wait to blast away the rocks of the hostile Namib Desert to make a cutting for the railway. He describes the "horror" he felt when he rode on horseback through this area for the first time: "nothing but rocks, sand and stone ... all life seems to have died away" (Schulze 1906: 5). A similar sensation was experienced by a passenger who travelled through quite a different landscape on the Usambara Railway in German East Africa:

> The untameable natural force of an unparalleled vegetation swallows all Kulturarbeit in shortest time if man does not perpetually force his will on to nature. The railway is an expression of this mastery, which demonstrates that the civilised man rules and will continue to rule. (Neubauer 1903: 575, cited in van Laak 2004: 125)

The *Kamerun-Post* referred to the example of North America when it stated, full of hope for the effect that railways would have in colonial Africa, that:

> It will not take long and the modern man of culture will feel at home in the interior of the "dark continent" and spend his "holidays" there as is already happening in the formerly feared homeland of the redskins. (*Kamerun-Post* 1912)

The quote of the traveller on the Usambara Railway hints at a third property of the colonial railway—additional to its use as a tool of conquest and as protection from a hostile environment—in that it inscribed a message directly on to the landscape. Once the train had passed and the space was devoid of colonists, the railway lines and accompanying telegraph poles still stood witness: "we took this land with our advanced technology, it is ours now and we are here to stay". The colonists had built countless 'monuments' in the landscape that reminded those who passed by of the supposed German superiority. Railways turned the footprints of the colonists into a permanent form; they tagged the African space as a colonised space.

African Encounters and Interventions

However, as Newell (2013: 37) reminds us, demarcation lines are not drawn quite as easily in reality. In much of the discourse, railways and telegraph were represented as German or European 'civilised' technology. Africans, on the other hand, were regarded as incapable of properly appreciating such technology. Baltzer (1916: 418) stressed that any Africans who were involved in operating the railways needed close supervision. Since most of the simple operations and maintenance works were carried out by African employees, no equipment that would need to be treated gently was supposed to be fitted to the trains. With African employees, "careful and precise treatment cannot be expected", Baltzer (392) stated. The common discourse about Africans, in this case, translated directly into recommendations for how to design the trains. But this also shows that a discourse that labels technology as exclusively European was, and is, misleading, as infrastructures were built, operated and used by Africans and Europeans alike. It was far too expensive to employ only Europeans for these tasks (Brode [1911] 1977: 77), so Africans built the railways and worked at telegraph stations and post offices (Thomas 1942: 55; Arthur Koppel Aktiengesellschaft 1907).[4] Africans sometimes sought such employment as it offered better conditions than, for example, working on an East African plantation (Sunseri 1998: 565). However, some were forced to build the infrastructure. In the case of the Otavi Railway in German Southwest Africa, construction came to a halt when the Herero left their work and joined the war against the Germans in 1904. When the Herero were defeated a few months later and slowly filled the concentration camps from early 1905, they were forced to take up construction work again, under worse conditions than ever. The war had finally enabled the colonists to take advantage of African labour as they pleased. While many prisoners died as a consequence of the harsh working conditions, the Otavi Railway itself was praised as the most cost-effective construction of its kind, thanks to the availability of indentured labourers (Dix 1907: 51; Kreienbaum 2012: 94–96).

Colonisers and the colonised encountered each other and negotiated their relationship through their interaction with colonial infrastructure, whether as users or as operators. Germans were eager to create and reinforce their status as the supposedly superior side, and tried to enforce this with a number of railway regulations. Users and operators were divided according to race and class. Race segregation also became an increasingly important topic for German colonists in other areas, such as, for example, the question of relationships and marriage between Europeans and Africans (Wildenthal 2001: 79). Although there were some exceptions, third class wagons were supposed to be used only by "coloureds" in order to adhere to the given "race differences" (Baltzer 1916: 424–440). Further regulations stated that only Africans could be transported in open freight trains. Servants in the dining cars had to be "coloureds", while those handling the cash needed to be "white" (ibid.). The discourse that constructed Africans as less human than Europeans, representing them as malicious and thievish, manifested itself in laws on colonial infrastructure and in the praxis of their daily use—a praxis that was secured by specific ordinances, further legitimising the exploitation of the colonised. The same railways that altered the perception of the outside space for the passengers also carried an altered space within them through the landscape; a controlled space that would segregate its users and operators according to the racist discourse that was prevalent in settler newspapers and other media. However, stories of resistance also exist, albeit a resistance that was carried on from outside the railway wagon.

Easy targets for African resistance were the telegraph lines that mostly accompanied the railway lines. Some of the destruction caused by African hands was not necessarily meant as sabotage, but was rather because of the usefulness of the cable as material for other goods, like jewellery, as Peglow (1942: 217) reports from Cameroon. In the Herero and Nama War, and during the Maji Maji War, African combatants deliberately cut telegraph lines to destroy their enemy's cable communications, which were vital to coordinate the movement of the colonial troops. Soldiers were deployed to repair and protect telegraph lines, but new destruction frequently occurred. These construction troops also posed a welcome target for the combatants. In German East Africa, the devastation was so severe that it took ten months to repair the lines after the Maji Maji War had ended (Kunz 1905: 12–13; Thilo 1942: 266–267). Settler newspapers in both German East Africa and German Southwest Africa covered the destruction of the cables, and also reported on the dangers posed by their maintenance (*Deutsch-Ostafrikanische Zeitung* 1905c; *Windhuker Nachrichten* 1907). But the real shock came to the colonists in German Southwest Africa with the destruction of railway lines and the blowing up of a railway bridge by the Herero. Bridgman (1981: 77) states that the cutting of the telegraph line in Swakopmund isolated the entire colony from communicating with the outside world. The Swakopmund station usually connected the colony to other parts of the world via a submarine cable in Walvis Bay, which also provided the settler press with the latest news (Mantei 2007: 107–108). Major Kunz (1905: 16) pointed out that the attacks on this infrastructure attested to the Herero's good "strategic understanding", and the *Deutsch-Südwestafrikanische Zeitung* commented on a telegram that reported on the destruction: "so the situation is serious, much more serious than we had guessed yesterday. We did not think that the Herero would proceed with such a vigorous strategy" (*Deutsch-Südwestafrikanische Zeitung* 1904: 1). It cannot be determined if infrastructures were targeted for purely strategic reasons or for their highly symbolic meaning, but in the same way that the railways were leaving a message in the landscape—probably unintended by its engineers—this message was now being contested in the course of warfare. The African message read: "This is our land, and we are taking it back".

CONCLUSION

Settler newspapers and their related infrastructures reflect the tensions and contradictions of the wider German colonial situation. Settlers were dependent on a positive relationship with the German homeland, but at the same time challenged the colonial policymakers, demanding a radically supremacist and exploitative approach to colonial projects. Through discourse the settlers constructed their economic objectives as a cultural mission while trying to prevent any intellectual activity and networking of Africans. Newspapers, railways and the telegraph were used by the colonists as tools to expand their appropriation of the land and to protect themselves against the African majority, which was a cause of anxiety for them. The importance that infrastructures had for the settlers spawned an intensive discourse that fed into wider public demand for their construction in the colonies. Yet, to operate these tools of appropriation the settlers needed African labour to keep them running, just as with other economic and political aspects of the German colonial project. This opened up new possibilities of intervention for Africans. Railways and the telegraph inscribed a message on the landscape that could be contested. While these infrastructures enhanced the speed and safety of transport and communication in the colonies, the effect and symbolism of their sabotage was a strong one. Africans built, operated and used railways and the telegraph, but also had a certain power to destroy them.

Not many stories of such resistance have survived in the records, as it was not in the colonists' interests to record incidents that would contradict their discursively constructed image about the inferior colonial Other. Neither did the settlers report stories in their newspapers that would have countered their narrative of a colonialism that was supposedly beneficial to the colonised. Settler newspapers, quick to complain about Africans, swept the thousands of dead bodies caused by German colonialism under the discursive carpet. Hardly any articles can be found that mention the concentration camps in German Southwest Africa or the many thousand deaths in the wake of the Maji Maji War in German East Africa. The number of stories from that time that are lost forever because their subjects have been written out of history will never be known. Discourse produces knowledge, but discourse also produces forgetting. Discursive colonialism shaped colonial space in the past, and to a certain degree it still shapes the perception of that space today.

NOTES

1. Letter of Samuel Maharero to Hendrik Witbooi that was intercepted and never reached its destination, around 20/01/1904. In: Dierks (1999–2005).
2. The broad term African is used in this chapter to refer to several societies or nations at once, or where the settler press uses the term "natives" without specifying which group of people they are referring to. Where possible, I use terms that are closer to the self-definition of the people in question.
3. All quotes from the settler newspapers are the chapter author's translation.
4. See, for example, the photographs in the coffee table book about the Otavi Railway (Arthur Koppel Aktiengesellschaft 1907).

REFERENCES

Anderson, B. ([1983] 2006). *Imagined Communities. Reflections on the Origin and Spread of Nationalism.* London: Verso.

Arthur Koppel Aktiengesellschaft. (1907). *Zur Erinnerung an den Bau der Otavibahn 1903–1906.* Berlin: Arthur Koppel Aktiengesellschaft.

Baltzer, F. (1916). *Kolonialbahnen mit besonderer Berücksichtigung Afrikas.* Berlin: G. J. Göschen'sche Verlagshandlung.

Beez, J. (2005). "Karawanen und Kurzspeere. Die vorkoloniale Zeit im heutigen Südtansania". In: Becker, F. and Beez, J. (Eds.) *Der Maji-Maji-Krieg in Deutsch-Ostafrika 1905–1907*, 17–27. Berlin: Ch. Links.

Bridgman, J. (1981). *The Revolt of the Hereros.* Berkeley: University of California Press.

Brode, H. ([1911] 1977). *British and German East Africa. Their Economic and Commercial Relations.* New York: Arno Press.

Bührmann, A.D. and Schneider, W. (2013). "Vom 'discursive turn' zum 'dispositive turn'? Folgerungen, Herausforderungen und Perspektiven für die Forschungspraxis". In: Wengler, J.H., Hoffarth, B. and Kumiega, L. (Eds.) *Verortungen des Dispositiv-Begriffs*, 21–36. Wiesbaden: VS.

Bundesarchiv Berlin-Lichterfelde R1001/4696. (1907). Governor of German East Africa to the Colonial Department of the Foreign Office Berlin, 21 April, 31.

Bundesarchiv Berlin-Lichterfelde R1001/4696. (1909). Governor of Togo to the Colonial Department of the Foreign Office Berlin, 9 December, 103.

Conrad, S. (2012). *German Colonialism. A Short History.* Cambridge: Cambridge University Press.

Deutsch-Ostafrikanische Zeitung. (1900). "Der Weihnachtswunsch Deutsch-Ostafrikas". *Deutsch-Ostafrikanische Zeitung*, 22 December, 1.

Deutsch-Ostafrikanische Zeitung. (1901). "Die Entscheidung naht". *Deutsch-Ostafrikanische Zeitung*, 23 February, 1–2.

Deutsch-Ostafrikanische Zeitung. (1902). "Zur Hebung der Eingeborenen-Kulturen". *Deutsch-Ostafrikanische Zeitung*, 18 January, 1.

Deutsch-Ostafrikanische Zeitung. (1903). "Zum Geburtstag unseres Kaisers". *Deutsch-Ostafrikanische Zeitung*, 24 January, 1.

Deutsch-Ostafrikanische Zeitung. (1905a). "Regulierung und Verschärfung der Prügelstrafe". *Deutsch-Ostafrikanische Zeitung*, 8 July, 1.

Deutsch-Ostafrikanische Zeitung. (1905b). "Beruhigendes und Aufklärendes zur Aufstandsfrage". *Deutsch-Ostafrikanische Zeitung*, 23 September, 1.

Deutsch-Ostafrikanische Zeitung. (1905c). "Telegraphenleitung Morogoro-Kilossa wieder betriebsfähig". *Deutsch-Ostafrikanische Zeitung*, 11 November, 2.

Deutsch-Südwestafrikanische Zeitung. (1904). "Mobilmachung". *Deutsch-Südwestafrikanische Zeitung*, 19 January, 1–2.

Deutsch-Südwestafrikanische Zeitung. (1907). "Mehr Rassegefühl". *Deutsch-Südwestafrikanische Zeitung*, 14 December, 5.

Dierks, K. (1999–2005). *Chronology of Namibian History*. Accessed 23 November 2016. http://www.klausdierks.com/Chronology/61.htm.

Dix, A. (1907). *Afrikanische Verkehrspolitik*. Berlin: Hermann Paetel.

Dresler, A. (1942). *Die deutschen Kolonien und die Presse*. Würzburg: Konrad Triltsch.

Gründer, H. (2012). *Geschichte der deutschen Kolonien*. Paderborn: Schöningh.

Hillebrecht, W. (2003). "Die Nama und der Krieg im Süden". In: Zimmerer, J. and Zeller, J. (Eds.) *Völkermord in Deutsch-Südwestafrika. Der Kolonialkrieg (1904–1908) in Namibia und seine Folgen*, 121–134. Berlin: Ch. Links.

Iliffe, J. (1979). *A Modern History of Tanganyika*. Cambridge: Cambridge University Press.

Jäger, S. (2011). "Diskurs und Wissen. Theoretische und methodische Aspekte einer Kritischen Diskurs- und Dispositivanalyse". In: Keller, R., Hirseland, A., Schneider, W. and Viehöver, W. (Eds.) *Handbuch Sozialwissenschaftlicher Diskursanalyse. Band 1: Theorien und Methoden*, 81–112. Wiesbaden: VS.

Kamerun-Post. (1912). "Eisenbahndurchquerungen Afrikas". *Kamerun-Post*, 9 November, 1.

König, W. (2007). *Wilhelm II und die Moderne. Der Kaiser und die technisch-industrielle Welt*. Paderborn: Ferdinand Schöningh.

Kreienbaum, J. (2012). "Guerrilla wars and colonial concentration camps. The exceptional case of German South West Africa (1904–1908)". *Journal of Namibian Studies*, 11, 83–101.

Kunz, H. (1905). *Die kriegerischen Ereignisse in den deutschen Kolonien im Jahre 1904*. Berlin: Ernst Siegfried Mittler und Sohn.

Lau, B. (Ed.) (1995). *The Hendrik Witbooi Papers*. Windhoek: National Archives of Namibia.

Lester, A. (2002). "British Settler Discourse and the Circuits of Empire". *History Workshop Journal*, 54, 24–48.

Mantei, S. (2007). *Von der "Sandbüchse" zum Post- und Telegraphenland. Der Aufbau des Kommunikationsnetzwerks in Deutsch-Südwestafrika (1884–1915)*. Windhoek: Namibia Wissenschaftliche Gesellschaft.

Manz, S. (2014). *Constructing a German Diaspora. The "Greater German Empire", 1871–1914*. New York: Taylor & Francis.

Marvin, C. (1988). *When Old Technologies Were New. Thinking About Electric Communication in the Late Nineteenth Century*. New York: Oxford University Press.

Massey, D. (2005). *For Space*. London: Sage.

Massey, D. (2013). "Doreen Massey on Space". *Social Science Bites*, 1 February. Available at: http://www.socialsciencespace.com/2013/02/podcastdoreen-massey-on-space/.

Müller, S. (2016). *Wiring the World. The Social and Cultural Creation of Global Telegraph Networks*. New York: Columbia University Press.

Neubauer, P. (1903). "Die Usambarabahn in Deutsch-Ostafrika". *Velhagen und Klasings Monatshefte*, 17(11): 575–582.

Newell, S. (2013). *The Power to Name. A History of Anonymity in Colonial West Africa*. Athens, OH: Ohio University Press.

Peglow, D. (1942). "Kamerun". In: Schmidt, W. and Werner, H. (Eds.) *Geschichte der Deutschen Post in den Kolonien und im Auslande*, 179–240. Leipzig: Konkordia-Verlag Reinhold Rudolph.

Redeker, D. (1937). *Die Geschichte der Tagespresse Deutsch-Ostafrikas: 1899–1916*. Berlin: Triltsch & Huther.

Schivelbusch, W. (1977). *The Railway Journey. Trains and Travel in the 19th Century*. Oxford: Blackwell.

Schröder, R. (1903). "Stimmen aus dem Publikum". *Landwirtschaftliche Beilage zur Deutsch-Südwestafrikanischen Zeitung*, 1 January, 3.

Schubert, M. (2003). *Der schwarze Fremde. Das Bild des Schwarzafrikaners in der parlamentarischen und publizistischen Kolonialdiskussion in Deutschland von den 1870er bis in die 1930er Jahre*. Stuttgart: Franz Steiner.

Schulze. (1906). "Zwischen Lüderitzbucht und Kubub". *Windhuker Nachrichten*, 1 November, 5–6.

Sebald, P. (2013). *Die deutsche Kolonie Togo 1884–1814. Auswirkungen einer Fremdherrschaft*. Berlin: Ch. Links.

Sunseri, T. (1998). 'Dispersing the Fields': Railway Labor and Rural Change in Early Colonial Tanzania. *Canadian Journal of African Studies*, 32(3), 558–583.

Thilo, D. (1942). "Deutsch-Ostafrika". In: Schmidt, W. and Werner, H. (Eds.) *Geschichte der Deutschen Post in den Kolonien und im Auslande*, 241–292. Leipzig: Konkordia-Verlag Reinhold Rudolph.

Thomas, E. (1942). "Deutsch-Südwestafrika". In: Schmidt, W. and Werner, H. (Eds.) *Geschichte der Deutschen Post in den Kolonien und im Auslande*, 24–107. Leipzig: Konkordia-Verlag Reinhold Rudolph.

van Laak, D. (2004) *Imperiale Infrastruktur. Deutsche Planungen für eine Erschließung Afrikas 1880 bis 1960*. Paderborn: Schöningh.

Wildenthal, L. (2001). *German Women for Empire, 1884–1945*. Durham: Duke University Press.

Windhoeker Anzeiger. (1898). [no title] *Windhoeker Anzeiger*, 10 November, 4.

Windhoeker Anzeiger. (1899). Stahlwindmotor 'Herkules', *Windhoeker Anzeiger*, 2 March, 5–6.

Windhuker Nachrichten. (1905). "Vortrag des Herrn Erdmann-Haris", *Windhuker Nachrichten*, 15 June, 5–12.

Windhuker Nachrichten. (1907). "Die Nachrichtenübermittlung in Südwestafrika", *Windhuker Nachrichten*, 12 September, 6.

Windhuker Nachrichten. (1909). "Die Pressefreiheit in den deutschen Kolonien", *Windhuker Nachrichten*, 17 March, 2–3.

Zantop, S. (1997). *Colonial Fantasies. Conquest, Family, and Nation in Precolonial Germany, 1770–1870*. Durham: Duke University Press.

Zimmerer, J. (2003). "Krieg, KZ und Völkermord in Südwestafrika. Der erste deutsche Genozid". In: Zimmerer, J. and Zeller, J. (Eds.) *Völkermord in Deutsch-Südwestafrika. Der Kolonialkrieg (1904–1908) in Namibia und seine Folgen*, 45–63. Berlin: Ch. Links.

Zimmerer, J. (2015). "Bismarck und der Kolonialismus". *Bundeszentrale für politische Bildung*, 20 March. Available at: http://www.bpb.de/apuz/202989/bismarck-und-der-kolonialismus?p=all.

Zimmermann, A. (2006). 'What do you really want in German East Africa, *Herr Professor?*' Counterinsurgency and the Science Effect in Colonial Tanzania. *Comparative Studies in Society and History*, 48(2), 419–461.

PART II

Representing Communities, Perpetuating Inequality

Legitimising Political Homophobia: Sexual Minorities and Russian Television News

Anna Khlusova

INTRODUCTION

Since March 2012, when the St. Petersburg Duma adopted a legislation that prohibited "homosexual propaganda" to minors, Russia has witnessed the rise of moral anxiety, with the LGBTQ community portrayed as threatening the country's traditional values. The passing of the St. Petersburg Law accelerated the process of demonising sexual minorities, subsequently paving the way for a federal bill banning the "propaganda of non-traditional sexual relations to minors", which the Russian Duma adopted in June 2013 (Article 19 Legal Analysis 2013). The legislation enjoyed an overwhelming backing from the population, with 88% of Russians supporting the ban (Levada-Center 2013).

Certainly, the adoption of the, so-called, anti-homopropaganda bill (Wilkinson 2013a) must be perceived as closely tied to the media, as the law initially targets media content and the alleged widespread queer visibility. More importantly, as argued in this chapter, the Russian mainstream media campaign to discredit and alienate sexual minorities

A. Khlusova (✉)
King's College London, London, UK
e-mail: anna.khlusova@kcl.ac.uk

© The Author(s) 2017
R. Sanz Sabido (ed.), *Representing Communities*,
DOI 10.1007/978-3-319-65030-2_6

has become a central feature of the increasingly intolerant and populist regime of moral regulation. Yet, the significance of national mass media in the stimulation of moral panic over LGBTQ people remains a largely understudied area.

This chapter seeks to fill this gap and, in this way, contribute to the debate about the reasons behind such popular support for anti-gay policies in contemporary Russia. It focuses specifically on the role of national television news in the mobilisation of homophobic narratives, for Russian television is still regarded as the primary way in which to reach and sway the majority of the population (Zassoursky 2009: 31). The fundamental question that is driving the discussion here is: how does television news discourse about homosexuality reproduce the negative stigma attached to LGBTQ people, justifying the political discrimination against this minority group?

To answer this question, this chapter builds upon the Critical Discourse Analysis (CDA) of 58 news reports covering the subject of homosexuality that were broadcast on the flagship national news programmes *Vesti* (Rossiya) and *Vremya* (Channel One) during 2013. It argues that sexual minorities are discursively constructed as stigmatised social subjects through scapegoating and negative stereotyping, establishing homosexuality as a threat to Russian national values as an Orthodox Christian and non-Western civilisation. Fuelled by patriotic feelings and a wide range of societal anxieties, this discursive manipulation frames the political contempt towards homosexuality not as a violation of LGBTQ human rights, but as an issue of morality and protection of Russia, its sovereign values and traditions. In fact, it legitimises the state's rhetoric, presenting the Kremlin's policies of moral vigilantism as the only suitable measure.

This discussion contributes to existing studies on homophobia in Russia (Essig 1999; Kon 1999, 2009; Wilkinson 2013a, b; Laruelle 2014), the significance of media as a deviance-defining tool (Kielwasser and Wolf 1991; Gross 1994, 2001; van Dijk 2015) and the debates surrounding the current Russian mass media environment (Lipman 2005; Dunn 2009; Beumers et al. 2009). The chapter ultimately aims to examine the role of Russian news media in the maintenance of social inequality based on sexual orientation.

THE LOGIC OF MORAL SOVEREIGNTY: MAPPING POLITICAL HOMOPHOBIA IN RUSSIA

In the light of the recent adoption of the so-called anti-gay legislation, LGBTQ people's right to equality in Russia has been largely undermined. Yet, Russian officials have sought to explain, in domestic and international fora, that the laws are non-discriminative to sexual minorities, but offer the most appropriate solution to the tensions that arise between the maintenance of the heterosexual family according to traditional Russian values, on the one hand, and the need to recognise LGBTQ rights, on the other (Wilkinson 2013b: 5). The short briefing note that introduces the bill states that "family, motherhood and childhood in their traditional understanding inherited from the ancestors" are values that require "special protection by the state" (Article 19 Legal Analysis 2013). Accordingly, Yelena Mizulina, co-author of the bill and head of the Committee on Women, Children and Families, explains:

> The aim of our bill is not to ban non-traditional sexual relations but to limit their propaganda when it is directed at children [...] LGBT people are trying to travel a long way immediately, to force everyone to like them immediately. (Mizulina 2013, my translation)

Conversely, critics of the anti-homopropaganda law have asserted that the implicit logic the Kremlin follows is, in fact, the logic of moral regulation, or what Wilkinson calls the logic of "prohibiting the sin, not the sinner" (2013a: 2). Being lesbian, gay, bisexual, transgender or queer is thus not a crime, as long as LGBTQ people adhere to societal norms in public (Wilkinson 2013a: 2). In addition to remaining highly problematic on a practical level, acceptance of such a proposition not only disregards human rights norms, but also the government's responsibility to protect them. Effectively, this regulation peddles tradition as a basis for the recognition of human rights norms, rather than admitting to their universality based on non-discrimination. Within this frame, the right to freedom of expression is denied to sexual minorities, and then framed as an issue of preserving the country's moral sovereignty, which is allegedly threatened by LGBTQ people and the liberal values foisted on Russian culture from outside (Kon 2009; Wilkinson 2013a).

The equation of homosexuality with Western values has been evident throughout the history of Russia's governing of sexual deviance (Essig 1999; Baer 2009; Kon 2009). Essig (1999: 6–7) writes that within the heteronormative ideology of communism, a "pervert" could never be a patriot; homosexuality, along with other non-procreative forms of sexual desire, was perceived as an indication of capitalist systems, a vestige of the destructive, corruptive influence of a bourgeois mentality. Under the Soviets homosexuality was indeed a crime not just against 'nature' but also against society, an aggressively anti-Soviet gesture and a "Western vice"

(Essig 1999; Kon 2009). The post-Soviet legalisation of homosexuality in 1993 brought same-sex desire out into the open, frustrating the conservatives and all those who felt betrayed by the democratic and market reforms of the 1990s (Kon 1999, 2009). In turn, this provided a fertile ground for the stimulation of a moral panic that blamed homosexuality for the societal crisis born out of a declining population, high abortion rates, child neglect and abuse, which, according to state officials, have infiltrated Russia (Chandler 2014). Yet again, homosexuality has played a symbolic part in establishing Russia's oppositional relation to Western modernity, leading to troubling consequences for the LGBTQ community.

Even prior to the introduction of anti-gay regulations, being public about one's homosexuality in Russia was an exception rather than the norm (Wilkinson 2013a: 6). The advent of the law, however, marked the state's desire to actively politicise homosexuality and to silence sexual minorities. In practice, it sets a dangerous precedent for the refusal of citizenship rights to any group that disobeys 'public morals', while also stimulating the use of a subjective moral judgement to suppress dissent of any kind. With the majority of Russians supporting the government's position on the matter and the resulting increase in violence against sexual minorities (LGBT Network 2013), it is vital to examine how the anti-homosexual narrative is perpetuated by the mass media, and how it resonates with wider social anxieties and historical discourses about homosexuality in Russia. For media stigmatisation has had, and will continue to have, tangible consequences and a human cost.

MEDIATED VISIBILITY AND MINORITY GROUPS

The media play a major role in the process of social definition, since it is in and through representations that we get "the broadest common background of assumptions about what things are, how they work and why" (Kielwasser and Wolf 1991: 25). Gross (2001: 36) writes that the mass media are especially powerful in constructing the meanings that are assigned to minority groups, which the majority of viewers have little opportunity to know first-hand. Considering that LGBTQ people do not possess significant material or political power bases, achieving visibility in the mainstream media is perceived to be crucial for their recognition (Kielwasser and Wolf 1991).

Still, attaining mediated visibility does not guarantee one's inclusion in the community. Quite the contrary, much of the research demonstrates that, generally, sexual minorities' positions and interests, when not symbolically annihilated, are discredited by means of scapegoating and negative stereotyping in order to maintain the existing heteronormative system (Fejes and Petrich 1993; Gross 1994, 2001). Quasthoff (1989), who analyses the news reporting of minorities, explains that stereotypes take on the form of rational judgement, exploiting simplification or generalisation to justify and maintain social inequality. Exposing stereotyping as signifying practice is central to this discussion since, according to Hall (1997: 257), this practice essentialises, naturalises and sustains social difference through deploying a strategy of 'splitting', in which the normal and acceptable is divided from the abnormal and unacceptable. The manner in which this strategy is employed usually replicates the biases and interests of the elites who define the public agenda to sustain prejudices against minority groups that present a threat to the status quo (Shoemaker 1987: 353). On a similar note, Critcher (2003: 131) stresses that "modern moral panics are unthinkable without the media", and claims that support from the public is not necessary, as the media "neither reflect nor create public opinion, they construct it" (137).

NATIONAL TELEVISION IN PUTIN'S RUSSIA

The criticism of the media as an integral tool for the 'deviance-defining elite' is essential when analysing how homophobic attitudes are constructed and perpetuated by Russian television news, particularly since media autonomy has been significantly undermined by Vladimir Putin's regime. Between 2001 and 2003 a series of procedures that were described by Fedotov (2006, cited in Beumers et al. 2009: 44) as the "means of legal compulsion", led to the monopolisation of the main national channels, while smaller channels, owned by private companies, were forced to avoid current affairs altogether.

Against this backdrop, the predominant assessment of contemporary Russian television—at least, as far as political communication is concerned—is extremely pessimistic (Becker 2004). The Russian government is perceived to have enforced a "neo-authoritarian media system" (Becker 2004: 147–150), where the obsession with control is a coherent strategy and the coverage of political topics is determined by informal guidelines passed down from the president's supporting staff (Dunn 2009; Lipman 2005). Indeed, the significance of television as an ideological tool for influencing public opinion seems to be a consistent notion in Russian political rhetoric, as indicated in an article by Dunn (2009: 48), when he states that "the mass media in Russia is more than the mass media. Especially television". As the largest media sector by far national television remains the main source of information about Russia and the outside world for the vast majority of the Russian population (Zassoursky 2009: 31). This is not to say that there are no alternative media spaces available, or other realities, stories and images that challenge the mainstream representations. It is, however, the mainstream story and elite-driven project of stigmatisation that is under scrutiny here. Thus, the following investigation takes an overt moral stance intended to expose and ultimately resist social inequality based on sexual identity, by examining Russian television news discourse that is both discriminatory and dangerous.

METHODOLOGY

The aims of this project justify the relevance of CDA as its methodological framework, for CDA is fundamentally "interested in the way discourse (re)produces social domination, that is, the power abuse of one group over others" (van Dijk 2015: 63). Within this paradigm, reality is understood as constructed by means of discourse, which is, in turn, shaped by several social forces. Language use, discourse, visual and verbal interaction belong to the micro-level of the analysis. Power, domination and inequality between social groups are typically terms that belong to a macro level of social order (van Dijk 2001: 355). The aim of CDA is to bridge the gap between micro and macro approaches to show how discourse is implicated in relations of power to produce and reproduce inequality (van Dijk 2001: 356).

Guided by the CDA framework, the following section classifies the micro-level discursive practices of the flagship national newscasts *Vesti* (Rossiya) and *Vremya* (Channel One), identifying the key tropes or themes that emerge in their portrayals and locating them in the context of wider socio-political and historical discourses about homosexuality in Russia.[1] This enables a critical analysis of how the political condemnation of homosexuality is legitimised in Russian television news and presented as common sense. In this case, Rossiya and Channel One are an obvious choice for the investigation considering both channels are state-owned and are Russia's most viewed and most influential news broadcasters (Khvostunova 2013).

Discursive Manipulation in Action: Key Tropes in Discussions of Homosexuality in Russian Television News

Considering the restrictions enforced upon national television in Putin's Russia, it is only natural that Channel One and Rossiya's news discourses replicate the government's perspective. Indeed, within micro-level instances of *Vremya* and *Vesti*'s discussions about sexual minorities, one can detect twin discourses on Russian national identity and homosexuality, whereby the latter is epitomised as a threat to the continuation of the former, stabilising the identity and the connotations attributed to the ethno-national discourse. This is not to suggest that homosexuality is described as the only threat to the Russian nation, but that it is positioned in a chain of equivalence with other arguments to establish same-sex desire as an Other to the Russian nation. The following examination reveals the key tropes that emerge in *Vremya* and *Vesti*'s discussions on homosexuality, each contributing in their own ways to its construction as the antithesis of Russian national identity. These tropes, however, have no clear-cut boundaries, but overlap on several levels.

'Corruption of Children' and 'Corruption of Traditional Family Values'

The first trope in *Vesti*'s and *Vremya*'s discussions on homosexuality is the notion of corruption of children. Their reports are saturated with verbal and visual negative portrayals that constitute same-sex desire as necessarily damaging the country's children, describing sexual minorities as sick, perverse, unnatural, irreligious, promiscuous, symbolically linked to paedophilia, or connoted in other ways as posing a threat to the nation's youth.

Indeed, out of the 58 reports under review, eleven focus the discussion on paedophilia, with five more referring to cruelty against children and four reporting on sexual assaults. Interestingly, only three out of the eleven news reports that mention paedophilia refer directly to a paedophilic act, with the remaining eight reports arbitrarily mentioning the term paedophile when discussing the subject of homosexuality. Within these reports, the terms paedophile and pervert are repeatedly collocated alongside the terms gay and homosexual, including phrases such as "homosexual-paedophile ... homosexual pervert" (*Vesti* 2013e) and "gay perverts" (*Vremya* 2013e). Consequently, the concepts of perversion and paedophilia are never far from the viewer's consciousness. Some examples include statements such as "Russian orphans have always attracted foreign homosexual perverts" (*Vesti* 2013e), "Our children were always available for all sorts of perverts that came to Russia" (*Vremya* 2013e) and "If we accept that [homosexuality], we can as easily accept polygamy, incest, paedophilia … We are assisting perverts!" (*Vesti* 2013b).

Connecting the discourse about childhood with notions of homosexual 'perversion' and 'immorality' provides those in positions of power with a discursive justification to validate a moral intervention on behalf of minors, thereby helping to frame the policies as necessary to protect children. As Critcher (2003: 155) points out, moral panics are irresistible when they are offered as threats to children. In the modern world, the notion of childhood is symbolically linked with social order (ibid.: 154). What happens to minors, or what they do, tells us what type of society we have become and are becoming: "'the child' has become a way of speaking about the society as a whole" (Jenks 1996: 130). Thereby, any attack on what the child is, or rather, what the child has developed into, "threatens to rock the social base" (ibid.: 131). Furthermore, specifically within the context of the contemporary demographic crisis, discussions about childhood in Russia have become particularly invested with an increasing sense of anxiety and panic (Chandler 2014). Presenting children as the victims of homosexual desire is an effective method of persuasion and stigmatisation, as it finds points of resonance with a wide range of public fears, from the moral degeneration of the nation's youth to the decrease in birth rates and the annihilation of traditional family values.

Indeed, the trope that is twinned with 'corruption of children' in *Vremya* and *Vesti*'s homosexual discourses is that of the 'corruption of traditional family values'. Russian post-communist traditionalism explicitly elaborates on the idea of the nation-as-family, establishing clear public and private roles for men and women, with the heterosexuality of the nation taken for granted (Kon 2009: 46). Indeed, the belief that the traditional (heterosexual) family is under threat constitutes a central narrative in the recent rhetoric of anti-homopropaganda laws.

Among the most striking lexical choices made by both *Vremya* and *Vesti*'s reports is that they distinctly describe LGBTQ people as the opposite of tradition by constantly referring to homosexuality as "non-standard sexual orientation" (*Vesti* 2013c), "non-traditional sexuality" (e.g. *Vremya* 2013d) or "deviation from the norm" (*Vesti* 2013h). This type of wording clearly sets up a symbolic boundary between the 'normal' and the 'deviant', the 'natural' and the 'pathological', the 'traditional' and the 'non-traditional' and, consequently, what is accepted and what is not.

Furthermore, the news reports under analysis are saturated with value-laden visual signs that stimulate the misrepresentation of homosexuals as immoral, perverse and promiscuous. News pictures are heavily encoded and constructed according to recognisable conventions, with much of the reviewed footage employing conventional representations of homosexuals as provocatively dressed and overly sexualised subjects (see Figs. 6.1 and 6.2), placed in spaces that typically connote promiscuity, such as nightclubs, bars and festivals. Certainly, these stereotypical images are not meant to document but rather to trigger the myth of LGBTQ promiscuity, and to centralise the concept of homosexuality around sexual desires.

These visual signs, impregnated with implicit allusions to the promiscuity of gays and lesbians, are usually employed to accompany the negative connotations of linguistic signs in voice-overs. For example, in *Vesti*'s

Fig. 6.1 Still from *Vesti* [TV news report] (Rossiya 1, 26 August 2013)

Fig. 6.2 Still from *Vesti* [TV news report] (Rossiya 1, 26 May 2013)

report on François Hollande's decision to legalise same-sex marriage in France, the verbal track "obviously, children are not important for the majority of homosexuals" (*Vesti* 2013h) is accompanied by the footage of men, presumably gay men, dancing provocatively in a nightclub (see Figs. 6.3 and 6.4). The same visual footage was used in several more of *Vesti*'s reports to accompany verbal tracks such as "700,000 people in Russia are officially recognised to be HIV positive. 65% of them are actually homosexuals" (*Vesti* 2013f) and "It will become illegal for France to adopt our children which, in the light of recent gay-marriage, is understandable" (*Vesti* 2013d). The overall connotative meaning of the visual material is therefore clear; sexualisation renders the homosexual subject as a one-dimensional being, entirely consumed by a sinful sexual desire and thus opposed to procreation, Christianity and family values.

By repeatedly succumbing to prejudiced media narratives that discredit same-sex relationships as abnormal, unnatural, non-procreational, hedonistic and untraditional, *Vremya* and *Vesti* set in motion a deviance

Fig. 6.3 Still from *Vesti* [TV news reports] (Rossiya 1, 29 May 2013; 26 August 2013; 25 November 2013)

amplification spiral through which homosexual subjects are signified as sources of moral threat and social degeneration, legitimising the relevance of traditionalist claims.

'MILITANT MINORITY'

In many ways, the underlying idea behind the abovementioned discussions is that sexual minorities are forcefully imposing their 'unnatural' values on society to corrupt and undermine 'natural' heterosexual values. Thus, another important trope in the overall anti-homosexual narrative is the representation of sexual minorities as a small, yet militant and powerful group that foists its values and lifestyle upon the majority. Therefore, the anti-gay laws are presented as a defence of this majority's rights.

The symbolic exclusion of sexual minorities from the Russian heterosexual norm is strengthened by clear verbal divisions between us and them, and between protagonists and antagonists, as revealed in the use

Fig. 6.4 Still from *Vesti* [TV news reports] (Rossiya 1, 29 May 2013; 26 August 2013; 25 November 2013)

of pronouns in expressions such as "our values" (e.g. *Vesti* 2013c), "we" (e.g. *Vremya* 2013d), "our country" (e.g. *Vremya* 2013d), and "our children" (e.g. *Vremya* 2013e) as opposed to "their values" (*Vesti* 2013d), "they" (e.g. *Vesti* 2013d) and "with them" (e.g. *Vremya* 2013c). The choice of pronouns suggests that the queer discourse of the television news has clear and stable addressees of Russian citizens (us), who are being told about the outsiders, the deviant social species (them). Within this argumentation, the political and popular condemnation of homosexuality in Russia is described not as being homophobic or discriminative, but as a natural and normal reaction aimed at the protection of 'our' values: "it is not homophobic, but is a natural desire to remain man and woman for *your* country, father and mother to *your* children" (*Vesti* 2013h) and "in *our* country it is very important to protect those values that are key for *our* society" (*Vremya* 2013c). Furthermore, when reporting on homosexuality or homosexuals, adjectives that denote aggressiveness and violence are frequently appropriated. *Vesti*'s choice of terminology is particularly troubling, with several news reports referring to homosexuals as the "boorish totalitarian minority ... aggressive Russian gays ... militant gays and lesbians" (*Vesti* 2013c) and "aggressive minority" (*Vesti* 2013d). *Vremya* generally tends to be subtler in its descriptions, yet there are several instances when LGBTQ activists are referred to as "angry crowd of gays and lesbians" (*Vremya* 2013c), and as a "scandalous movement" (*Vremya* 2013a).

CHAIN OF EQUIVALENCE: HOMOSEXUALITY = SOCIAL PATHOLOGIES = WESTERN VICE

Homosexuality is not the only element in Channel One's and Rossiya's news reports that is constructed as a moral threat to the nation. Yet, it is one of the key elements that are effectively classified together in a chain of correspondence that seeks to create a frontier between the desired conceptualisations of the Self and the Other. The use of a chain of correspondence can be clearly recognised in the identification of homosexuality with a number of social pathologies, such as prostitution, tobacco addiction, alcoholism and suicide. In this respect, four news broadcasts mention the increase in tobacco addiction alongside reports on recent anti-homopropaganda legislation. For example, *Vesti*'s news report from 25 January is framed by the headline "Duma on tobacco and gays. Prohibit all!" (2013a), presenting homosexuality and tobacco addiction as harmful desires that must be monitored by the government for the protection of the country's welfare.

Another noteworthy example that demonstrates this logic is *Vesti*'s report on the international criticism of Russian anti-gay laws. The verbal commentary states,

> If the US Secretary of State proclaims that gay rights are human rights, we can understand the spread of pornography, drug addiction and prostitution as Western human rights' achievements. They demolish and destroy traditions. For example, there is no such concept as a homosexual couple, we need to create it. Church condemns sodomy? So we need to stop it. [...] They can leave these values to themselves. (*Vesti* 2013d)

There is nothing that pornography, drug addiction, Western human rights, prostitution and homosexuality share, other than being defined here as threats to Russian national values and to the desired conceptualisation of Russian morality. Moreover, it is clear that, in this chain of equivalence, "these values" are equated with homosexual values, which in turn are associated with liberal Western values. The implication here is that there is a sharp contrast between Russia and the West, and that the notion of gay and lesbian rights is highly incompatible with the Russian nation, its politics and history.

The desire to disdain the LGBTQ minority by linking it to the notions of diseases, perversion and social pathologies is not exclusive to Russian television discourse, as scholarship on (mis)representations of homosexuality in the Western mass media reveals similar traits (Gross 1994, 2001; Fejes and Petrich 1993; Moritz 1994). Yet, what is unique to Russian television news is the salient dichotomy in its recognition of homosexuality not only as an illness and a social degeneration, but also as a fashionable socio-cultural trait inflicted by the West. Indeed, Russian news discourse identifies two categories of homosexuals. The first category is constituted by 'genuine' gays and lesbians, who are often seen to want to be reverted to the 'correct' and 'natural' heterosexual norm, as in the statement "Many homosexuals want to return to normal life, become heterosexual, like 95–99% of our citizens" (*Vesti* 2013g). These homosexuals can therefore be tolerated. By contrast, the second category includes those homosexuals who are following imported trends, and are therefore metaphorically represented as traitors to the Russian nation. In the news reports that cover the protests against the recent anti-gay legislation, LGBTQ activists are described in the verbal track as following "fashionable European tolerance" (*Vremya* 2013c); whereas, homosexuality is narrated as "becoming public and fashionable" (*Vesti* 2013d) and "constantly receiving support from the [Western] mass media" (*Vesti* 2013d).

As discussed in the previous section, the construction of the notion of homosexuality as a Western vice first appeared in Russia during the Soviet period. Yet, in the light of post-communist transitions and the resurgence of the Russian Orthodox Church, the relevance of this assembly of meaning has been renewed and continues to have a powerful impact on the position of sexual minority groups. According to Baranovsky (2000: 451), a residual 'superpower' complex and the frustration of its inability to modernise the country along with some foreign models, resulted in Russia's instinctive impulse to depart from Western ideologies, and to re-establish itself as a special player 'not-like-the-others'. Since Russia cannot proclaim its economic or political superiority as a nation-state, it attempts to establish its unique international position through claims of moral superiority (Laruelle 2014: 2).

The attitudes expressed in *Vremya*'s and *Vesti*'s reports reassert the Kremlin's attempts to promote its own voice of moral conservatism, instilling the 'Russian Idea' by leading opposition to Western human rights norms in general and LGBTQ rights in particular. Out of the 58 news items in the dataset, 37 broadcasts refer to events occurring outside Russia, with the majority of reports focusing on public protests against the implementation of certain liberal policies in Europe. The discursive elements of these reports aim to denounce the hypocrisy of most Western elites, who favour more liberal values than the majority of their citizens. In this context, the discourse of Russian morality is disseminated through statements such as "Hyper-liberal Western values turned out to be unacceptable not only for Russia—but for pro-western Georgia. [...] And generally, it just looks as if in Europe entirely everyone is for the bright same-sex future" (*Vesti* 2013d); "Socialist France is so fascinated by the topic [of same-sex marriages] that it has forgotten about the economy and everything else [...] This is the price of crazy priorities. Not everyone agrees with them there" (*Vesti* 2013c); and "Experts generally agree that the fight for traditional values [in Europe] is probably already lost" (*Vremya* 2013b).

By repeatedly stressing the harmful effects of liberal policies on European society and its values, television news media advances a narrative in which Russia embodies the 'traditional' values that the West has lost. The legitimacy of anti-homopropaganda legislation is thereby justified by the necessity to maintain Russian moral sovereignty.

THE ULTIMATE 'OTHER'

The interpretation of homosexuality through the prism of 'Russianness' and 'Otherness' allows Channel One's and Rossiya's news discourses to define normality in terms of Russian national identity, Orthodox Christianity and heterosexuality, as well as its countertype, which encompasses secularism, Western liberal values, homosexuality and LGBTQ rights. This binary opposition is shaped throughout the narrative and is evident in transitivity patterns and in lexical and semiotic choices. Homosexual discourse is constructed under the themes of 'corruption of children and family values', 'militant minority', 'Western vice' and, as such, as a 'moral' or 'national threat', while the image of the state is

positively enhanced as the righteous opposite. Within the CDA framework the positive representation of the Self is perceived to be as important as the construction of deviance in the meaning-making processes of
stigmatising discourses (van Dijk 2015: 73). Thus, *Vesti*'s and *Vremya*'s
news coverage must be understood to be as much about the representation of the Russian government and its interventionist agencies, as it
is about homosexuals themselves. The positive image of the state is tied
to, and reinforced through, the themes of 'protection of family values',
'protection of children' and 'guardians of the national identity', which
are implicitly and explicitly communicated in the verbal and visual tracks.
The portrayal of government officials in general, and of Vladimir Putin
in particular, as agents who are carrying out figurative and material
actions aimed at the protection of societal values, traditions and parent-
hood, includes statements such as "saved the child from foreign gays"
(*Vesti* 2013e), "protecting citizen's rights and interests" (*Vremya* 2013c),
"politicians will take additional measures to protect these [traditional
family] values" (*Vesti* 2013d, e) and "Russia should be able to identify,
expose and punish perverts, protecting children" (*Vesti* 2013e).

By appealing to the patriotic feelings of the Russian population,
Vremya's and *Vesti*'s reports constitute the political condemnation of
homosexuality as shorthand for the protection of the national identity
and moral values, reaffirming the Kremlin's homophobic rhetoric of
moral intervention, and positioning the viewers as consenting subjects.
Consequently, through this discursive manipulation, the news broadcasts
manufacture an ideological consensus about the hierarchy of sexuality,
the inferiority of homosexuals and the righteousness of political discrimination against sexual minorities, to which the Russian population is pre-
disposed to surrender while enjoying the alienation from the Other.

Conclusions

In a context characterised by the Kremlin's turn to moral conservatism,
the recent enactment of anti-homopropaganda legislation and the subsequent spate of discrimination against sexual minorities, the issue of homophobia in Russia has gained a new level of significance. To acquire a
more nuanced understanding of Russian hostility towards homosexuality
this chapter has addressed the problem by investigating the connection
between Russian news broadcasts—Channel One's *Vremya* and Rossiya's
Vesti—and prejudice against the LGBTQ community.

The analysis of these news reports has shown that discourses about homosexuality in Russian television news media can and must be identified as nothing less than homophobic propaganda aimed at perpetuating heteronormative attitudes and legitimising political discrimination against LGBTQ minority groups. Indeed, the analysis of discursive practices employed by *Vesti*'s and *Vremya*'s reports reveals the unmistakable contempt that is expressed against non-heteronormative sexualities. By capitalising on wider societal fears, gays and lesbians are: defined as abnormal, unnatural and untraditional; verbally and visually connoted as aggressive, perverse and degenerate; symbolically represented as a moral threat to family and children; and otherwise discredited as an Other by means of negative and rigid stereotypes. Additionally, queer sexuality, which is seen as a direct effect of Western influence, is narrated as inherently alien to Russia.

This stereotypical portrayal of homosexuality acts as the signifying practice that constructs the symbolic frontier between 'us' and 'them', between 'normalcy' and 'deviance' and, as such, naturalises homosexuality as the negation of Russian national identity, 'othering' it as a means to fix a desired conceptualisation of Russian morality. It is through this symbolic division that Channel One's and Rossiya's news discourses disguise heteronormative logic as common sense, creating a collective consciousness of homosexual inferiority that helps to maintain the status quo of the existing gender system and justifies the need for anti-gay legislation.

The exposed affinity between the attitudes expressed in the news broadcasts and the political rhetoric of the Russian government confirms that *Vesti*'s and *Vremya*'s discussions about the LGBTQ community must be understood as the direct mediation of the state's ideology, and the discursive mobilisation of the political homophobic project.

NOTE

1. All the translations are provided by the author.

REFERENCES

Article 19 Legal Analysis (2013). "Russia: Federal laws introducing ban of propaganda of non-traditional sexual relationships". *Article 19*, 27 June. Available at https://www.article19.org/resources.php/resource/37129/en/russia:-federal-laws-introducing-ban-of-propaganda-of-non-traditional-sexual-relationships.

Baer, J. (2009). *Other Russias: Homosexuality and the Crisis of Post-Soviet Identity*. New York: Palgrave Macmillan.

Baranovsky, V. (2000). "Russia: A Part of Europe or Apart from Europe?" *International Affairs*, 76(3): 443–458.

Becker, J. (2004). "Lessons from Russia: A neo-authoritarian media system". *European Journal of Communication*, 19(2): 139–163.

Beumers, B., Hutchings, S.C. and Rulyova, N. (eds.) (2009). *The Post-Soviet Russian Media: Conflicting Signals*. New York, Routledge.

Chandler, A. (2014). *Democracy, Gender, and Social Policy in Russia: A Wayward Society*. Basingstoke: Palgrave Macmillan.

Critcher, C. (2003). *Moral Panics and the Media*. Milton Keynes: Open University Press.

Dunn, J.A. (2009). "Where did it all go wrong? Russian television in the Putin era". In: Beumers, B., Hutchings, S. and Rulyova, N. (eds.) (2009). *The Post-Soviet Russian Media: Conflicting Signals*, 42–56. New York: Routledge.

Essig, L. (1999). *Queer in Russia: A Story of Sex, Self, and the Other*. London: Duke University Press.

Fejes, F. and Petrich, K. (1993). "Invisibility, homophobia, and heterosexism: Lesbians, gay men and the media". *Critical Studies in Mass Communication*, 10(4): 396–422.

Gross, L. (1994). "What is wrong with this picture? Lesbian women and gay men on television". In: Ringer, R. (ed.) *Queer words, queer images: Communication and the construction of homosexuality*, 143–156. New York: New York University.

Gross, L. (2001). *Up From Invisibility: Lesbians, Gay Men, and the Media in America*. New York: Columbia University.

Hall, S. (1997). *Representation: Cultural Representations and Signifying Practices*. London: Sage.

Jenks, C. (1996). *Childhood*. New York: Routledge.

Khvostunova, O. (2013). "A Brief History of the Russian Media". *The Interpreter*, 6 December. Available at http://www.interpretermag.com/a-brief-history-of-the-russian-media/.

Kielwasser, A.P. and Wolf, M.A. (eds.) (1991). *Gay People, Sex, and the Media*. London: Harrington Park Press.

Kon, I.S. (1999). "Sexuality and politics in Russia (1700–2000)". In: Eder, F.X., Hall, L.A. and Hekma, G. (eds.) *Sexual cultures in Europe. National Histories*, 197–218. Manchester: Manchester University Press.

Kon, I.S. (2009). "Homophobia as a Litmus Test of Russian Democracy". *Sociological Research*, 48(2): 43–64.

Laruelle, M. (2014). "Beyond Anti-Westernism: The Kremlin's Narrative about Russia's European Identity and Mission". *Ponars Eurasia Policy Memo*, 2(326): 1–6.

Levada-Center (2013). "The fear of the other. The problem of homophobia in Russia". *Levada-Center Public Opinion Poll*, 15–18 January. Available at http://www.levada.ru/12-03-2013/strakh-drugogo-problema-gomofobii-v-rossii.

Lipman, M. (2005). "Constrained or Irrelevant: The Media in Putin's Russia". *Current History*, 104(684): 319–324.

Mizulina, Y. (2013). "Propaganda, not gays, annoys people. Interview by Ekaterina Vinokurova". *GazetaRu*, 10 June. Available at http://www.gazeta.ru/politics/2013/06/10_a_5375845.shtml.

Moritz, M.J. (1994). "Old strategies for new texts. How American television is creating and treating lesbian characters". In: Ringer, R.J. (ed.) *Queer words, queer images: Communication and construction of homosexuality*, 122–142. New York: New York University Press.

LGBT Network (2013). "Violation of rights and discrimination against LGBT people in Russia". *Russian LGBT Network*, September 2012–August 2013. Available at http://lgbtnet.ru/ru/content/narusheniya-prav-i-diskriminaciya-lgbt-v-rossii-sentyabr-2012-avgust-2013-gg.

Quasthoff, U. (1989). "Social Prejudice as a Resource of Power: Towards the Functional Ambivalence of Stereotypes". In: Wodak, R. (ed.) *Language, Power and Ideology: Studies in Political Discourse*, 181–196. Amsterdam: John Benjamin Publishing Company.

Shoemaker, P. (1987). "The communication of deviance". In: Dervin, B. (ed.) *Progress in communication science*, 151–175. Norwood, NJ: Ablex.

van Dijk, T.A. (2001). "Critical Discourse Analysis". In: Tannen, D., Schiffrin, D., and Hamilton, H. (eds.) *Handbook of Discourse Analysis*, 352–371. Oxford: Blackwell.

van Dijk, T.A. (2015). "Critical Discourse Studies: A Sociocognitive Approach". In: Wodak, R. and Meyer, M. (eds.) *Methods of Critical Discourse Analysis*, 63–85. Third Edition. London: Sage.

Vesti (2013a). "Duma o tabake i geyakh: vse zapretit". Rossiya *24*, 25 January. Available at http://www.vesti.ru/doc.html?id=1115136#.

Vesti (2013b). "Gei i lesbiyanki vstanut v ochered' za det'mi". Rossiya *1*, 15 February. Available at http://www.vesti.ru/doc.html?id=1034783&cid=9.

Vesti (2013c). "V Den' materi frantsuzy potrebovali zapretit' gey-braki". Rossiya *1*, 26 May. Available at http://www.vesti.ru/doc.html?id=1088329#.

Vesti (2013d). "Duma rassmotrit vo vtorom chtenii zakon o zaprete propagandy gomoseksualizma". Rossiya *1*, 29 May. Available at http://www.vesti.ru/doc.html?id=1089490.

Vesti (2013e). "Astakhov spas rossiyskogo rebenka ot inostrannykh geyev". Rossiya *24*, 1 July. Available at http://www.vesti.ru/doc.html?id=1099969#.

Vesti (2013f). "Gosduma mozhet vvesti pozhiznennyy zapret na donorstvo dlya geyev". Rossiya *1*, 26 August. Available at http://www.vesti.ru/doc. html?id=1122212.

Vesti (2013g). "Gomoseksualistam mogut zapretit' byt' donorami". Rossiya *24*, 26 August. Available at http://www.vesti.ru/doc.html?id=1121969.

Vesti (2013h). "Seksual'nyye opyty starushki-Yevropy". Rossiya *1*, 25 November. Available at http://www.vesti.ru/doc.html?id=968389.

Vremya (2013a). "V Parizhe sotni tysyach demonstrantov protestovali protiv usynovleniya detey odnopolymi sem'yami". Channel One, 14 January. Available at http://www.1tv.ru/news/world/223912.

Vremya (2013b). "Frantsuzskaya politsiya razognala uchastnikov aktsii protesta protiv odnopolykh brakov slezotochivym gazom". Channel One, 25 March. Available at http://www.1tv.ru/news/world/229187.

Vremya (2013c). "Obnazhennyye feministki i demonstratsii geyev stali fonom vizita Vladimira Putina v Niderlandy". Channel One, 14 April. Available at http://www.1tv.ru/news/polit/230800.

Vremya (2013d). "GD prinyala zakon o shtrafah za propagandu netradizionnih seksualnih otnoshenii sredi detei". Channel One, 11 June. Available at http://www.1tv.ru/news/polit/235026.

Vremya (2013e). "Nad mal'chikom, rozhdennym surrogatnoy mater'yu-rossiyankoy, izdevalis' izvrashchentsy iz raznykh stran". Channel One, 1 July. Available at http://www.1tv.ru/news/world/236434.

Wilkinson, C. (2013a). "Putting traditional values into practice: Russia's anti-gay laws". *Russian Analytical Digest*, 5(138): 5–7.

Wilkinson, C. (2013b). "Russia's anti-gay laws: the politics and consequences of a moral panic". *Disorder of Things*, 3(4): 1–11.

Zassoursky, I. (2009). "Free to get rich and fool around". In: Beumers, B., Hutchings, S.C. and Rulyova, N. (eds.) *The Post-Soviet Russian Media: Conflicting Signals*, 29–42. New York: Routledge.

CHAPTER 7

Interrogating Representations and Misrepresentations of Violence: The Contested Identities of Generation 1.5 Somalis in Melbourne

Elizabeth Lakey

INTRODUCTION

Muslim communities across the globe are no strangers to hyperbolic representation. In particular, Somalis have often been characterised as violent in the media. Many reasons have been given to justify this characterisation, from the harsh environment of Somalia to, perhaps most importantly, the strong clan system.

Most Somalis aged between 18 and 30 living in Melbourne were born either in Somalia or en route to another country. These Generation 1.5ers are described as being "caught in the middle" of two cultures. Initially the term Generation 1.5 was used by Rumbaut and Ima in the 1980s to describe immigrant youth who were not born in the United States. However, since Rumbaut and Ima's initial use of the label, educators and

E. Lakey (✉)
Graduate School of Humanities and Social Sciences, University of Melbourne, Parkville, Australia
e-mail: elizabeth.lakey@unimelb.edu.au

© The Author(s) 2017
R. Sanz Sabido (ed.), *Representing Communities*,
DOI 10.1007/978-3-319-65030-2_7

117

researchers have used the name in varying ways (see Frodesen 2002). Generation 1.5 comprises individuals born in one country and taken by their migrating parents to another country, where they settle with their family. They often have close ties to the culture and country of their birth, which means that they occupy a unique position; they straddle cultures, and can offer deep insights into both their birth and adopted countries. This chapter investigates the portrayal of young Somali Australians as violent in both the academic literature and the popular media, and takes into account their own reflections on this misrepresentation.

All the data presented in this chapter pertains to reflections on violence by Generation 1.5 gathered from in-depth interviews conducted between 2012 and 2014 with 24 Somalis living in Melbourne, aged between 18 and 30 years old. In addition, focus groups, discussions and interviews were held with 15 community members, including parents, young people, professionals and older people.

Interrogating Representations and Misrepresentations of Violence

There is no doubt that the dominant representation of Somalia has been that of an unusually violent and anarchic place. It is depicted as a bloody and dangerous nation, even by scholars who are traditionally seen as sympathetic to Somali interests. Lewis, for example, describes the Somali expansion northwards, up to the nineteenth century, as dominant in the history of the Horn of Africa. This migration was accomplished at great cost to other resident populations, involving "considerable displacements of other populations, and the Somali sphere was only extended by dint of continuous war and bloodshed" (Lewis 2002: 19).

The media perform a central role in shaping the way society as a whole sees different groups. This can influence attitudes towards these groups, affect their civil rights and even influence government policy towards them (Happer and Philo 2013; David 2009). This, in turn, may affect the relationship between individual members of those groups and wider society (Cottle 2004). Other authors have noted the tendency of media coverage to position ethnic minorities as problematic others to a white, normative self (Shohat and Stam 1994). In March 2009 the Australian Human Rights Commission released a report regarding African Australians' experiences of rights and access to key services. One finding of this paper concerned media debates focusing on "the numbers, 'integration potential' and settlement needs of African Australians". According to the report, the Australian media "usually focuses on crime or on political commentary about African Australians—and has often been negative or critical, and sometimes misleading" (Australian Human Rights Commission 2009: 7). The following examples relate to violence that has been ascribed to Somalis in Australia, which illustrate the argument that Australian Somalis have been misrepresented through the use of false or misleading statistics.

Writing in the *Sunday Herald Sun* in 2008, journalist Liam Houlihan claimed that in the twelve months since June 2006, 283 Somali-born people committed a crime. Using 2006 census population data, this equates to roughly one in every nine Somalis. His article provoked a public outcry, and much attention was directed to "ethnic crime" in the following days. However, as Media Watch pointed out two weeks later, the journalist made a serious mistake in his reading of the crime results released by Victoria Police. He counted the number of offences committed by members of the Somali-born population, rather than the distinct number of offenders. If a Somali-born person was alleged to have committed three offences, in his reading of the statistics, this counted as three separate offenders. Using the statistics correctly, we can see that only 115 alleged offenders were Somali-born: that is, one in every 23 Somalis (Media Watch 2008). While still greater than the number of Australian-born offenders (one in every 31), this statistic is significantly closer to it than the one originally reported by Houlihan (2008).

In 2012 there was widespread anger from the African community when Victoria Police released ethnic crime statistics. These purported to show that Sudanese and Somali-born Victorians were about five times more likely to commit a crime than other Victorians: "The police statistics show the rate of offending among the Sudanese community is 7109.1 per 100,000, while for Somali people it is 6141.8 per 100,000. The figure for the wider community is 1301.0 per 100,000" (Oakes 2012). At a forum organised by African youth representatives and attended by members of Victoria Police, the youth challenged the decision to release the statistics and argued that they were "incomplete" (Reech 2012).

The 2013/2014 crime statistics released by Victoria Police show that the crime rate per 100,000 population was 7489.5 (Victoria Police 2014: 4). This is, in fact, higher than the rates of crime attributed to Sudanese and Somali-born Victorians in 2012. It is not known how the police arrived at the 2012 statistics, although their official release states that all the data originates from the LEAP database (ibid.).

Young Muslims have been increasingly represented in the media as having the potential to become radicalised. One highly charged area of concern in Australia is the risk of young people becoming attracted to the ideology of the Islamic State (ISIS). In April 2015 a Somali-born Australian was killed while fighting for ISIS. Sharky Jama had been a successful model for over two years, and was well liked and respected within the Melbourne Somali community when he decided to travel to Syria (Schliebs 2015). His death was reported in the context of growing numbers of Jihadis leaving Australia to fight in Syria and other places. However, relatively few media outlets followed the story or reported on the response from within the Somali community in Melbourne. Sharky's father, Dada Jama, said he would speak out with the Somali community and pass on the message to "look after their kids" (ABC News 2015). Community leaders have spoken about forming groups against extremism within the Somali community in Melbourne and have urged the government to scrutinise closely the plans of any Australians travelling to areas where ISIS is known to operate (ibid.).

A 2015 report released by the Lowy Institute states that the previous Abbott government's "troubled relations" with Australian Muslim communities hampered efforts to prevent radicalisation, and that the significant numbers of Australians fighting in Iraq and Syria represent "a serious national security threat" (Zammit 2015: 2, 16). The same report points out that the surge in the number of Australians joining Al Shabaab, following the Ethiopian invasion of Somalia in 2006, dissipated "following the disruption of a support network in Melbourne and Al Shabaab's dramatically reduced popularity in the Somali diaspora" (ibid.: 8). The prominence of the perceived threat of radicalisation in Australia is not supported by the Lowy Institute's findings.

The increased media attention on radicalisation and those 'at risk' of being radicalised is not confined to Australia. For example, Travis Dixon and Charlotte Dixon have documented the way that terrorism was reported extensively over the last decade in America. Using the UCLA Communication Studies Digital News Archive, he sampled 146 cable and network news programmes that aired between 2008 and 2012 to find that Muslims were reported as "terrorists" more often than other groups of people who committed similar offences (Dixon and Williams 2015).

FINDINGS: REFLECTIONS ON VIOLENCE BY GENERATION 1.5

This section focuses on the reflections from Somali interview participants on the perception and representations of the Somali community as
violent. These examples reflect their lived experience. For instance, the
following quote is a reconstruction of a conversation with a young man
who did not want to be recorded:

Elizabeth: What can you tell me about violence in the Somali community in Melbourne?

X: I don't want to talk about this issue, because it gets taken
out of context and looks very bad for us, for my community.

Elizabeth: Can you explain a bit more what you mean?

X: I don't want to say anything about it because, even if we do
have some violence problems in our people in Melbourne,
I don't think it's right to focus on that. Every group of
people has some problems, even if they're rich and white.
I think that when we talk about it all the time we are making
sure that that's the thing that people remember about us.

The conversation continued in a similar vein for a few minutes, with a
gentle probing into why this young man did not want to engage with
the issue of violence in the Somali community. He said that he believes
there is violence in every group of people because "there are good and
bad people everywhere". Conscious that the questions were causing him
distress, the conversation turned to other topics. His sense of unease was
very strong, providing a clear indication that this constitutes a significant
personal issue for some young Somalis.

Relations with Law Enforcement Officers

There is a significant body of work that deals with youth and police relations, particularly ethnic minority youth. Some studies have suggested
that minority youth have a more troubled relationship with police and
tend to report more personal negative experiences with police officers (Brunson and Weitzer 2009). It has also been well documented that
police have a tendency to mistrust young black males (Piliavin and Briar
1964; Black and Reiss 1970; Hurst et al. 2000). More recent scholarly

work has been devoted to examining the complex ways in which citizens manage their behaviour towards the police. In particular, Weitzer and Brunson (2009) uncovered the contours of male youth's strategic responses to the police in an inner-city neighbourhood with high crime rates in the United States. Discussing minority male relationships with the police, Robin Engel suggests that the wider the gap between the social backgrounds of the police officers and the minority youths, the more likely it is for mutual displays of disrespect to emerge. Engel states that "it is possible that particular types of citizens (e.g. young minority males) may act in disrespectful or otherwise resistant ways to symbolise their perceptions of injustice" (Engel 2003: 477). One young man explained that the police expect Somalis to be criminals, so there is no point telling them otherwise:

X: They're always on the look out for us, especially if we're in a group of friends together. Sometimes I wonder if we should do something bad just to see what happens. I know they're going to question us anyway, so maybe we should make it worth the hassle?

The conversation continued for some time in an attempt to unpack the statement "I know they're going to question us anyway, so maybe we should make it worth the hassle". This young man believed that he would be targeted because of his ethnicity and that this would probably result in negative consequences for him, regardless of his innocence or guilt. He said that he was sometimes tempted to "play up" to this increased police attention because then, at least, he would "deserve" this attention. However, his friends had always talked him out of such behaviour, warning that the result would be damaging for him and his family.

The idea that young Somalis are unfairly targeted by the police was very common among the respondents:

Bashir: There is always, always, always someone from our community in trouble with the police. It's obvious it's because we are Somali.

Bilan: It's still hard because, we're not trained to trust the police, you know? The boys expect bad things will happen if they go there, and sometimes I think that's probably true.

When pressed about what she meant by "not trained to trust the police", Bilan explained that law enforcement was something to be feared in

Somalia, and that many parents of young people had a visible attitude of mistrust.

Bilan: Our parents are afraid of the police. I knew that even from a very young age. They would cross over the street to avoid them, and you could tell that they were very nervous.

The behaviour that Bilan observed in her parents serves to reinforce the way that power is expressed in society through multiple layers of relations. People are always conceiving of themselves in terms of the categories that are available to them. Bilan's parents consider themselves as untrustworthy in the eyes of the police, and believe that the authorities are suspicious of them because they are seen as very dangerous. This move encourages Bilan to ask herself whether she also needs to be wary of the police, even in Australia. Generation 1.5 Somalis in Melbourne grow up in a space where they are forced to view themselves in terms of the prevalent categories that have been constructed about them, and to negotiate their identity formation and expression against the backdrop of embedded power relations in society. This is also due to the fact that the police force in Somalia has not functioned cohesively since the outbreak of the civil war. There was a Somali Police Force prior to the civil war, however, once hostilities escalated, many of the police returned to their hometowns to stay safe (Baumann et al. 2003: 69–70). Indeed, many of my respondents described how their parents were fearful of the police in Somalia as they were unregulated and unpredictable in their behaviour.

However, I do not suggest that young Somali Australians do not have grounds for fearing members of the police force in Australia. There have long been questions about how police officers interact with young African Australian males in particular. In 2013 a case brought against Victoria Police by six young African Australian men was settled outside court the day before it was due to be heard. The young men accused Victoria Police of widespread racial profiling and alleged that police officers were stopping them for unwarranted searching and questioning. As part of the case, they requested a statistician, Professor Ian Gordon, to analyse police notes. He found that young African Australian men living in Flemington and North Melbourne were stopped two and a half times more than their counterparts who were not of African descent (Donovan 2013).

Police diary notes that were to be used as evidence in the case showed that police had described African Australian males as "criminals loitering in the area". "Unable to provide police with reason of why they were there or what they were doing. Nervous in police presence" was the explanation given by police officers for approaching an African Australian teenager and asking them to justify why they were in a public place. This is in disagreement with the law, which requires the police to have a legitimate reason to interfere with a person's freedom of movement (Seidel and Hopkins 2013). Additionally, Professor Gordon's analysis of police statistics found that, in fact, young men of African descent committed significantly less crime than other populations in Flemington and North Melbourne (Donovan 2013).

In 2015 Daniel Haile-Michael and Maki Issa (2015), two of the men who brought the original case against Victoria Police, released a report titled "The more things change, the more they stay the same". They spoke with young people in Sunshine, Flemington, Noble Park and Dandenong about their experiences with the police and found that negative experiences were still common public occurrences that caused isolation, fear and anxiety.

It seems that young Somali Australians tend to see themselves as the type of people who will be targeted by the police and are likely to end up in jail. As an illustration of these anxieties I once witnessed some tension between a group of Somali young men and police officers in Footscray in September 2013. There was a group of around eight young men, aged approximately between 17 and 25 years old, in high spirits, laughing, talking and pushing each other around as a joke. Two uniformed police officers, one male and one female, were approaching along the footpath. They were heading in the direction of the group of boys, but it was not clear if they intended to speak with them or not. As soon as the group noticed the officers, the laughter died away. The group dispersed immediately, in twos and threes. Some went into the station, others walked away in the same direction as the police officers were heading, and two even crossed the road against the lights to avoid having to speak with them. At that moment, I was with a friend, a young Somali woman who is active in the community, who told me that this type of reaction is not uncommon. I was amazed that it was preferable to jay-walk in front of police officers rather than be found in a seemingly innocent group of friends. However, she explained that in the minds of young Somali men, anything is better than having contact with a police officer. After all, once they are across the road, they can always run away if necessary. I spoke to some of my participants about this incident and many believed it is better to disappear rather than risk a confrontation. They thought similarly about ticket inspectors on public transport. I have seen young Somalis exit a train as ticket inspectors have boarded it, or pass through carriages in an attempt to exit successfully at the next stop.

The anxiety felt by members of minority groups during interactions with police officers has been well documented (Chan 1997; Mills 2008; Hall et al. 1978). The desire to avoid contact with law enforcement may be a result of the experiences that migrants have had of police in their countries of origin. This was the case for the interview respondents, although, rather than their direct experience of the police force in Somalia, they referenced their parents' feelings and experiences of police interaction. Other examples of members of ethnic minorities attempting to escape when confronted by police have been described, even when the police investigation concerns minor breaches, such as traffic infringements (Chan 1997: 26).

Iman, one of the interview participants, explained that in his work as a social worker he had dealt with many young men who felt that the police targeted them unfairly:

Iman: I talk to heaps of these guys, you know? They feel like they're trying to live their life and when they hang out in the mall, or go out with their friends, there's always someone watching them and the police get involved if there's a big group of them.

Absame, another participant, believes that part of the problem for Somali youth comes down to a lack of understanding of the law and of Australia's bureaucratic processes, and of the difficulty they have in accessing a network of professionals (lawyers, social workers and doctors, for example) who can help their children:

Absame: Some of the young guys act violent and sometimes he have [sic] problems with maybe the ticket inspectors and sometimes he acted like... we accused him of acting like he was above the law: driving without licence, you know, things like normal teenagers do—there's too many young Somalis who are in jail. They are in jail for some easy things which, if they had some people to fix it, or if their parents knew more about the law, or if their parents could help them... It's a very, very big disadvantage.

These Somali youth are exposed to a form of inherent structural violence. Poor representation and low understanding of the structures of the legal system, for instance, can lead to an inflated proportion of Somalis appearing in crime statistics. This, in turn, may reinforce notions of inherent violence in Somalis, perpetuating the conditions for a cyclic reproduction of events (Nolan et al. 2014: 19–20). The incidents mentioned above of police and journalists producing inaccurate statistical data about the proportion of Somalis who commit crimes, are also very relevant here. The reinforcement of such inaccuracies contributes to the entrenchment of prejudiced ideological categories that affect the young people themselves and encourage others to view them in specific ways.

Representation by the Media

While the size of the Somali community in Melbourne is not large compared to other Somali communities (especially in the United States, for example), there has been substantial media focus on Horn of Africa populations in Melbourne, and indeed on the Somali community in particular. Within the community mixed reactions to the media scrutiny were found. For example, one Somali community leader said he did not mind the media focus because it drew attention to the Somalis in Melbourne, which in turn could highlight the work of many community organisations. He hoped this might also lead to social, multicultural, educational programmes being developed and targeted at the Somali community. However, many of the young respondents felt very differently. They believed they were targeted unfairly by the media and indeed were profoundly affected by their representation in the media.

Many of the respondents discussed how Muslims are often described as such when the news media report on a crime they have committed, connecting their criminal behaviour with their identification as Muslim:

Omar: I read an article a couple of years ago on the *Herald Sun*, and it was two young men that I actually knew they were Ethiopian. They were non-Muslim. And they got intoxicated and they were harassing people, I can't remember exactly what the article was on. But they got categorised as young Muslim youth who weren't used to this culture, and alcohol and the lifestyle. But there was actually a lot of alcohol back in Ethiopia and even in Somalia... there was alcohol back home. It's not something new but they were getting categorised as Muslims who never drank alcohol in their life, but now that they're here they get introduced to alcohol, they don't know how to handle it. So I was like, "Yeah, I recognise these guys and they're not Muslim, so you can't say there's no alcohol in their culture".

Omar is referring to a situation where Islam was used directly as an explanation for poor behaviour. The assumption that the young men were Muslim and that this explained their unfamiliarity with alcohol carries two levels of falsity. In the first, explicit level, the news coverage was incorrect about the Muslim origins of the youths. In the second instance, although Islam does not tolerate alcohol, the respondents said there was alcohol in Somalia (where the population is almost universally Muslim). This means that the young people would have been exposed to alcohol before.

This type of reporting seems, at first glance, to be a reasonable and even sympathetic account of events. However, making such essentialist statements about Islam and what it permits only serves to homogenise the entire community to a mass of people who are tightly bound by Islam, never experimenting or doing anything that falls outside a literal interpretation of the religion. Such statements are not likely to be made about Catholics, or Christians more broadly, for example.

The respondents understood the way that the media shapes public opinion, and did not condemn the general public for their perceived tendency to believe what appears in the popular media. Indeed, many of them told me that they believe most people are time-poor and simply do not have the resources to seek out alternatives to popular media. The idea of "lazy reporting" was also a common theme in the interviews. There were various reasons offered to explain why reporters rarely get the full story, from the idea that bad news sells and this is what the reporters want to produce, to the more nuanced understanding that some reporters may be scared of Muslims because of the bad press that already surrounds them.

Cabaas: I find it really hard, you know, because the reporters, other than SBS don't want to come here and find out what we're all about. I really think they might be scared of us because of our difference and that they are affected by all the negative stuff they hear on the news. Which makes it like some kind of circle we'll never break out of.

The response above shows the belief of the respondents that there is a cycle whereby reporters are reluctant to get close to Muslim communities in Australia, and this reluctance leads to shallow and inaccurate reporting, which in turn fuels a further distance between Muslims and the mainstream Australian community. The respondents believed that their misrepresentation in the media means they are mistrusted by the mainstream Australian public.

"Radicalisation"

When presenting the examples of violent acts perpetrated by Somalis, the notion of Generation 1.5 becoming "radicalised" was also discussed. The term radicalisation has become almost synonymous with the term terrorism and is central to counter-terrorism policy making (Kundnani 2012: 3). It is described as being a process, however there is considerable variation in academic literature with regard to its exact causes and manifestations (Nasser-Eddine et al. 2011: 13). The term is used here to describe the process through which an individual is exposed to extremist views, and is considered to be willing to deploy extreme acts—often deemed to be acts of terrorism—to promote their views.

None of the respondents volunteered the term radicalisation during the interviews or focus groups without it being introduced into the conversation. The term that is so often used by academics, reporters and members of government was not in the lexicon of the Generation 1.5ers interviewed, although they did understand how loaded and negative a term it is, so it is perhaps not surprising that none chose to apply the term to themselves. However, many wished to discuss events such as the counter-terrorism raids made by Federal and Victoria Police in 2009, 2012 and 2013 in Melbourne. Multiple operations took place over this time and there were reports of Somali "terror cells" operating in Melbourne (Stewart and Wilson 2009). Many respondents wanted to discuss reports that *dugsis* may be teaching extremist doctrines. *Dugsis* are cultural schools that are similar to a Sunday School, but include elements of education, such as Arabic grammar and letter formation (Berns-McGown 1999: 104). They were also worried by reports that groups such as Al Shabaab are recruiting young men. Interestingly, the local media reports that they mentioned (mainly radio and TV news bulletins) very rarely linked *dugsis* directly with terror attacks. In fact, some of the reports were about the calls from within the Somali community to regulate *dugsis* in Melbourne (Aly 2013; Shand 2013).

The young people's collective memory of media reports about *dugsis* teaching terrorism was not supported by the local media reports accessed in the search for more information regarding reports that terrorists were infiltrating *dugsis*. It was striking how heartfelt the young people were in their concern about the way *dugsis* were being portrayed in the media, and how their memories were similar regarding these reports. However, one must be conscious of the need to remain "sufficiently critical" of the construction of collective memories (Maynes et al. 2008: 62). Roy (1999) has also shown how strong emotions can alter and reconstruct memory. The young people clearly had strong feelings about their representation in the media, and it is possible that their strong emotion coloured their memory, leading to what Passerini (2005: 4) describes as "distortions or 'false memory'". Thus, the respondents were particularly sensitive about how *dugsis* are perceived.

In general, there was a strong sense of injustice around these events and the ways in which they were reported and, in some focus groups, this led to some heated discussions:

Hani: I was overseas when this news happened in Australia, and I came back and heard it and I was gobsmacked. I was like, "Seriously? Kids learning Qur'an leads to terrorism?" I found that to be the most stupid thing... the most stupid reporting. If they actually came in and saw what the kids were learning, they would never conclude to that. Never!

Ismahaan: I think everyone had the same feeling of "Oh my God, you're kidding me". Just disbelief. It was ridiculous.

Amal: And come on! We're the ones doing the teaching! It's not some guy who has come from Somalia. It's us! We grew up here. When I saw the reports on TV I couldn't understand it, it was all foreign to me. And it's really strange to see it on TV and think "Oh, that's what people think of me".

The above exchange illustrates the shock felt by the young people and the distance they place between their practising of Islam and the way it has been interpreted. Nobody in any focus group or interview discussed radicalisation as a real threat from the Somali community. Some young people believed that the threat in general has been grossly overestimated:

Kadiye: I never knew anyone who was approached to go and fight, or to do any terror acts.

Said: There is always somebody saying that we can't be trusted and that we will fight for the terrorist cause, but I don't meet any-one who actually feels this way. Sure, we think what is happen-ing in Somalia is very bad news. But our home is here now, and we are not going to risk everything our parents have done for us to go to a war that doesn't belong to us.

Said was not unusual in mentioning a sense of responsibility towards his parents and the sacrifices they have made. Said spoke about belonging *here*, in Australia, and he uses his allegiance to Australia to explain why the war had nothing to do with him.

In addition, participants often referred to issues of categorisation over the course of the interviews and the discussion groups, expressing annoy-ance at the fact that they are usually represented as "the bad guy":

Naado: And it's just another hit, another jab, you know? Now they say the Somali community teaches terrorism at school and tries to influence children. It's basically like the bogey-man. They make it bigger and bigger every time they do reportage.
Kadiye: People, you know, they got to be scared of something. So maybe it just has to be us?
Cabass: Every time I'm watching like a detective show or something and the bad guy is Muslim—he's always Muslim! I think about how it's shown as good guys versus bad guys. And if you want to be a good guy, then you have to have a bad guy to fight against.

These comments suggest that some respondents relate the practice of categorising and labelling others with their personal experiences and the broader context of terrorism and fear that is frequently promoted by the media. They worried that the media fuelled fear, with little or no evi-dence to support their own claims.

Conclusion: Key Findings

The young people offered many reflections on the types of violence they faced on a daily basis. These included problematic relationships with law enforcers and difficulty gaining adequate representation if they were in trouble with the law. In terms of news discourses about radicalisation, the respondents reported that they had been affected negatively by the media coverage of terror raids, as those reports seemed to indicate that there is a problem with the Somali community in Melbourne. The girls who taught at the *dugsis* were especially surprised and disappointed by reportage suggesting that what was being taught in *dugsis* in the Australian context was dangerous.

The respondents have been affected by numerous forms of relational power, including those imposed through legal, administrative, economic and military structures. As migrants or refugees, they are placed on the receiving end of many expressions of power that are both explicit (such as the process of gaining entry to a country, and reporting as part of visa conditions) and implicit (such as the difficulty in entering the labour market, learning new languages or making oneself understood). These conditions are worsened by the fear of terrorism that is projected by the media on to Muslims, resulting in documented forms of abuse against them.

The Generation 1.5 Somali Australians who participated in this research have a strong sense that their identity is something that is available for public consumption and critique. Because of their visible ethnic and religious differences, and the increasing scrutiny that is focused on individuals who share their characteristics, they felt unfairly judged by members of the mainstream Australian public. Many described the disadvantages they faced in their status as refugees, as well as the challenge of expressing their identity openly and without fear of repercussions. However, they stopped short at suggesting that the problems faced by the Somali community could lead to a radicalisation of young people. The respondents did not believe that the Somali community in Melbourne posed a real threat. Instead, they believe that the danger has been overestimated for various reasons. Some pointed out that it is difficult to identify Somalis from other dark-skinned Africans. Others believe that the negative reportage about their community is purely designed to sell newspapers and attract TV viewers. Others pointed out that there is a natural human need to have something to fear and, unfortunately, for many people, their community occupied that position.

The representation of Generation 1.5 as prone to violence appears in conflict with their actual expression of identity. This generation of Somalis seems no more likely to engage in violent behaviour than the average Australian of the same age. However, when violence does occur, it is subject to much more scrutiny than when it takes place in a mainstream setting.

REFERENCES

ABC News. (2015). Sharky Jama, Melbourne Male Model, Reportedly Killed Fighting with Islamic State in Syria. *ABC News*, 16 April. Available at http://www.abc.net.au/news/2015-04-16/sharky-jama-dfat-will-not-confirm-reports-australian-model-death/6396112.

Aly, W. (2013). Concern over Madrassas in Australia. In *RN Drive: Radio National*, 24 September. Available at http://www.abc.net.au/radionational/programs/drive/concern-over-madrassas-in-australia/4978340.

Australian Human Rights Commission. (2009). African Australians: A Report on Human Rights and Social Inclusion Issues. Discussion Paper. Human Rights and Equal Opportunity Commission, Sydney: AHRC. Available at https://www.humanrights.gov.au/sites/default/files/content/africanaus/AFA_2009.pdf.

Baumann, R., Yates, L. and Washington, V. (2003). 'My clan against the world': US and coalition forces in Somalia, 1992–1994. Fort Leavenworth, Kansas: Combat Studies Institute Press.

Berns-McGown, R. (1999). *Muslims in the Diaspora: The Somali Communities of London and Toronto*. Toronto: University of Toronto Press.

Black, D. and Reiss, A. (1970). Police Control of Juveniles. *American Sociological Review*, 35, 63–77.

Brunson, R.K and Weitzer, R. (2009). "Police Relations with Black and White Youths in Different Urban Neighborhoods". *Urban Affairs Review*, 44(6), 858–885.

Chan, J. (1997). *Changing Police Culture: Policing a Multicultural Society*. Cambridge: Cambridge University Press.

Cottle, S. (2004). *The Racist Murder of Stephen Lawrence: Media Performance and Public Transformation*. London: Praeger.

David, C.C. (2009). Intergroup attitudes and policy support: How prejudice against minority groups affects support for public policies. *International Journal of Public Opinion Research*, 21(1): 85–97.

Dixon, T.L. and Williams, C.L. (2015). The Changing Misrepresentation of Race and Crime on Network and Cable News. *Journal of Communication*, 65(1): 24–39.

Donovan, S. (2013). Victoria Police Settles Racial Profiling Case. *ABC News*, 18 February. Available at http://www.abc.net.au/news/2013-02-18/police-agree-to-new-procedures-to-combat-racism/4524770.

Engel, R. (2003). Explaining Suspects' Resistance and Disrespect toward Police. *Journal of Criminal Justice*, 31, 475–492.

Frodesen, J. (2002). At What Price Success?: The Academic Writing Development of a Generation 1.5 'Latecomer'. *The CATESOL Journal*, 14(1), 191–206.

Haile-Michael, D. and Issa, M. (2015). *The More Things Change, the More They Stay the Same: Racial Profiling across Melbourne*. Kensington: Flemington and

Kensington Community Legal Centre. Available at http://www.policeac-countability.org.au/wp-content/uploads/2015/07/More-Things-Change_report_softcopy.pdf.

Hall, S., Critcher, C., Jefferson, T., Clarke, J., and Roberts, B. (1978). *Policing the Crisis: Mugging, the State, and Law and Order.* London: The Macmillan Press Ltd.

Happer, C. and Philo, G. (2013). The role of the media in the construction of public belief and social change. *Journal of Social and Political Psychology*, 1(1): 321–336.

Houlihan, L. (2008). Fears Our Crime Being Imported. *Sunday Herald Sun*, 9 March. Available at http://www.hiiraan.com/news2/2008/mar/fears_our_crime_being_imported.aspx.

Hurst, Y., Frank, J. and Browning, S. (2000). The Attitudes of Juveniles Towards the Police. *Policing*, 23(1): 37–53.

Kundnani, A. (2012). Radicalisation: the journey of a concept. *Race & Class*, 54(2): 3–25.

Lewis, I.M. (2002). *A Modern History of the Somali.* Ohio: Ohio University Press.

Maynes, M.J., Pierce, J.L. and Laslett, B. (2008). *Telling Stories: The Use of Personal Narratives in the Social Sciences and History.* London: Cornell University Press.

Media Watch. (2008). Crime Stats. *Australian Broadcasting Corporation*, 24 March. Available at http://www.abc.net.au/mediawatch/transcripts/s2197803.htm.

Mills, J. (2008). Racing to Refuge: Ethnicity, Gendered Violence, and Somali Youth in San Diego. PhD Thesis. University of California, San Diego.

Nasser-Eddine, M., Garnham, B., Agostino, K., and Caluva, G. (2011). Countering Violent Extremism (CVE) Literature Review. *Australian Government.* Canberra: Department of Defence.

Nolan, D., Farquharson, K., Marjoribanks, T. and Muller, D. (2014). The Ausud Media Project 2011–2013: Final Report. Centre for Advancing Journalism: University of Melbourne. Available at http://arts.unimelb.edu.au/__data/assets/pdf_file/0006/1760163/Report_AuSud_Media_Project2014.pdf.

Oakes, D. (2012). African Youth Crime Concern. *The Age*, 20 August. Available at http://www.theage.com.au/victoria/african-youth-crime-concern-20120819-24glt.html.

Passerini, L. (2005). Introduction. In: Passerini, L. (Ed.) *Memory and Totalitarianism*, 1–20, London: Transaction Publishers.

Piliavin, I. and Briar, S. (1964). Police Encounters with Juveniles. *American Journal of Sociology*, 70: 206–214.

Reech, T. (2012). African Communities Confront Police over Crime Statistics. *The Gazelle*, 27 October. Available at http://ausudmediaproject.wordpress.com/2012/10/27/african-communities-confront-police-over-crimestatistics.

Roy, B. (1999). *Bitters in the Honey: Tales of Hope and Disappointment across the Divides of Race and Time*. Fayetville, AR: University of Arkansas Press.

Schliebs, M. (2015). Ex-Model Sharky Jama Killed as Jihadi Toll Totals 20. *The Australian*, 16 April. Available at http://www.theaustralian.com.au/in-depth/terror/exmodel-sharky-jama-killed-as-jihadi-toll-totals-20/news-story/a7767a3be77c7689075371a2deca8cdf.

Seidel, P. and Hopkins, T. (2013). No One Should Be Stopped by Police Just Because They're Black. *The Age*, 19 February. Available at http://www.smh.com.au/comment/no-one-should-be-stopped-by-police-just-because-theyre-black-20130218-2end5.html.

Shand, A. (2013). "Madrassa Lessons Worry Somalis". *The Australian*, 24 September, 43.

Shohat, E. and Stam, R. (1994). *Unthinking Eurocentrism: Multiculturalism and the Media*. Routledge: London.

Steward, C., and Wilson, L. (2009). Police Swoop on Melbourne Homes after Somali Islamists' Terror Plot Exposed. *News.com.au*, 16 August. Available at http://www.news.com.au/news/police-swoop-on-melbourne-homes-after-somali-islamists-terror-plot-exposed/news-story/121bbc5a4f5024642b9b01c26b928f8d.

Victoria Police. (2014). Crime Statistics 2013/2014. Available at http://www.police.vic.gov.au/content.asp?a=internetBridgingPage&Media_ID=72176.

Weitzer, R., and Brunson, R.K. (2009). Strategic Responses to the Police among Inner-City Youth. *The Sociological Quarterly*, 50: 235–256.

Zammit, A. (2015). *Australian Foreign Fighters: Risks and Responses*. Sydney: Lowy Institute. Available at https://www.lowyinstitute.org/sites/default/files/australian-foreign-fighters-risks-and-responses.pdf.

CHAPTER 8

News Coverage of a Women's Hunger Strike Against "Chauvinist Violence"

Ruth Sanz Sabido

INTRODUCTION: PROTESTING AGAINST CHAUVINIST VIOLENCE

On 9 February 2017 a group of eight women set up a tent in Puerta del Sol, in the centre of Madrid, and commenced a hunger strike to demand the reformation of the Spanish Law that deals with gender-based violence (*Ley Integral de Violencia de Género*). The group of women are part of the Ve-la luz Association, which was founded in 2009 in the Spanish northwestern region of Galicia, to defend what they describe as "a clear position against battery: to prevent, to support, to denounce" (Ve-la luz 2017a, my translation). The Association is mainly comprised of "survivors of gender-based violence and/or abuse and relatives" and their mission is "to fight for a system that fosters the freedom of women and children who have experienced gender-based violence and/or abuse" (ibid.). Since its foundation, the group has engaged in actions that have ranged from local initiatives to support victims, to broader activities to raise awareness and seek support from the public administration, making (in their own words) a "firm response, peaceful but emphatic, against the

R. Sanz Sabido (✉)
Canterbury Christ Church University, Canterbury, UK
e-mail: ruth.sanz-sabido@canterbury.ac.uk

© The Author(s) 2017
R. Sanz Sabido (ed.), *Representing Communities*,
DOI 10.1007/978-3-319-65030-2_8

135

neglect experienced by women and children before, during and after the process" (ibid.).

Prior to the beginning of the hunger strike the Spanish Parliament had proposed the creation of a subcommittee to deal with gender-based violence. The women complained that this subcommittee planned to go ahead without including any representatives of the community of victims, and demanded to be present at the meetings. Channelled through the gathering of these eight women in Puerta del Sol, we find two interlinked communities: one, the immediate and visible, though temporary, community formed by the women in the public square and the citizens that joined them at various points during the strike; and two, the symbolic, largely invisible and often silent community that is constituted by the victims, whose rights the Association works to defend.

In February 2017, just before they began the hunger strike, the Association published a message on their website stating that the fight against "chauvinist terrorism" ("*terrorismo machista*") should be treated "as a state matter" (Ve-la Luz 2017b, my translation). They pointed out that, under the current law, battered women and their children felt unprotected and abandoned, and "every day we witness, through news stories, how women and children are killed by their partners, ex-partners or fathers" (ibid.). Their message, which also included a petition for signatures in support of this cause, demanded that the government should "create an emergency cabinet" that focuses on treating chauvinist violence as an "absolute priority". The government, they argued, has the duty of "stopping this massacre that leaves/maintains women and children as living dead until they are eventually murdered" (ibid.). This call for urgent action, and for a serious commitment to take effective measures to protect the victims, proposed a 25-point manifesto to achieve two related aims: first, to ensure that battered women and their children receive adequate protection; and second, to make other forms of sexist violence more visible. They argued that the law should consider every type of chauvinist violence and act upon each of them accordingly, drawing on specialised knowledge. The first point in this list of 25 demands stated that the government should

> pass an integral law on chauvinist violence, that acknowledges the existence of "femicides" and includes the existing 2004 law as one of its sections. It should also include the law against the sex trade and exploitation, as well as other related laws, so that there is one specific law that uses specialised

knowledge of these various realities and deals with each type of chauvinist violence. (ibid.)

The manifesto also demanded that women who are affected by gender-based violence must be recognised as victims and must be provided with the same help and assistance that is available for victims of "Terrorism" (ibid.; capital T and quote marks in the original). In addition, women whose children were murdered in the context of gender-based violence should also be recognised as victims, as should any individuals living with the battered women when the aggression or murder took place. Amongst other crucial points, the Association asked for appropriate protection, economic support and psychological assistance to help victims move away from their aggressors from the moment they present a formal complaint. They also called for adequate public investment in training for professionals, so they can provide congruous support at all stages of the challenges that the victims encounter, including the "recovery phase (psychological help), transition (obtaining temporary accommodation), setting up a new home (requiring contact with banks), finding work and gaining economic independence (employment) and feeling safe (local police)" (ibid.). Furthermore, the group of women criticised the legal system for being contaminated with chauvinist stereotypes, and demanded that judges, police officers, civil servants and any professionals involved in the process should be trained on gender awareness and assessed on the support they provide.

In their message, the Association also asked for the revision of certain judicial procedures, such as: filming the statements of minors so as to avoid their re-victimisation in court; not forcing women and children to face mediation with their aggressors (where visiting rights and custody disputes exist); and not making children see their assailants during visits or shared custody which, according to the Association, should be terminated as soon as there are indications of abuse (Ve-la Luz 2017b). In fact, the 25-point manifesto focused to a great extent on the children who witness the aggression, including those who become direct targets of violence at the hands of their father (often as a means to hurt their mother), and those who are left orphaned when their mother is murdered. The Association denounced the terrible situation where orphans of gender-based violence are forgotten and left in a state of economic and emotional neglect. It demanded, furthermore, that the state should provide these children with a full orphan's pension and—in the absence of their mother—that their development and interests are safeguarded.

The women's hunger strike lasted 28 days, from 9 February to 8 March 2017, at which point, coinciding with International Women's Day, the two main Spanish political parties (Partido Popular and Partido Socialista) announced that the women were guaranteed a place on the subcommittee that would deal with this problem, and that a working group would be created for one year (EP 2017a; EP 2017b; Europa Press 2017a; Europa Press 2017b; *Público*/Agencias 2017). During the month of the hunger strike the women experienced a variety of health issues, while also having to fight the local council. They did, however, receive the support of citizens who joined them at various times, attended 'concentrations' (or static demonstrations) in the central square of Madrid, or signed their names in support of the women's manifesto.

METHODOLOGY AND SAMPLE

This chapter examines the news coverage of the hunger strike conducted by this group of women, placing this protest action in the context of news reporting on gender-based violence in Spain. The analysis approaches this type of violence as a public health matter, opposing any arguments that contend that these issues belong only to the private or familial sphere. The argument is that the patriarchal order not only lies at the heart of gender-based violence, but that it also guarantees both its continued (relative) invisibility in the news media, and the perpetuation of ineffective legal measures that are meant to address it.

The research presented here builds on previous studies on the news coverage of gender-based violence, by conducting a discourse analysis of a nationally representative sample of news articles, all of which examine a widely discussed social issue—gender-based violence—by focusing on a specific event—the hunger strike—thereby providing a coherent and purposeful body of data. The sample of newspaper coverage includes all the articles published about the hunger strike in the online versions of six national newspapers from 9 February 2017, when the strike began, until 8 March 2017, when it ended: *ABC* (right wing), *El Mundo* (centre right), *El País* (centre), *La Razón* (right wing), *La Vanguardia* (centre) and *Público* (left wing). The keywords "*huelga de hambre*" (hunger strike) and "Sol" were used to conduct the search in each newspaper's website, resulting in a sample of 87 articles that mentioned the event (the name of the Association itself was not used as a search term, because different authors and newspapers spelt its name differently). The sample presents the following distribution across newspapers: *ABC* (12), *El Mundo* (5), *El País* (4), *La Razón* (1), *La Vanguardia* (52) and *Público* (13).

The Association's success or failure in becoming visible within the news media depended on (and was indicative of), on the one hand, the news organisations' standard reporting practices around protest events and, on the other hand and more specifically, on the newspapers' attitudes towards gender-related issues. The analysis not only offers an insight into the news coverage of a particular protest event conducted by a group of women in the centre of Madrid, but also sheds light on the extent to which gender-based violence is reported as a manifestation of existing patriarchal imbalances of power. The women's manifesto highlights the current systemic deficiencies that, in their own words, are the direct result of chauvinist stereotypes and practices that have permeated the public administration (Ve-la Luz 2017b). The chapter therefore considers whether the women's manifesto is discussed in the news coverage and, where it does appear, examines two related aspects: one, the extent to which the perpetration of violence against women is presented as a patriarchal issue that targets women due to the very fact that they are women; and two, the extent to which the newspapers provide a critique of the deficient institutional structures that fail to provide adequate legal, economic and health support for the victims.

In the sample that forms the basis of this study, these issues are made visible by the fact that a group of women conducted a hunger strike in a public space such as the famous Puerta del Sol in Madrid, thereby commanding attention in order to invoke some action (Solesbury 1976). By not focusing on the coverage of a concrete case of gender-based violence, the approach used here enables us to consider the extent to which the issue is represented, not in terms of any specific episodic features related to a particular violent incident, but in terms of the *public debates* the strike elicits. These debates may include: the broader structural reasons that explain this type of violence; the extent to which social awareness is raised and a socially responsible analysis is offered; the critiques of existing procedures and institutions; alongside a discussion of what needs to change to solve the problem and to provide the victims with proper support networks.

GENDER-BASED VIOLENCE IN THE SPANISH NEWS MEDIA

In Spain, violence between intimate partners or ex-partners, and particularly those that end in murder (most often with the murder of the wife or ex-wife), was often described in the media as *crímenes pasionales* (crimes of passion), a term that suggests that the deaths were caused by momentary fits of rage or jealousy in the privacy of the home. These crimes were therefore presented as isolated events that played on the romantic idea that love kills (Gregoratto 2017), which meant that the causes of the violence were primarily related to the condition of the couple's private life, removing any suggestions that men's violence against women could possibly be explained by much deeper structural problems. The linguistic classification for these aggressions evolved and began to be presented as *violencia doméstica* (domestic violence). While preferable to that of crimes of passion, this label has also raised some questions about the types of acts and contexts to which it refers. More recently, the use of the term domestic violence has ceded increasing amounts of space to *violencia de género* (gender-based violence), leading to further debates about how appropriate these classifications are and the extent to which they may obscure the realities and the structural issues behind each case.

As outlined above, several terms have been used to describe this type of violence, including domestic violence, gender-based violence and violence against women (Archer 2000; Dobash and Dobash 1979). Although these are overlapping concepts, it is important to distinguish between (1) gender-based violence, which refers to violence that is directed against a person on the basis of their gender (EIGE 2014); (2) violence against women, which describes "any act of gender-based violence that results in or is likely to result in physical, sexual or mental harm or suffering to women" (UN General Assembly 1993); and (3) domestic violence, which is violence that takes place in the domestic sphere, involving intimate partners, former partners or other family members, and is therefore not necessarily based on the aggressor's or the victim's gender (Walby et al. 2014). These classifications often become blurred. For instance, violence is often considered gendered on the basis that it is directed against women, due to patriarchally driven power relations of inequality, and performances of masculinity and femininity (Jakobsen 2014). In addition, these notions also overlap when domestic violence is gender-based or specifically targeted at women as a manifestation of patriarchal values, sometimes leading to inaccurate and ineffectual definitions in public discussions. In this chapter an additional term is often used: chauvinist violence, which is a literal translation from the Spanish *violencia machista*. The notion of *machismo*—sexism or male chauvinism—is rooted in the traditional Hispanic perspective of male pride and superiority over women. *Violencia machista* therefore acts as a synonym for gendered or gender-based violence against women, in that it is violence committed by men against women as a way to establish and maintain their male or *macho* superiority over women. Throughout this chapter these terms are used according to the ways in which they appear in the original texts.

Despite these terminological variations, the positive development is that men's violence against women has, over the last 20 years, become increasingly visible in the news media. While similar trends have also taken place in other countries (see, for example, Gillespie et al. 2013), it took one case of gender-based violence for news practices to take a new turn in Spain. This violence had already acquired more attention since the end of the 1970s, when women began to take back some control over their own lives with the advent of democracy and an emerging, though very limited, degree of economic independence.

However, it was in 1997, when 60-year-old Ana Orantes was murdered by her ex-husband, that gender-based violence moved out of the private domain, where it had traditionally been hidden, to acquire public exposure. In this case, at two different points, the media played a crucial role. The first of these occasions was two weeks before her killing, when Orantes took part in a regional television talk show, in which she and other women described their experiences of battery. She talked about the beatings and the forced sexual relations that her husband had inflicted on her for 40 years, and the fact that their children had also been abused. Forty years of beatings ended in divorce, two years before her murder. However, a court ruling dictated that their dwelling would need to be shared with her aggressor, despite her constant complaints to the authorities about his violent behaviour. The beatings continued during those two years, and worsened after she spoke on television.

Perhaps because Orantes had appeared on television two weeks earlier, her killing became newsworthy beyond its immediate local sphere. This was the second moment when the media played an essential role in placing domestic violence on the public agenda; the news of her murder was widely covered by the Spanish media, sparking several demonstrations and political reactions. The transition of domestic violence from the private to the public sphere, and its widespread symbolic visibilisation in the media, was inadvertently facilitated by Orantes' decision to take a significant step by appearing on television. But it was because the news media took an interest in her story that the wider issues began to be discussed more frequently.

The outrage brought about by her murder was not shared by certain sectors, which attempted to redefine the event in more traditional terms. One of the clearest examples was when Francisco Álvarez Cascos, Vice-President of the Government at the time, publicly stated that Orantes' murder had been "an isolated case, the work of an eccentric" (Álvarez 2013; El Khattat and Roman 1997, my translation). His framing of the murder ignored the realities of thousands of women, as well as the gender-based issues that are central to understanding these realities. The spokesperson for Unión Progresista de Fiscales (Progressive Prosecutors' Union), Carlos Castresana, criticised Álvarez Cascos' statement as "absolutely unfortunate", and pointed out that, in fact, "this is not an isolated case, they are cases that take place regularly and, unfortunately, women tend not to report them because they see that there is no adequate response from the institutions when formal complaints are made" (El Khattat and Roman 1997, my translation).

Indeed, attitudes such as that presented by Álvarez Cascos were met with counter-discourses that worked to put the broader issue on the public agenda. A Spanish news article pointed out that Orantes was the 59th woman who had been killed by their partner that year, but

> the worst part, the most terrible part, … is that Ana Orantes' murder is not extraordinary. It is implacably in keeping with the cold statistics: every month, five women are murdered by their husbands or partners in Spain. One dead person every six days. […]

> Ana Orantes' death will not be the last one. There will be more. One fact: in 1996 there were 16,500 complaints from women against their abusive husbands.

> But the majority of these complaints end up in mere trials for misdemeanour. And, when they are convicted, abusers are often fined or put under house arrest. (Hernández Velasco 1997, my translation)

The public step that she took to denounce her husband eventually cost Orantes her life, but also led to the beginning of a more serious national debate around gender-based violence. Many developments have taken place in this respect since then, such as the reformation of the Penal Code in the first instance, followed by the 2004 Integral Law against gender-based violence, the same one that Ve-la Luz wants to improve. The emergency telephone service 016 was introduced for victims, relatives and friends, to seek help without leaving any trace on the family's phone bill. Statistically, before Orantes' murder, women who were killed by their husbands were counted as parricides, thereby ignoring the gender-specific characteristics of their murders. If the murder was committed by a boyfriend or an ex-partner, they were not included in those statistics. There was no gender distinction and the issue was generally ignored, legally and socially. The news media have, since then, reported on every woman that has been killed by a partner or an ex-partner, and news broadcasts are often headed by any new cases or updates on the latest ones, keeping count of how many women have been murdered since the beginning of each particular year, while sometimes comparing the running statistics with previous years. Despite these developments women's associations, such as Ve-la luz, continue to highlight the pervading inefficiencies of the system, which fails on several essential grounds: first, preventing the violence through adequate gender-aware education; second, providing adequate assistance for surviving women and children; and finally, protecting orphaned children.

Ultimately, news coverage of gender-based violence may arguably have an effect on the extent to which women may be encouraged or discouraged to take the necessary steps to leave the abusive environment, through their perception of the extent to which they would be helped or put further at risk if they were to make this decision. The media and the various public administration services need to alleviate the women's fears and direct them towards safe routes that they can use to protect themselves and their children. The news coverage of this issue therefore has a direct impact on the health and safety of individuals, families and communities (Carlyle et al. 2008: 169). As such, it is important that the news media presents gender-based violence as a public rather than a private problem. One of the key discursive practices that may foster public disengagement from media representations of this type of violence is, precisely, the characterisation of the story as a private relationship issue (Kozol 1995: 648–649), which only serves to perpetuate archaic approaches to this systemic patriarchal issue.

Indeed, the media's sense of social responsibility should stop them from perpetuating representational strategies that protect male power, by making the issue look trivial, or as though it is merely a private matter, or by blaming the women for the abuse (ibid.: 648). Previous studies have shown that newspaper framing of this type of violence tends to be episodic (Carlyle et al. 2008), that is, it focuses on the descriptive details of the event, promoting individualistic ways of understanding and failing to provide in-depth analyses that place the event in relation to the broader picture (Iyengar 1991). So, even when the news media do a better job at helping to make the problem visible, they still often fail to provide adequate socio-political contextualisation and analysis that challenges the patriarchal context in which this violence happens, according to which men should dominate women. By describing the event itself, the structural issues that underpin it are left undisturbed, even if all similar events are reported cumulatively on a regular basis.

The ensuing analysis focuses, not on any specific news stories about gender-based violence, but on another type of event, a hunger strike that was inherently public. With this approach, the chapter examines the news coverage of gender-based violence by focusing on a related event that happened, undeniably, in the public sphere. The women who took part in this hunger strike did so in the conviction that gender-based violence is also, in fact, a public issue and its social roots must be addressed by developing and applying efficient public measures. From this perspective, the following discussion examines whether the news coverage of the women's hunger strike was episodic, in keeping with the protest paradigm (Chan and Lee 1984; Detenber et al. 2007; Harlow and Johnson 2011; McLeod and Hertog 1999), or whether the fact that it was a (public) protest event led to a more thematic and useful social analysis of the core issue. As such, it considers the extent to which the Association's demands were put at the centre of the discussions, or whether news reports were dominated by other voices and agendas. The following sections focus on three of the key aspects that motivated the women's hunger strike: (1) to make their fight visible beyond the confines of Puerta del Sol and to garner support to implement their manifesto; (2) to recognise that gender-based violence is a consequence of the patriarchal system and, as such, should be treated as a state matter; and (3) to effect a number of changes to the law and to the ways in which the public administration treats the victims, with a particular focus on the children.

Newsworthiness and Episodic Politicisation of the Hunger Strike

The organisers of any protest event want their actions and demands to become visible in the public domain and to receive as much support as possible (Solesbury 1976). The group of women of Ve-la Luz also wanted to promote their message beyond the confines of Puerta del Sol. The news coverage of protest events has been widely discussed by media scholars, who have pointed out that it is not only the amount of coverage (the extent to which the protest event is selected to become news), but also the quality of the coverage (how the selected event is described) that need to be considered in this type of analysis (Wolfsfeld 1997). The protest paradigm presents a range of characteristics that are frequently observed in the coverage of protest events, such as: the trivialisation and marginalisation of protestors; the negative description of protest events not as legitimate or debatable issues, but as violent confrontations that provide a spectacle of protest; the reliance on official sources, bystander portrayals and invocations of public opinion, rather than the protest organisers themselves; and the focus on noise, that is, on issues that serve to hide the reasons that fuel the action (Detenber et al. 2007). In addition, actions conducted by larger or more established organisations receive more attention, which leads to "cumulative inequality" (Wolfsfeld 1997). However, the protest paradigm thesis has not been embraced universally, and some studies have found that journalists have sometimes challenged it (see, for example, Wouters 2015).

In any case, the news coverage of protest, as happens with news production practices more generally, involves processes of selection, exclusion, emphasis and elaboration (Entman 1993). Central to this practice is the concept of news values, which refers to the factors that determine the likelihood that an event has of being selected and distorted throughout the publication process (Galtung and Ruge 1965; see also Harcup and O'Neill 2001). The analysis of the sample of news articles revealed a varied picture with regard to the total amount of coverage that the hunger strike received in each newspaper, and the point at which the event became newsworthy for each of the sampled publications. The first newspapers to report on the women's hunger strike, the day after it began, were *Público* and *La Vanguardia*. For *Público*, not only was the coverage immediate, but the piece was also selected as one of the highlights of the day within the paper itself (Salvador 2017). In the case of *La Vanguardia*, the item was also highlighted in their daily summary of news articles the following day, when they referenced artists who had publicly shown their support for the women of Ve-La Luz (Vanguardia 2017). For both *Público* and *La Vanguardia*, it was the women's hunger strike itself, and the demands that they put forward, that made the event newsworthy.

Meanwhile, the event was covered by *El Mundo* for the first time on 14 February, five days after it had started, indicating that eight women were camping at Puerta del Sol "indefinitely" to demand that "this type of aggression" becomes a state matter, and that "victims should be part of the subcommitte for a state pact on gender-based violence, which starts on Thursday in Congress" (Díaz 2017, my translation). Therefore, it was both the event itself and the problem that it sought to address that were newsworthy, even though they covered it later than the first two publications.

For *El País*, the event was only covered on 18 February, nine days after the strike began (Burgos 2017). While the article began by explaining that the strike had actually been on since 9 February, it was at that point, when actress Pamela Palenciano did her show "*No sólo duelen los golpes*" ("What hurts is not only the beatings"), that the women's strike became, for this publication, newsworthy. The show, a monologue about gender-based violence and "the marriage between capitalism and the patriarchy" (ibid., my translation), had been advertised on social media by the actress 24 h earlier. Palenciano, a victim of gender-based violence herself, decided to support the group of women by offering to stage her act next to the activists' tent at Puerta del Sol. Arguably, the strike itself had not been newsworthy for *El País*, but it was the connected performance and subsequent concentration of people that attracted its attention.

ABC covered the strike in depth for the first time on 21 February, having only mentioned it briefly at the end of another article on 19 February. This first reference appeared in an article that covered the unrelated trade union demonstrations that took place in Madrid on 19 February:

> The only thing that has grown is […] inequality. And even more so with women. They have coincided at Sol, precisely, with a group that has spent ten days on hunger strike against gender-based violence. They [the trade unionists] let them have their stand so they could send out their message:

"One woman is murdered every three days in Spain". And that also has to change. (Atlas España 2017a, my translation)

This first cursory mention was followed up by another article, two days later, a brief piece that led with the murder of another woman, indicating that this was "the twelfth victim of chauvinist violence in the year so far" (Atlas España 2017b, my translation). For this reason, the article stated,

> Dozens of people got together and sang last night at Puerta del Sol in Madrid. They did it alongside the eight women who started a hunger strike there eleven days ago. This is their way of protesting againt gender-based violence, and of trying to turn it into a state matter. (ibid.)

This was the entire length of the piece, which only mentioned the women's strike in superficial terms.

Finally, based on the publications that were sampled, *La Razón* was the newspaper that not only reported the strike the latest but also covered it the least. In fact, the event itself never really became newsworthy, and was reported only once, on 28 February, to emphasise the fact that the local council—which has been run since 2015 by Ahora Madrid, a post-indignados left-wing group—had fined the activists three times for placing a tent "to protect themselves from the cold" (Pérez 2017, my translation). The news story was not about a group of women who were fighting for an in-depth review of laws and procedures related to gender-based violence, but that the local council had targeted them—a fact that they selected and emphasised as politically ironic without engaging with the real issues at any point.

Overall, the analysis suggests that not only were the majority of newspapers late in covering the women's hunger strike and their demands, but that some publications also decided to focus on aspects of the event that did not help to promote the Association's demands or provide an in-depth analysis of the issue itself. This is not only applicable to aspects that made the hunger strike newsworthy to begin with, but also to those that maintained it in the agenda during the month that the women camped at Sol. The distribution of articles that mentioned the strike in each publication (see above) is indicative of the level of interest presented by the newspapers. For example, we notice that *La Vanguardia* released 52 articles that mentioned the women's hunger strike (60% of the total coverage), significantly more than the other newspapers. While

La Vanguardia's relative amount of coverage may be understood positively from the perspective of the Association's struggle, a closer examination reveals more nuanced findings. Out of those 52 articles, only five were exclusively dedicated to the hunger strike, its development and its demands (a total of 11 articles if we consider all the sampled newspapers).

The remaining articles in *La Vanguardia* only mentioned the strike briefly when reporting on other stories (such as general discussions of debates that took place in Parliament, or references to demonstrations that were not related to this particular cause), or dealt with it from other perspectives. For example, eight articles focused on the fact that the local council had fined the women, and reported on various politicians' reactions to the penalties. In fact, this theme was the most frequent in the analysis, and it is the only one that appeared in all publications, with a total of 17 pieces dedicated to it across all newspapers (*ABC*, 4; *El Mundo*, 2; *El País*, 1; *La Razón*, 1; *La Vanguardia*, 8; *Público*, 1). This data points towards the discursive politicisation of the hunger strike in ways that were not necessarily useful for the women's cause. In these cases the hunger strike was not newsworthy for what it intended to achieve, but because it provided the local opposition to Ahora Madrid with a political weapon at local, regional and national levels.

More positive approaches included the coverage of different forms of support that were received by the women from other citizens who joined them, and from those who attended various demonstrations at Puerta del Sol. In addition, there were other demonstrations organised by other associations in various parts of Spain, and support expressed by politicians and trade unions. Two newspapers, *Público* and *La Vanguardia*, showed some interest in the women's deteriorating health, and all newspapers but *La Razón* covered the Association's decision to end the strike on 8 March, International Women's Day. Precisely on that day, and in the run up to it, *La Vanguardia* published four articles that referred to the strike by placing it, more broadly, in the context of women's struggles for equality. One of those articles compared the eight women at Sol to the "13 roses", a group of 13 women who were killed in 1939, after the Spanish Civil War, for opposing fascist repression (Europa Press 2017c). In the words of Jaime Cedrún, Secretary General of Comisiones Obreras in Madrid, both groups of women were "an example of the women's struggle" (ibid., my translation).

More worrying was the headline, also produced by *La Vanguardia*, stating that the Police would analyse "the murderers' minds" in order to prevent new aggressions. The article suggests that understanding their "criminal minds" would help to prevent further attacks, and even though it uses the term *violencia machista*, it seems to suggest that it is an individual mental and contextual problem, failing to situate it in a broader patriarchal context (EFE 2017a). Another article by *La Vanguardia* reported on Cristina Cifuentes, Regional President of Madrid, who welcomed the Real Madrid basketball team after winning the King's Cup. The celebration took place at Puerta del Sol, and the unrelated reference to the women's strike was that "a group of women that has protested against chauvinist violence with a hunger strike since 9 February, also drew attention to itself" (EFE 2017b, my translation). These articles illustrate how a higher amount of coverage, such as the one presented by *La Vanguardia*, is not necessarily indicative of a more committed and socially responsible approach to the issues. The following sections delve further into the ways in which some of the women's key demands were discussed within the sample.

"Chauvinist Terrorism" and "Femicide": A State Matter

The Association's manifesto included some key terminological choices that were motivated by a desire to put the patriarchal system at the centre of the problem. So, for example, their message referred to gender-based violence as *terrorismo machista* (chauvinist terrorism), and demanded that "chauvinist violence be treated as a state matter" (Ve-la Luz 2017b, my translation). In addition, the first demand in the 25-point manifesto was that "the women who are affected by gender-based violence must be recognised as victims, and they must be provided with the same help and assistance that is available for victims of 'Terrorism'" (ibid., capital T in the original). They added that "women whose children were murdered in the context of gender-based violence", and "those who live with the battered women when the aggressions and/or murders take place" must also be recognised as victims, in the same way that individuals who are directly related to victims of terrorism are treated as such (ibid.). In the Spanish context terrorism had normally been associated with ETA's actions in their pursuit of Basque separatism, and more recently with Islamist activities, such as the 2004 train bombings in Madrid. We therefore observed two uses of the term terrorism in the manifesto: one, to describe violence against women; and two, to refer to the more widely used reference to acts of political violence.

Referencing terrorism in the context of male chauvinism is not new. The expression sexist terrorism has been used in both academic (see, for example, Caputi and Russell 1992) and journalistic milieus. For example, in 1997 a news article published by *El Mundo* reported on a demonstration that took place in Granada to protest against the murder of Ana Orantes (see above). The article, which used expressions such as *violencia familiar* (family violence) and *violencia machista* (chauvinist violence), was placed in a section of the newspaper titled *terrorismo doméstico* (domestic terrorism). The article stated that protesters, who pointed at the judiciary system as "'accomplices' of family crimes", demonstrated against "chauvinist violence, which they described as 'terrorism'" (El Khattat and Roman 1997).

Despite previous uses of the term terrorism in this context, it is not frequently applied to this type of violence. If we compare the use of certain expressions in the Association's online message with the terminology that is employed in the news articles, we notice various degrees of contrast between them. In most cases, newspapers only mention the term terrorism when the articles discuss the need to provide the victims of gender-based violence with similar forms of support to those received by the victims of terrorism (e.g. Atlas España 2017c; Díaz 2017; Guillén 2017; EFE 2017c). The wording is quite similar across these articles and is in keeping with the Association's manifesto when it refers to victims of political violence. In fact, the most frequent reference to terrorism alludes to those victims, and the demand that the state should match this support for victims of gender-based violence, as illustrated by the following excerpt:

> Amongst other measures, they demand an integral law of chauvinist violence that acknowledges the existence of femicide, and recognises that victims must be provided with the same help and assistance that is available for victims of terrorism. (EFE 2017d, my translation)

By contrast, gender-based violence is only described as terrorism on eight occasions by two of the sampled newspapers (*La Vanguardia*, 7; *Público*, 1). One of those articles was published by *Público* on 19 February, stating that:

> The eight women who are on strike against the "terrorism of chauvinist violence" are members of that Galician organisation [Ve-la luz], which defends and supports women and children that survive gender-based violence and abuse. (Santos 2017, my translation)

The quotation marks also appear in the original article, indicating that they are quoting directly from the Association's own message. Indeed, this was a constant across all the articles that included this reference to terrorism. For instance, *La Vanguardia* quoted a trade unionist stating that murders caused by gender-based violence should be considered as "acts of 'terrorism'" (Europa Press 2017d), and a similar approach was taken when they reported on a demonstration that took place at the beginning of the hunger strike:

> Some of the mottoes that could be seen on placards and heard from the loudspeaker expressed that gender-based violence should be described as "terrorism" and that abusers "are not crazy" but they are murderers. Some placards said "You, chauvinists, are terrorists" or "Beating, never". (Europa Press 2017e, my translation)

La Vanguardia also emphasised the women's own statement that "chauvinism has killed more than ETA in Spain" (Agencias 2017, my translation). The women stated that they would not leave the strike until all 25 demands had been met, including that the victims should receive provision similar to the victims of terrorism because, they pointed out, "numbers speak for themselves" and "to this day, chauvinism has killed more than ETA" (ibid.). Indeed, these numbers appeared in another article by the same newspaper. Carmen Sarmiento, who won an award for her commitment to women's rights in her work as a journalist, pointed out in her acceptance speech that "the most universal crime is the one that is committed against women", stating that "7.5 million women were raped in the world last year" and "there are one hundred million women fewer than there should be"; just in Spain, she added, "since 2003, 883 women have been killed, more victims than caused by ETA's terrorism" (Europa Press 2017f, my translation). Since 2003 ETA had killed 15 people; since its foundation in 1968 it had killed 829 people (El Periódico n.d.). Similar references were made to "gender-based terrorism" as the "bloodiest expression of inequality and a consequence of a patriarchal society" (EFE 2017e, my translation), and as the "terrorism that is doing the most damage to Spanish democracy" (Europa Press 2017c, my translation). On every occasion, the use of this term in this particular context appeared as direct quotes from politicians or spokespersons, or with direct reference to the Association's original message. Unlike the first use of the term, this meaning was never part of the newspapers' own narratives.

Femicide

One of the key demands that the Association put forward was "to pass an Integral Law of chauvinist violence, that acknowledges the existence of 'femicide'" (Ve-la Luz 2017b, my translation). Radford and Russell (1992: xi), who recount that they used the term femicide for the first time in 1976, define it as "the misogynist killing of women by men", often after the women had endured various forms of violence over a long period of time. However, they point out that this violence is directed at women at least in part because they are women, so the domestic element is not a universal factor (for example, random victims of sexual assault and prostitutes are also femicide victims). Russell (1992) argues that naming an injustice provides a means of thinking about it, so it is important to use this term to raise awareness and sensitise the public and policy makers (see also Campbell and Runyan 1998).

In the sampled articles, the term *feminicidio* appeared sparingly, and was only used by four of the newspapers (e.g. Atlas España 2017c; Díaz 2017; EFE 2017c; Salvador 2017). Most articles made direct references to the manifesto, or to statements made by Gloria Vázquez, the Association's spokesperson, as shown in the following excerpt:

> The manifesto includes several measures to fight against chauvinist violence, such as protocols that "guarantee the adequate protection, provide the same support that is given to victims of terrorism, or introduce the notion of femicide", as Vázquez explains. (Díaz 2017, my translation)

This excerpt reappears in very similar forms several times in the sample, regardless of the newspaper, which indicates a generalised reliance on news agency material. In other instances, we find quotes by politicians such as, for example when *La Vanguardia* stated that Dolors Montserrat, Secretary of Health, Social Services and Equality, criticised the government (of which she was part) for failing "to quantify the number of 'femicides', as women are killed because of the fact that they are women" (EFE 2017f, my translation). This statement, which offers a direct though superficial explanation of this type of violence, appears in a politicised context of confrontational party politics, as part of a debate in which Partido Popular and Podemos politicians clashed over the budget assigned to prevent violence against women.

"An Invisible Reality": The Orphaned Children

The Association's manifesto is far from exclusively focused on women, for at least ten of the 25 demands that they presented related directly to the children: children who have witnessed the beatings in the domestic sphere; children who have also been beaten; children who are involved in divorce and custody battles or in legal processes against their abusers; and children who are orphaned when the abuser kills their mother. Despite the emphasis that the association puts on the improvements that need to be made to the law to safeguard the interests of the children, who they argue should also be considered as victims, the news articles largely fail to match their declared interests.

None of the sampled articles focused entirely on the problems faced by the orphans and the ways in which the system fails to protect them in their mother's absence. Some of the articles that reported on the hunger strike only mentioned the orphans superficially or in passing, when listing some of the demands the Association had made. This was done in a similar fashion to the description of other demands, following a standard reference to the manifesto that was replicated in several articles. On this theme, articles pointed out that the Association demanded that "the orphans who are victims of chauvinist violence should receive the full orphan's pension" (e.g. EFE 2017h; EFE 2017i, my translation), or that there should be "an improvement in the protection of the orphans" (*Público* 2017). Furthermore, on 8 March, five of these articles were similar across five of the sampled newspapers, having been sourced directly from a news agency (EP 2017a; EP 2017b; Europa Press 2017a; Europa Press 2017b; *Público*/Agencias 2017). Therefore, the level of in-depth analyses and variety of perspectives was very limited. There was, however, some space for critical remarks, including statements that pointed towards the need for "improved protection of the orphans, who are 'brushed aside and made invisible' by the system" (EFE 2017g, my translation), or those that used statistics to highlight the problem:

They are fed up. Literally. They are fed up with words and more words, with protocols, with meetings, with politicians condemning it through Twitter, with minutes of silence [...] while the murders of women by their partners or ex-partners continue to happen. And they have taken to the streets, also literally, against gender-based violence, which has ended the lives of 886 women in 13 years, accounting for one-fourth of all the murders that were committed in the country. This year so far [up to 24 February 2017], it has already ended the lives of 15 women (in addition to one baby and the daughter of one of the murdered women) and has left six orphans. (López 2017, my translation)

On one occasion, a reference was made to a relative's testimony about her experience of looking after orphaned children, such as Martina Gómez, a member of Ve-la Luz whose sister was killed "by chauvinist violence over one year ago":

"she would still be alive had the protocols been efficient", she insists. She is the guardian of two teenagers who were left without a mother by a shotgun taken up by their father, right in front of them. [...]

Her sister asked for advice the same morning she was killed. [...] "She warned them [at Casa de la Mujer, Women's Home, at the local council in Lugo] that her husband had pointed a gun at her but they did not refer her to the Civil Guard". After the murder, Gómez remembers the negligence of the public administration, the lack of attention that they paid to her family, something that still continues. (Rodrigo 2017, my translation)

Gómez also argued that her nephews had been given an inadequate pension, since it was calculated based on the contributions that the deceased parent made during their working life. She also criticised the psychological help they received:

in total, my nephews have had the right to attend ten sessions with a psychologist after the death of my sister, when this is something that will stay with them for the rest of their lives, so they should have the right to indefinite psychological attention. (ibid.)

If references to the demands that relate to orphans are generally scarce and superficially descriptive, real examples that help to illustrate their predicament are practically non-existent within the sample, with this particular testimony being one of the few exceptions.

As regards the children, the Association is also particularly concerned about the custody battles, which often end in shared custody orders that force the children to spend time with their abusive fathers. Despite the emphasis that the group of women put on the issue of custody, only six articles mentioned the terms *custodia* (custody) or *potestad* (legal authority), while a small number of articles referred to the danger of letting children "go to abuser's homes" (Agencias 2017). One article was quite exhaustive in listing all the demands that related to the children in the manifesto (Burgos 2017), although this appeared as a concatenation of demands without further analysis. The remaining ones provided shorter versions of those demands (EFE 2017c; EFE 2017j), while one article included a video that stated that "children should have the same assistance as their mothers, as abusers perpetuate the violence against the mothers through the children" (Europa Press 2017g). The Association's argument that shared custody should be overturned the moment there is evidence of abuse was therefore scarcely covered or discussed in the analysed sample.

Conclusion

Chauvinist violence, a form of violence that men perpetrate against women due to their incapacity to cope with their partner's power and independence, does not respond to any individual male's pathology, but is rooted in the patriarchal dynamics of gender inequality (Gregoratto 2017). Despite the positive developments that have taken place over the last 20 years, there is still much room for improvement, not only in the provision of adequate support for the victims, but also in the treatment of this problem by the news media.

The analysis indicates that, even though there is a relative amount of attention being given to chauvinist violence, this is uneven amongst publications and inconsistent in its quality, even when the coverage provided by any one newspaper is considered. This is particularly clear from *La Vanguardia*, which offered the highest amount of coverage within the sample, but this visibility was not always effective. In many cases, some of the content within the articles was rather similar, limiting the options for in-depth critique and debate, while in some cases they were altogether counter-productive, as illustrated by the piece that suggested that the root of chauvinist violence was in the murderer's "criminal mind", detaching the violence from the deeper social inequalities that actually underpinned it.

The aim of this chapter was to examine the news coverage of chauvinist violence, not by focusing on specific cases of violence, but on a protest event whose inherent purpose was to put this social health problem on the public agenda. The analysis of this one event, which spanned one month, showed how the broader problem, rather than any individual cases that may be episodically framed and isolated, was politicised by all the newspapers, for example, by using the fines imposed by the local council as ammunition to attack their respective ideological opponents. Meanwhile, summaries of the 25 points that the Association put forward in their manifesto were covered, to varying degrees, in most newspapers, although it was noticeable, once again, that the formulations used to report on these demands tended to be quite rigid, superficial and similar in several articles. Furthermore, the level of attention given to the Association's demands was uneven. While their claims that chauvinist violence should become a state matter, and that the 2004 law needed to be amended, were often acknowledged, the details of what actually needed to change were inadequate. Particularly evident was the continued invisibility of the orphans, despite the Association's efforts to counteract precisely this problem.

Overall, there were mixed approaches to the news coverage of chauvinist violence, with evidence of some positive developments in the space that is given to address this problem as a public issue. However, it can be argued that most newspapers not only failed to cover the strike and its demands in a timely and effective fashion (from the activist's perspective), but the depth of the coverage generally also let this group of women down. It was not the hunger strike and the women's demands that drove the coverage and became newsworthy in most cases, but there was a tendency to emphasise secondary elements, distracting from the main problem. The articles that provided an analysis of the failures of the current system, and a consistent acknowledgement of the patriarchal context that underpinned it, remain a minority. This suggests that, despite the relative visibility that was given to the women's hunger strike, there remains a need for a deeper commitment to address the problem of chauvinist violence in the public realm.

References

Agencias (2017). "Diez mujeres y un hombre se unen a la huelga de hambre contra la violencia de género". *La Vanguardia*, 6 March. Available at: http://www.lavanguardia.com/local/madrid/20170306/42573596050/mujeres-hombre-suman-huelga-sol-violencia.html.

Álvarez, I. (2013). "Ana somos todas". *El Correo*, 12 February 2013. Available at: http://www.elcorreo.com/vizcaya/20130212/mas-actualidad/sociedad/somos-todas-201302111539.html.

Archer, J. (2000). "Sex differences in aggression between heterosexual partners: a meta-analytic review". *Psychological Bulletin*, 126: 651–680.

Atlas España. (2017a). "La vida se encarece, salarios y pensiones no suben". *ABC*, 19 February. Available at: http://www.abc.es/espana/abci-vida-encarece-salarios-pensiones-5329060989001-20170219015006_video.html.

Atlas España. (2017b). "Música en la Puerta del Sol contra la violencia machista". *ABC*, 21 February. Available at: http://www.abc.es/espana/abci-musica-puerta-contra-violencia-5330809433001-20170221012004_video.html.

Atlas España. (2017c). "Una asociación conta la violencia machista, denunciada por la policía por ocupar demasiado espacio en su acampada en la Puerta del Sol". *ABC*, 28 February. Available at: http://www.abc.es/espana/abci-asociacion-conta-violencia-machista-5341168524001-20170228014041_video.html.

Burgos, S. (2017). "De mayor, quiero estar viva". *El País*, 18 February. Available at: http://elpais.com/elpais/2017/02/18/mujeres/1487437602_069568.html.

Campbell, J. and Runyan, C.W. (1998). "Femicide". *Homicide Studies*, 2(4): 347–352.

Caputi, J. and Russell, D.E.H. (1992). "Femicide: Sexist Terrorism against women". In: Radford, J. and Russell, D.E.H. (Eds.) *Femicide: The Politics of Woman Killing*, 13–21. New York: Twayne.

Carlyle, K.E., Slater, M.D. and Chakroff, J.L. (2008). "Newspaper Coverage of Intimate Partner Violence: Skewing Representations of Risk". *Journal of Communication*, 58(1): 168–186.

Chan, J.M. and Lee, C.C. (1984). "The journalistic paradigm on civil protests: A case study of Hong Kong". In: Arno, A. and Dissanayake, W. (Eds.) *The News Media in National and International Conflict*, 183–202. Boulder, CO: Westview.

Detenber, B.H., Gotlieb, M.R., McLeod, D.M. and Malinkina, O. (2007). "Frame intensity effects of television news stories about a high-visibility protest issue". *Communication & Society*, 10(4): 439–460.

Díaz, B. (2017). "En huelga de hambre para luchar por 'un país sin violencia machista'". *El Mundo*, 14 February. Available at: http://www.elmundo.es/sociedad/2017/02/14/58a1fd3ce2704ef2358b458a.html.

Dobash, R.E. and Dobash, Russell P. (1979). *Violence against Wives*. New York: Free Press.

EFE (2017a). "Entender la mente de los asesinos machistas para prevenir nuevas agresiones". *La Vanguardia*, 23 February. Available at: http://www.lavanguardia.com/vida/20170223/42254954419/entender-la-mente-de-los-asesinos-machistas-para-prevenir-nuevas-agresiones.html.

EFE (2017b). "Cifuentes, al Real Madrid: 'Mi corazón no puede ser más blanco'". *La Vanguardia*, 20 February. Available at: http://www.lavanguardia.com/local/madrid/20170220/42179754120/cifuentes-al-real-madrid-mi-corazon-no-puede-ser-mas-blanco.html.

EFE (2017c). "Mujeres en huelga de hambre exigen un gabinete de crisis contra el maltrato". *La Vanguardia*, 12 February. Available at: http://www.lavanguardia.com/vida/20170212/414276241660/mujeres-en-huelga-de-hambre-exigen-un-gabinete-de-crisis-contra-el-maltrato.html.

EFE (2017d). "Las mujeres en huelga de hambre comparecerán el lunes en el Senado". *La Vanguardia*, 1 March. Available at: http://www.lavanguardia.com/vida/20170301/42439024664/las-mujeres-en-huelga-de-hambre-compareceran-el-lunes-en-el-senado.html.

EFE (2017e). "CCOO denuncia la firma de 163.000 contratos precarios entre mujeres en 2016". *La Vanguardia*, 7 March. Available at: http://www.lavanguardia.com/local/madrid/20170307/42617887637/ccoo-denuncia-la-firma-de-163000-contratos-precarios-entre-mujeres-en-2016.html.

EFE (2017f). "Montserrat pide unidad contra la violencia machista, una 'cuestión de Estado'". *La Vanguardia*, 15 February. Available at: http://www.lavanguardia.com/politica/20170215/4245646557/montserrat-pide-unidad-contra-violencia-machista-una-cuestion-de-estado.html.

EFE (2017g). "Mujeres en huelga de hambre urgen al Senado pacto contra violencia machista". *La Vanguardia*, 6 March. Available at: http://www.lavanguardia.com/vida/20170306/42584269690/mujeres-en-huelga-de-hambre-urgen-al-senado-pacto-contra-violencia-machista.html.

EFE (2017h). "Once personas se suman a la huelga de hambre contra la violencia machista". *La Vanguardia*, 4 March. Available at: http://www.lavanguardia.com/vida/20170304/42545815101/once-personas-se-suman-a-la-huelga-de-hambre-contra-la-violencia-machista.html.

EFE (2017i). "CCOO y UGT exigen en la calle soluciones a la pobreza y precariedad laboral". *La Vanguardia*, 19 February. Available at: http://www.lavanguardia.com/vida/20170219/42154295720/ccoo-y-ugt-exigen-en-la-calle-soluciones-a-la-pobreza-y-precariedad-laboral.html.

EFE (2017j). "Sindicatos muestran su apoyo a mujeres en huelga de hambre en Puerta del Sol". *La Vanguardia*, 21 February. Available at: http://www.lavanguardia.com/vida/20170221/42200814480/sindicatos-muestran-su-apoyo-a-mujeres-en-huelga-de-hambre-en-puerta-del-sol.html.

EIGE (2014). "What is gender-based violence?". *European Institute for Gender Equality*, 28 February. Available at: http://eige.europa.eu/content/what-is-gender-based-violence.

El Khattat, M. and Roman, S. (1997). "Granada protesta al grito de 'Ana somos todas'". *El Mundo*, 20 December. Available at: http://www.elmundo.es/elmundo/1997/diciembre/20/nacional/manifestacionana.html.

El Periódico (n.d.). "Los 829 muertos del trágico historial de ETA". *El Periódico*, n.d. Available at: http://www.elperiodico.com/es/lista-victimas-ETA.shtml.

Entman, R.M. (1993). "Framing: Toward clarification of a fractured paradigm". *Journal of Communication*, 43(4): 51–58.

EP (2017a). "Las mujeres en huelga de hambre dejan su protesta porque consideran logrado su objetivo". *El País*, 8 March. Available at: http://politica.elpais.com/politica/2017/03/08/actualidad/1488960434_357446.html.

EP (2017b). "Las mujeres en huelga de hambre en la Puerta del Sol abandonan su protesta tras casi un mes". *ABC*, 8 March. Available at: http://www.abc.es/espana/madrid/abci-mujeres-huelga-hambre-puerta-abandonan-protesta-tras-casi-201703080108_noticia.html.

Europa Press (2017a). "Las mujeres en huelga de hambre en la Puerta del Sol abandonan la protesta al lograr su objetivo". *El Mundo*, 8 March. Available at: http://www.elmundo.es/madrid/2017/03/08/58bf535846163f23098b4648.html.

Europa Press (2017b). "Las mujeres en huelga de hambre en la Puerta del Sol abandonan su protesta tras casi un mes al ver logrado su objetivo". *La Vanguardia*, 8 March. Available at: http://www.lavanguardia.com/vida/20170308/42633905202/las-mujeres-en-huelga-de-hambre-en-la-puerta-del-sol-abandonan-su-protesta-tras-casi-un-mes-al-ver-logrado-su-objetivo.html.

Europa Press (2017c). "CCOO compara a las activistas de la huelga de hambre de Sol con 'Las 13 Rosas', 'ejemplo de la lucha de las mujeres'". *La Vanguardia*, 8 March. Available at: http://www.lavanguardia.com/vida/20170308/42671439413/ccoo-compara-a-las-activistas-de-la-huelga-de-hambre-de-sol-con-las-13-rosas-ejemplo-de-la-lucha-de-las-mujeres.html.

Europa Press (2017d). "UGT y CCOO reclaman un pacto de estado contra la violencia machista y apoyan a las 8 mujeres en huelga de hambre en Sol". *La Vanguardia*, 21 February. Available at: http://www.lavanguardia.com/vida/20170221/42203968593/ugt-y-ccoo-reclaman-un-pacto-de-estado-contra-la-violencia-machista-y-apoyan-a-las-8-mujeres-en-huelga-de-hambre-en-sol.html.

Europa Press (2017e). "Tres mujeres acampan en Sol y se declaran en huelga de hambre indefinida para exigir protección a víctimas de machismo". *La Vanguardia*, 14 February. Available at: http://www.lavanguardia.com/vida/20170214/4232118427/tres-mujeres-acampan-en-sol-y-se-declaran-en-huelga-de-hambre-indefinida-para-exigir-proteccion-a-victimas-de-machismo.html.

Europa Press (2017f). "Carmen Sarmiento recibe el Clara Campoamor por 'referente del periodismo comprometido con derechos de las mujeres'". *La Vanguardia*, 8 March. Available at: http://www.lavanguardia.com/vida/20170308/42661776159/carmen-sarmiento-recibe-el-clara-campoamor-por-referente-del-periodismo-comprometido-con-derechos-de-las-mujeres.html.

Europa Press. (2017g). "Activistas: 'La ley de violencia de género es inútil'". *ABC*, 5 March. Available at: http://www.abc.es/sociedad/abci-activistas-violencia-genero-inutil-5348380621001-20170305010306_video.html.

Galtung, J. and Ruge, M. (1965). "The structure of foreign news: The presentation of the Congo, Cuba and Cyprus crises in four Norwegian newspapers". *Journal of Peace Research*, 2(1): 64–90.

Gregoratto, F. (2017). "Why Love Kills: Power, Gender Dichotomy, and Romantic Femicide". *Hypatia*, 32(1): 135–151.

Guillén, J.J. (2017). "'Las mujeres de Sol' acuden al Senado para pedir un pacto contra la violencia machista". *Público*, 6 March. Available at: http://www.publico.es/sociedad/mujeres-sol-acuden-senado-pedir.html.

Gillespie, L.K., Richards, T.N., Givens, E.M. and Smith, M.D. (2013). "Framing deadly domestic violence: Why the media's spin matters in newspaper coverage of femicide". *Violence Against Women*, 19(2): 222–245.

Harcup, T. and O'Neill, D. (2001). "What is news? Galtung and Ruge revisited". *Journalism Studies*, 2(2): 261–280.

Harlow, S. and Johnson, T.J. (2011). "Overthrowing the protest paradigm? How the *New York Times*, *Global Voices* and Twitter covered the Egyptian revolution". *International Journal of Communication*, 5: 1359–1374.

Hernández Velasco, I. (1997). "Ana Orantes: la muerta número 59 de este año". *El Mundo*, 18 December. Available at: http://www.elmundo.es/elmundo/1997/diciembre/18/nacional/malostratos.html.

Iyengar, S. (1991). *Is Anyone Responsible? How Television Frames Political Issues*. Chicago: University of Chicago Press.

Kozol, W. (1995). "Fracturing domesticity: Media, nationalism, and the question of feminist influence". *Signs: Journal of Women in Culture and Society*, 20: 646–667.

López, C. (2017). "La lucha contra la violencia machista se traslada a las calles de España". *La Vanguardia*, 24 February. Available at: http://www.lavanguardia.com/vida/20170224/42262394522/la-marea-violeta-crece.html.

McLeod, D.M., and Hertog, J.K. (1999). "Social control, social change and the mass media's role in the regulation of protest groups". In: Demers, D. and Viswanath, K. (Eds.) *Mass Media, Social Control and Social Change: A Macrosocial Perspective*, 305–330. Ames, IA: Iowa State University Press.

Pérez, L. (2017). "El Ayuntamiento multa a las mujeres maltratadas que protestan en Sol". *La Razón*, 28 February. Available at: http://www.larazon.es/local/madrid/el-ayuntamiento-multa-a-las-mujeres-maltratadas-que-protestan-en-sol-JD14608098.

Público (2017). "'Las mujeres de Sol' acuden al Senado para pedir un pacto contra la violencia machista". *Público*, 6 March. Available at: http://www.publico.es/sociedad/mujeres-sol-acuden-senado-pedir.html.

Público/Agencias (2017). "Las 'mujeres de Sol' abandonan la huelga de hambre tras conseguir su objetivo". *Público*, 8 March. Available at: http://www.publico.es/actualidad/mujeres-sol-abandonan-huelga-hambre.html.

Radford, J. and Russell, D.E.H. (1992). *Femicide: The politics of woman killing*. New York: Twayne.

Rodrigo, B. (2017). "Mi hermana seguiría viva si los protocolos contra violencia machista hubiesen sido eficaces". *El Mundo*, 23 February. Available at: http://www.elmundo.es/sociedad/2017/02/23/58af2d8e468aeba3068b45b9.html.

Russell, D. (1992). "Introduction". In: Radford, J. and Russell, D.E.H. (Eds.) *Femicide: The Politics of Woman Killing*, 3–12. New York: Twayne.

Salvador, C. (2017). "Ocho mujeres hacen huelga de hambre en el centro de Madrid por la violencia machista". *Público*, 10 February. Available at: http://www.publico.es/sociedad/huelga-hambre-violencia-machista-ocho.html.

Santos, C. (2017). "Miles de personas acuden a Sol en apoyo a las ocho feministas en huelga de hambre". *Público*, 19 February. Available at: http://www.publico.es/sociedad/violencia-machista-cientos-personas-acuden.html.

Solesbury, W. (1976) "The environmental agenda". *Public Administration*, 54: 379–397.

UN General Assembly (1993). "Declaration on the Elimination of Violence against Women". *United Nations General Assembly*, A/RES/48/104. Available at: http://www.un.org/documents/ga/res/48/a48r104.htm.

Vanguardia (2017). "Ocho mujeres en huelga de hambre en Puerta del Sol contra violencia machista". *La Vanguardia*, 10 February. Available at: http://www.lavanguardia.com/vida/20170210/414224202156/ocho-mujeres-en-huelga-de-hambre-en-puerta-del-sol-contra-violencia-machista.html.

Ve-la luz (2017a). "Quiénes somos". *Asociación Ve-La Luz*, 6 February. Available at: http://www.asociacionvelaluz.es/quienes_somos/.

Ve-la luz (2017b). "Ve-la luz solicita que sea cuestión de estado, la lucha contra el Terrorismo Machista". *Asociación Ve-La Luz*, n.d. Available at: http://www.asociacionvelaluz.es/_noticias/2017/02/06/ve-la-luz-solicita-que-sea-cuestin-de-estado-la-lucha-contra-el-terrorismo.

Walby, S. Towers, J. and Francis, B. (2014) "Mainstreaming domestic and gender-based violence into sociology and the criminology of violence". *The Sociological Review*, 62(S2): 187–214.

Wolfsfeld, G. (1997). *Media and Political Conflict: News from the Middle East*. Cambridge, UK: Cambridge University Press.

Wouters, R. (2015). "Reporting demonstrations: On episodic and thematic coverage of protest events in Belgian television news". *Political Communication*, 32(3): 475–496.

CHAPTER 9

Egresses: Countering Stereotypes of Blackness and Disability Through Horrorcore and Krip Hop

Mikko O. Koivisto

MONSTROUS REPRESENTATIONS OF BLACKNESS AND DISABILITY

In the 1960s there were attempts within the field of psychiatry to pathologise Civil Rights activism (Metzl 2009). This idea is articulated in a 1968 article from *Archives of General Psychiatry*, which presents the notion of 'protest psychosis', a mental disorder that supposedly causes "hostile and aggressive feelings" and "delusional anti-whiteness" (Bromberg and Simon, cited in Metzl 2009: Preface, para. 16). The pathologisation is also evident in an advertisement for the antipsychotic drug Haldol (McNeil Laboratories 1974), which includes the headline "Assaultive and belligerent?" above an image of an African American man showing "clenched, Black Power fists" (Metzl 2009: Preface, para. 18). The Civil Rights era overlapped with the transformation of schizophrenia diagnoses from being a white female ailment to being a black male disorder. Metzl argues that this change implicitly functioned as an extension of the prison system in order to confine people with

M.O. Koivisto (✉)
School of Arts, Design and Architecture, Aalto University, Espoo, Finland
e-mail: mikko.koivisto@aalto.fi

© The Author(s) 2017
R. Sanz Sabido (ed.), *Representing Communities*,
DOI 10.1007/978-3-319-65030-2_9

163

little or no criminal history, but who seemed to pose a threat to public security (Metzl 2009). Fifty years after the Civil Rights movement, tensions between ethnicity and mental disability remain, albeit in new configurations.

In Europe and the United States anxieties over race, ethnicity and nationality escalated again in 2015 and 2016. Since the Second World War, Western countries have gone through an immense process of self-reflection in an effort to understand why the most wealthy and developed countries in Europe had failed to prevent the rise of racism and xenophobia, which ultimately led to the mass execution of millions of civilians, first citizens with disabilities and eventually ethnic minorities, most notably Jews (Agamben 1998). Meanwhile, the United States, having helped to fight Nazism and Fascism in Europe, was forced to come to terms with its own biopolitics and thanatopolitics over the non-white bodies within its own population. Some years before the beginning of the European refugee crisis in 2015, and before the overtly racist and xenophobic presidential campaign of the republican candidate Donald Trump in 2016, the Black Lives Matter movement emerged as a response to the killing of African Americans by law enforcement officers (Garza 2014).

Black Lives Matter draws attention to the enduring precariousness and structural devaluation of the lives of Black Americans in the United States. The movement was initiated in 2011 by Alicia Garza, Opal Tometi and Patrisse Cullors as a response to the acquittal of George Zimmerman, a neighbourhood watch coordinator who had been charged for the murder of the seventeen-year-old African American man Trayvon Martin. While the creation of Black Lives Matter was a response to this specific homicide, it also resonated with the long history of anti-Black racism in the United States.

Recently, some leaders in the movement have expressed their concerns regarding the effects that their work has had on the activists themselves. In 2016 a twenty-three-year-old activist, MarShawn McCarrel, committed suicide in front of the statehouse in Columbus, Ohio. Even though the reasons behind his decision to take his own life remain unclear, McCarrel's death sparked a discussion in which several leaders of the movement reported experiencing mental distress, such as depression and anxiety (Lowery and Stankiewicz 2016).[1] Furthermore, a lead organiser from Cleveland reported that he had also attempted suicide, and another from St. Louis said that "there are so many folks [among Black Lives Matter activists] who are on the brink of killing themselves" (ibid.).

While there is no simple causation between mental disability and active participation in Black Lives Matter, it is striking that activists feel that working in a movement that defends the lives of black people can have a disabling effect that ultimately jeopardises their lives.

While some mental disabilities increase the likelihood of suicidal behaviour, they do not significantly increase the likelihood of engaging in violent behaviour towards other people. On the contrary, individuals with mental disabilities are significantly more likely to become victims of violent crimes in comparison with non-disabled people (Diefenbach 1997: 289). Despite not posing an actual threat to public safety, individuals with mental disabilities make up almost twenty-five per cent of all the victims who are fatally shot by police in the United States (Lowery et al. 2015). The proportion of African Americans who are victims of police shootings is also almost twenty-five per cent (Lowery et al. 2015).

Representations of black men and representations of people with mental disabilities in the media and popular culture embody the similar traits of violent behaviour and unpredictability and, in representations where blackness and mental disability overlap, they tend to amplify and reinforce each other (Metzl 2009). In this chapter, I discuss how incorporating these stereotypes into a first-person narrative could produce 'egresses' from those very stereotypes.

Delineating 'Egress'

Some disability studies scholars have explored the possibilities of employing autobiographical narratives either as a research practice (Derby 2013) or as a research subject (Price 2011). Specialised concepts and definitions have been developed for distinguishing forms of life writing, such as autopathography (Couser 1997), autosomatography (Couser 2009) and counter-diagnosis (Price 2011). Despite the variety of perspectives and ways of conceptualising autobiography, the shared view is that this form of writing has potential for critiquing the dominant discourses about disability, which are overwhelmingly objectifying (Derby 2009; Eisenhauer 2012; Price 2011). However, the perspective through which this critique is imposed is rather exclusive since it is, predominantly, the perspective of a white, middle-class woman with a college degree who has access to disability studies theories and concepts, as well as to political and activist communities of people with disabilities. The first person narratives discussed in this chapter are, however, produced by black male artists with a working class background and, in the case of Bushwick Bill, without the resources provided by disability studies and activism. In this sense, the artists can be considered to be egressing the dominant discourses of disability memoirs.

The *American Heritage Dictionary of the English Language* defines egress, when used as a noun, as "(1) the act of coming or going out; emergence; (2) the right to leave or go out: *denied the refugees egress*; (3) a path or opening for going out; an exit". When used as a verb egress means "to go out; emerge" (Egress, 2014).

Egressibility is a pivotal notion in accessible architecture and urban planning, designating the capacity of infrastructure to provide safe exit, or egress, for people with disabilities. Egress can also be employed as a theoretical tool for problematising representational infrastructures of disability. In addition to physical structures, such as walls, stairs and ramps, infrastructure also refers to the social, discursive and cultural structures that impact the ways, and the extent to which, subjects can navigate in different cultural spaces and settings. For example, in the context of higher education Price (2011) uses the notion of infrastructure with reference to different aspects of educational spaces, such as the classroom: "infrastructure comprises not only its tables and chairs, its technologies, and its participants, but also the beliefs, discourses, attitudes and interchanges that take place there" (Price 2011: 61).

To develop egress as a theoretical concept this chapter presents a framework that builds on two notions: the notion of 'potentiality', which draws particularly on Agamben's work on this concept; and Foucault's concept of 'counter-conduct'. Following Aristotle, Agamben approaches potentiality as a mode of being that exceeds the dichotomy of being and non-being. Potentiality is always coupled with impotentiality; it is always as much an unactualised capacity to be as it is an unactualised capacity not to be (Agamben 1999). The notions of ability and disability can also be viewed through this formulation. Ability is not simply a presence of potentiality, nor is disability an absence of potentiality. Disability is, in fact, a potentiality, that is, a positive presence of a capacity not-to (do or be):

> What is essential is that potentiality is not simply non-Being, simple privation, but rather the existence of non-Being, the presence of an absence; this is what we call "faculty" or "power". (Agamben 1999: 179)

The concept of counter-conduct was introduced by Foucault (2004) in his 1977–1978 lecture series at Collège de France for designating certain strategies that are used to resist the effects of power by moving beyond mere disobedience or overt resistance. He uses this notion to describe the stances that a subject of power can assume in order not to be obedient while still avoiding accusations of non-compliance. Counter-conduct also refers to forms of resistance that are not explicitly or even consciously political (Foucault 2004). As an example of counter-conduct, Foucault mentions certain responses to Christianity in Europe, including asceticism and mysticism. Neither of these approaches denies faith in a Christian god, but they reject the Church and its teachings, claiming that ascetic or mystic practices offer a more direct and profound relationship with god, thus countering ecclesiastical power (Foucault 2004). In an earlier lecture series, from 1973–1974, Foucault (2006) provides an account of a process that could be identified as counter-conduct, even though he does not use the concept at that point. He describes nineteenth-century hysterics as "the true militants of antipsychiatry" (Foucault 2006: 254), as they eventually brought down hysteria-centred psychiatry by providing the symptoms that the diagnoses expected from them.[2] This led to the collapse of psychiatric theory, as it became increasingly difficult to judge whether any given symptoms were caused by an illness or by the psychiatric intervention itself (Foucault 2006).

Representational egresses can be described as forms of counter-conduct in the sense that they involve assuming and utilising the very tropes of—and seemingly aligning with—mainstream representations. Egress refers to a stance that preserves its potentiality; performing or constituting an egress does not imply a total and absolute escape from a representation but, rather, a stance that is informed by the potentiality to exit. As noted above, the meanings given to egress are the "act of coming out", the "right to come out" and a "path or opening for going out" (Egress 2014), and in accordance with these meanings I attempt to theorise egress as a way to constitute a relationship between the oppressive discursive structures and the disabled subject, which enables the latter to resist confinement.

This chapter examines the capacity of discursive representations to confine subjects by imposing limitations not only on the ways in which non-disabled people perceive people with disabilities, but also on how people with disabilities perceive themselves and their own subjectivities. As a response to this capacity for discursive and representational confinement, it is necessary to develop strategies to evade and resist it. The notions of potentiality and counter-conduct can help to delineate the mechanisms of this confinement and theorise ways to counter it. The following sections attempt to show how certain representations may function as egresses from a representational tradition of racialisation, criminalisation and sub-humanisation of individuals with mental disabilities.

MUSIC AND BLACK SUBJECTIVITY

The precariousness of black life in the United States is one of the themes that black American music has persistently conveyed through its recorded history. "Crazy Blues", written by Perry Bradford and recorded by Mamie Smith, was the first commercial blues recording performed by an African American artist (Smith 1920). "Crazy Blues" employs an abandoned woman's blues narrative form, which became a major genre within the recorded blues of the 1920s. Gussow (2002) discusses how "Crazy Blues" can be read as a social text, as a documentation of the racial tensions in early twentieth-century American society. His interpretation of "Crazy Blues" suggests that blues songs sung by women do not necessarily describe the experience of being abandoned by an unfaithful lover but, instead, the experience of precariousness that was part of the everyday lives of black people in the Jim Crow South. Gussow points out that "Crazy Blues" can be read as the story not of a woman who has been abandoned, but of a woman who is afraid that her man might be murdered (Gussow 2002). This reading is based on several minor cues in the lyrics, but especially on the last verse of the song, which serves as a plot twist in the story. First, there is the refrain, which is repeated several times during the song:

> Now I've got the crazy blues
> Since my baby went away
> I ain't had no time to lose
> I must find him today.

But the last verse does not mention the man at all:

> I'm gonna do like a Chinaman, go and get some hop
> Get myself a gun, and shoot myself a cop
> I ain't had nothin' but bad news
> Now I've got the crazy blues.

Interestingly, in the verse preceding the last refrain, the narrator is about to commit suicide:

> I went to the railroad, set my head on the track
> Thought about my daddy, I gladly snatched it back.

After abandoning the idea of killing herself, she claims that she will "do like a Chinaman, go and get some hop/Get myself a gun, and shoot myself a cop".[3] The cop does not appear in the song before the last verse, and the introduction of this character at this point—and its immediate killing—remains rather puzzling, considering the first half of the song. Gussow argues that this twist in the story denotes a collective phantasy of vengeance towards the oppressor, in effect, the American society that the cop symbolises.

The theme in "Crazy Blues" is also taken up and developed in the song "Mad Mama's Blues", recorded by Josie Miles (1924), and written by movie director and songwriter Spencer Williams under the pen name Duke Jones. The song lacks the abandoned woman framework of "Crazy Blues" and concentrates, instead, on the narrator's homicidal fantasy, for which there seems to be no apparent cause:

> Now I could see blood running
> Through the streets
> Now I could see blood running
> Through the streets
> Could be everybody
> Layin' dead right at my feet
> ...
> I took my big Winchester
> Down off the shelf
> I took my big Winchester
> Down off the shelf
> When I get through shooting
> There won't be nobody left

In "Mad Mama's Blues" we see a narrative that lacks the type of psychological rationale in "Crazy Blues". The entire song consists of the narrator describing how she would like to kill everybody and destroy the city with firearms and explosives—without disclosing any motive or explanation for her desire.

The tradition of first person narration and stories of killing have been preserved in rap music. Biggie Smalls (real name Christopher Wallace)—more formally known as the Notorious B.I.G., and often regarded as one of the most influential rappers in the history of hip hop—published only one album, *Ready to Die* (1994), before his death at the age of twenty-four in a drive-by shooting. His second studio album, *Life After Death* (1997), was published posthumously, only sixteen days after his death. Throughout *Ready to Die* (1994), Biggie constantly refers to his own death, as well as the death of his many adversaries—for instance, "Gimme the Loot" ends, like Smith's "Crazy Blues", with a reference to shooting cops. Songs that refer to Biggie's death include: "Ready to Die", "Everyday Struggle"—which opens with the refrain "I don't wanna live no more, sometimes I hear death knocking on my front door"—and "Respect", in which Biggie recounts his encounter with death before his birth: "umbilical cord's wrapped around my neck/I'm seeing my death and I ain't even took my first step".

The album unfolds a story of a young man rising from poverty and violence towards success and wealth. At least, this is what the storyline looks like, until the last track of the album, "Suicidal Thoughts", which is not a conventional song with verses and choruses. It opens with a ringing phone, which wakes Biggie's friend and producer Puff Daddy (Sean Combs): "Hello? … Do you know what time it is?". However, there is no answer until he, frustrated, asks "what the fuck is wrong with you?", after which Biggie starts his monologue:

> When I die, fuck it, I wanna go to hell
> Cause I'm a piece of shit, it ain't hard to fucking tell
> It don't make sense going to heaven with the goodie-goodies,
> Dressed in white—I like black Timbs and black hoodies

In the middle part of the monologue, Biggie fantasises about killing himself:

> I swear to God I wanna just slit my wrists and end this bullshit
> Throw the Magnum to my head, threaten to pull shit,
> and squeeze
> Until the bed's
> Completely red
> I'm glad I'm dead
> A worthless fucking buddha head

This is immediately followed by a peculiar reflection as a response to his self-destructive desires:

> The stress is building up
> I can't, I can't believe suicide's on my fucking mind
> I swear to God I feel like the dead is fucking calling me
> Nah, you wouldn't understand

Inevitably, towards the end, Biggie expresses that he cannot go on:

> I reach my peak
> I can't speak
> Call my nigga Chic
> Tell him that my will is weak
> I'm sick of niggas lying, and sick of bitches hawking
> Matter of fact, I'm sick of talking

The last line is followed by the sound of a gunshot and a loud thump caused by Biggie's body falling on the floor. Puff Daddy, who has repeatedly tried to interrupt Biggie during the monologue, continues to call him: "Ayo, Big? Ayo, Big?" His voice fades out with the sound of Biggie's weakening heartbeat, while the recorded female voice from the operator instructs, "Please hang up, and try your call again".

The last track of the album, therefore, shifts the tone of the album. *Ready to Die* initially appears to state the will to die in a game of get rich or die trying, that is, a readiness to die *for* something. However, by the end of the album, the message is one about being determined to die regardless of the circumstances. While the entire album explores the meaning, objectives and motivations to die—and to let others die—as well as the significance of death in the economics of the drug trade, the final moment of death is detached from these social meanings.

Horrorcore and Krip Hop

Both Krip Hop and horrorcore rap are forms of hip hop culture, but they differ significantly from each other. Horrorcore is a loosely defined stylistic and thematic form of mainstream rap, often considered as a subgenre of gangsta rap, whereas Krip Hop is not a genre or a style, but refers exclusively to music produced by members of the Krip Hop Nation.[4]

Krip Hop Nation, a movement and a collective founded and led by disability activist and artist Leroy F. Moore Jr., is bound together by the clearly articulated political and philosophical stance shared by its members. Moore et al. (2016) state that Krip Hop is based on the following set of standards:

1. Use politically correct lyrics.
2. Do not put down other minorities.
3. Use our music to advocate and teach not only about ourselves, but also about the system we live under.
4. Challenge mainstream and all media on the ways they frame disability.
5. Increase the inclusion of voices that are missing from within the popular culture.
6. Recognize our disabled ancestors, knowing that we are built on what they left us, and nothing is new, just borrowed.
7. Know that sometimes we fail to meet the above standards but we are trying (Moore et al. 2016: 310).

The decision to name the movement Krip Hop Nation addresses the problematic nature of the concept 'nation', which, as Agamben (1998) reminds us, "derives etymologically from *nascere* (to be born)" (Part 3, Chap. 2, para. 3). Against this history of the term nation, and against the history of nationalism, Krip Hop Nation points to the problems involved in the definition of a group of people—*a people*, as a unified whole—and disrupts the racist underpinnings of the term by applying it to a group of individuals who do not share the same cultural identity, ethnic background or language, but have in common the experience of living as/in disabled bodies. Through its name Krip Hop Nation constitutes a rhetorical egress, abandoning the normative concept of nation and challenging the practices of police brutality and ethnic profiling that it informs.

Moore has contributed to disability activism and culture through a variety of methods, such as poetry, journalism, music, performance art and lecturing. A longstanding and pivotal theme in his work is the mistreatment of people with disabilities by law enforcement officers and the legal system (Moore et al. 2016). In (2012) Krip Hop Nation published, with 5th Battalion, the compilation album *Broken Bodies PBP— Police Brutality & Profiling Mixtape*, which was strongly motivated by the arrest and subsequent prosecution and conviction of an eighteen-year-old autistic man, Reginald Latson. The opening track of the album, "Neli Latsons Story", is written and performed by punk-hop duo Kounterclockwise, formed by Deacon Burns and Kaya Rogue. The song is a chronological, first-person narrative depicting Latson's arrest. It starts with a chorus:

> Now I'm headed to prison
> Charged with having autism
> And defending myself from being beaten
> Swallowed whole in the belly of an unjust system
> Stuck in isolation

The following verse starts with Latson waiting for the library to open, when a police officer approaches him and states that he "fit[s] a description/of a black male with a gun looking suspicious":

> Never found a weapon but still he kept pushing it
> "Where's the gun?"
> Talking about my mother, grandmother, and my sister—even Obama
> Calling us all monkeys

While the news media tend to portray the victims of police brutality from a distance, through a third-person perspective, Kounterclockwise's song reverses this representational strategy by portraying the injustice through a first-person narration, thereby providing a representational egress from dominant narratives.

Bushwick Bill—and the genre he represents, horrorcore—might be considered a target of the critique posed by Krip Hop Nation on the mainstream hip hop industry, insofar as he uses openly misogynist rhetoric and pairs violent behaviour with mental disability. However, the excessive and overdriven exploitation of the most extreme stereotypes of blackness, disability and violence might function, on another level, as a resistance to, or egress from, the very stereotypes it employs. As Bailey (2011) suggests, we should "go beyond the ineffective dichotomy of positive and negative representation... In the liminal spaces of hip hop the re-appropriation of ableist language can mark a new way of using words that departs from generally accepted disparaging connotations" (Bailey 2011: 142).

Bushwick Bill, whose real name is Richard Shaw, was born in Jamaica in 1966, moved to New York City and, later, to Houston, Texas, where he joined the Ghetto Boys in 1986.[5] After a series of changes in the line-up, the group eventually comprised of Willie D (William Dennis), Scarface (Brad Jordan) and Bushwick Bill. The group contributed to the commonplace rhetorical practice in rap music of claiming to be mentally ill for a two-fold meaning: first, as a reference to one's aptness to engage in violence and crime; and second, to be able to produce excessively violent lyrical content. The song "Mind of a Lunatic" (Geto Boys 1989) is a prime example of what would eventually be called horrorcore, a sub-genre of gangsta rap, which incorporates imagery, themes and narrative elements from horror literature and cinema (Strauss 1994). Even though the Geto Boys have been accused of misogyny and the perpetuation of negative stereotypes of African Americans, Willie D contests this simplistic reading in a recent interview by stating that the Geto Boys

> gonna speak about injustice all over the world. Cause the same dirty-ass shit that cops are doing out here in the US, that same thing is going on in other countries. Every country, they got some group of people that they oppress. Every single country got that shit going on. Now it's just that in this country [whistles] it's just so much more fucking pervasive. (Willie D, in Lubovny 2016)

The cover of the third album by the Geto Boys, *We Can't Be Stopped* (1991), consists of a photograph of the group members, with the band name and the album title printed over it in bright blue block letters. In the picture, Bushwick Bill is sitting on a hospital bed, which Willie D and Scarface are pushing along what appears to be a hospital corridor. The latter two are dressed in casual gear, while Bushwick Bill is wearing a hospital gown and a black baseball cap. His right eye appears to be injured, and he is holding a mobile phone to his ear. The events preceding this photograph are described in Bushwick Bill's first solo album, *Little Big Man*, two years later.

Little Big Man (Bushwick Bill 1992) used many of the Geto Boys' stylistic and thematic strategies, such as graphic depictions of murder and sexual violence, but it also included more personal insights to his disabilities: dwarfism, depression and vision impairment. The album title, for instance, refers to his dwarfism, while several songs point to his mental disability, such as "Call Me Crazy", "Skitso" and "Chuckwick", a song that introduces Bushwick Bill's alter ego, which is based on the murderous doll Chucky in the *Child's Play* horror movie franchise. Throughout the album the rapper describes numerous instances when he became an object of ridicule and abuse because of his height. Bushwick Bill also presents fantasies of avenging these ableist remarks. "Call Me Crazy", for instance, begins with an anonymous person telling jokes about Bushwick Bill and his height: "He can't even piss, he can't even piss without rounding all the way back, squeezing his little dick… little nasty motherfucker". These jokes provoke laughter among a crowd of listeners, before Bushwick Bill enters the scene and apparently shoots everyone who is mocking him (Bushwick Bill 1992).

The song that illuminates the events preceding the cover photo of *We Can't Be Stopped* is "Ever So Clear", an autobiographical narrative covering Bushwick Bill's life from birth to the present. He recounts how he "damn nearly didn't make it on my date of birth" and "see, people got it bad from jump street/and being short is just another strike against me/I used to get funny looks 'cause I was small". Later, despite his success as a recording artist, he feels that friends and "bitches" tend to take advantage of him. He describes his disappointment at his relationships with women, and the eventual escalation of his frustration:

> And it's gettin outta hand, gee
> 'cause nobody seems to understand me
> Reminiscing got me feelin kinda low
> I broke out the Ever-Clear and then I drunk some more
> Until it was all gone
> Now I'm lookin for somebody to take my pain out on
> But not just anybody, gee
> I'ma take that on to Mica 'cause she's the closest to me
> Full of that Ever-Clear and high on that buddah
> Get to the house all I'm thinkin bout is shooting her
> 'cause shooting her would be sweet
> But you know what'd be sweeter? if I make her shootin me
> Call me crazy, but that's what I'm thinking (Bushwick Bill 1992).

He intrudes in Mica's house, hands his gun to her and insists that she must shoot him. As she refuses, he attacks her in an attempt to provoke her. She still does not comply, so he grabs her baby and threatens to hurt him if she refuses to fulfil his request:

She still wouldn't grab the gun
And at that time I wasn't thinking about no one
Damn near crazy I went and grabbed the baby
Held him by the door and said I'ma throw his ass out, ho
She went to crying, somebody stop him
I said: you better grab the muthafuckin gun or I'ma drop him
She snatched the baby out of my hands
We started fighting, punching, scratching, and biting
When we fell on the bed, check this shit
All kinds of crazy shit was goin through my head
So I ran and got the gun and came back to her
Loaded it up and handed the gat to her
I grabbed her hand and placed the gun to my eye muscle
She screamed stop and then we broke into another tussle
Yo, during the fight the gun went off quick
Damn! Aw shit, I'm hit (Bushwick Bill 1992).

The juxtaposition of this narrative of an actual incident of (mainly) suicidal violence, with images drawn from horror films, creates a disconti-
nuity in the album's structure and style. The song discusses violence, but
without deploying the horrorcore tropes that are used in the majority of
the album's songs.

In Bushwick Bill's most recent album, *My Testimony of Redemption*
(2009), which reflects the religious convictions that he developed after
his previous albums, he abandons the violent themes of his earlier work.
In an interview in 2015 Bushwick Bill was asked about his current views
on his earlier explicit lyrics. He stated that he had been disappointed
and disturbed when people claimed that they had committed homicides
inspired by his music. He insisted that his lyrics were not to be perceived
as a glorification of violence and crime (Bushwick Bill, in Monarch
2015). Nevertheless, he stated that even though he had moved away
from his earlier style, he did not see horrorcore as ultimately incompatible with his Christian faith:

Just 'cause I read the Bible don't mean that there's no horrorcore raps
from the Bible … When you get a chance read Deuteronomy 28 and tell
me what you think a rap would be like if I was to rap about the blessings
and the curses. Because in one of the curses in Deuteronomy is said your
woman will bear a child in secret and eat it and not even share it with you.
You can't tell me that wouldn't be a horrorcore lyric. (Bushwick Bill, in
Monarch 2015)

Furthermore, as a response to the interviewer's question "Does it, in fact, feel good to be a gangsta?" (referring to the song by Geto Boys (1992) "Damn It Feels Good to Be a Gangsta"), Bushwick Bill egresses a confining subject position by stating that

> Yes it does because my definition of a gangsta is not a ruthless dictator. ... Okay, to break it down in short: Stephen Biko—gangsta; Mandela—gangsta; Malcolm X—gangsta; Martin Luther King—gangsta. It's like people who go against the grain to make things happen for good. That's a gangsta. A gangsta doesn't necessarily have to be a derogatory statement". (Bushwick Bill, in Monarch 2015)

Conclusion

This chapter has delineated an approach to deconstructing stereotypical representations by concentrating on two distinct forms of hip hop culture. This juxtaposition of horrorcore and Krip Hop addresses the problems of countering stereotyping and representational confinement by performing a series of multiple, overlapping and even conflicting egresses. For example, Bushwick Bill undoubtedly egresses conventional representations of little persons. His work egresses the conventions of horrorcore by placing a song like the autobiographical "Ever so clear" among the otherwise mainly fictional and gory horrorcore songs. He also egresses the image of a horrorcore rapper by openly embracing Christianity, and egresses the stereotype of a born-again Christian by describing the Bible as a source of horrorcore lyrics.

Krip Hop, on the other hand, egresses from the tendency of mainstream rap to use disparaging language towards minority groups, such as people with disabilities. It also egresses from mainstream media depictions of police brutality, in which victims are objectified, by rewriting the usual narratives that we see in the news with first person accounts. Finally, Krip Hop Nation egresses the racist and xenophobic connotations of nation by using this concept in a completely different manner.

Representational egress is applied here in an analysis of hip hop, but the notion could be employed in a variety of contexts and discourses. It can help to theorise ways in which to respond to oppressive discursive structures to evade dichotomies such as acceptance and refusal, obedience and defiance, and interior and exterior. It can also open up possibilities for creating and maintaining a state of not-yet-responding, lingering on the threshold of an egress.

NOTES

1. McCarrel only left a message on Facebook a few hours before his suicide: "My demons won today. I'm sorry" (Lowery and Stankiewicz 2016).
2. His description was probably a response to attempts at labelling his work as being part of the anti-psychiatry movement.
3. Hop apparently refers to opiates.
4. Krip refers to the historically derogatory word crip (derived from crippled) used by many member of the disability community in a self-affirmative manner. In Krip Hop the word is spelt with a k to avoid confusion with the Los Angeles street gang Crips.
5. The original spelling of the group's name.

REFERENCES

Agamben, G. (1998). *Homo Sacer: Sovereign Power and Bare Life*. Stanford, CA: Stanford University Press.

Agamben, G. (1999). *Potentialities: Collected Essays in Philosophy*. Stanford, CA: Stanford University Press.

Bailey, M. (2011). 'The Illest': Disability as Metaphor in Hip Hop Music. In Bell, C.M. (Ed.) *Blackness and Disability: Critical Examinations and Cultural Interventions*, 141–148. Münster: LIT Verlag.

Bushwick Bill. (1992). *Little Big Man* [CD]. Houston, TX: Rap-a-Lot Records.

Bushwick Bill. (2009). *My Testimony of Redemption* [CD]. Houston, TX: Much Luvv Records.

Couser, G.T. (1997). *Recovering Bodies: Illness, Disability, and Life-writing*. Madison, WI: University of Wisconsin Press.

Couser, G.T. (2009). *Signifying Bodies: Disability in Contemporary Life Writing*. Ann Arbor, MI: University of Michigan Press.

Derby, J. (2009). *Art Education and Disability Studies Perspectives on Mental Illness Discourses*. Dissertation. The Ohio State University.

Derby, J. (2013). Accidents Happen: An Art Autopathography on Mental Disability. *Disability Studies Quarterly*, 33(1).

Diefenbach, D.L. (1997). The portrayal of mental illness on prime-time television. *Journal of Community Psychology*, 25(3): 289–302.

Egress. (2014). In *The American Heritage Dictionary of the English Language*. Available at https://www.ahdictionary.com/word/search.html?q=egress.

Eisenhauer, J. (2012). Behind Closed Doors: The Pedagogy and Interventionist Practice of Digital Storytelling. *Journal of Curriculum and Pedagogy*, 9: 7–15.

Foucault, M. (2004). *Society Must Be Defended: Lectures at The Collège de France 1975–1976*. London: Penguin.

Foucault, M. (2006). *Psychiatric Power: Lectures at The Collège de France 1973–1974*. New York, NY: Palgrave Macmillan.

Garza, A. (2014). *A HerStory of the #BlackLivesMatter Movement*. Available at http://blacklivesmatter.com/herstory/.

Geto Boys. (1989). *Grip It! On That Other Level* [CD]. Houston, TX: Rap-a-Lot Records.

Geto Boys. (1991). *We Can't Be Stopped* [CD]. Houston, TX: Rap-a-Lot Records.

Geto Boys. (1992). *Uncut Dope: Geto Boys' Best* [CD]. Houston, TX: Rap-a-Lot Records.

Gussow, A. (2002). *Seems Like Murder Here: Southern Violence and the Blues Tradition*. Chicago, IL: University of Chicago Press.

Krip Hop Nation & 5th Battalion. (2012). *Broken Bodies PBP—Police Brutality & Profiling Mixtape* [CD].

Lowery W., Kindy, K., Alexander, K.L., Tate, J., Jenkins, J. and Rich, S. (2015). Distraught People, Deadly Results. *Washington Post*, 30 June. Available at http://www.washingtonpost.com/sf/investigative/2015/06/30/distraught-people-deadly-results/.

Lowery, W. and Stankiewicz, K. (2016). 'My demons won today': Ohio activist's suicide spotlights depression among Black Lives Matter leaders. *The Washington Post*, 15 February. Available at https://www.washingtonpost.com/news/post-nation/wp/2016/02/15/my-demons-won-today-ohio-activists-suicide-spotlights-depression-among-black-lives-matter-leaders/?utm_term=.471cba1ac13f.

Lyubovny, V. (2016). *Willie D: Bushwick Bill Getting Shot for Threatening to Throw Baby Out Window*, 28 June. Available at https://www.youtube.com/watch?v=Uhesu3mqikU&t=40s.

McNeil Laboratories. (1974). *Archives of General Psychiatry*, 31(5): 732–733.

Metzl, J. (2009). *Protest Psychosis: How Schizophrenia Became a Black Disease* [Kindle version]. Boston, MA: Beacon Press.

Miles, J. (1924). *Mad Mama's Blues* [Phonograph record]. New York, NY: Edison Records.

Monarch, B. (2015). *Monarch Podcast Ep. 001—Bushwick Bill*. 28 May. Available at https://www.youtube.com/watch?v=XN90awrQqgk.

Moore, L.F., Gray-Garcia, L. and Thrower, E.H. (2016). Black & Blue: Policing Disability & Poverty Beyond Occupation. In Block, P., Kasnitz, D., Nishida, A. and Pollard, N. (Eds.) *Occupying Disability: Critical Approaches to Community, Justice, and Decolonizing Disability*, 295–318. New York, NY: Springer.

Notorious B.I.G. (1994). *Ready to Die* [CD]. New York, NY: Bad Boy Records.

Notorious B.I.G. (1997). *Life After Death* [CD]. New York, NY: Bad Boy Records.

Price, M. (2011). *Mad at School: Rhetorics of Mental Disability and Academic Life*. Ann Arbor, MI: University of Michigan Press.

Smith, M. (1920). *Crazy Blues* [Phonograph record]. New York, NY: Okeh Records.

Strauss, N. (1994). When Rap Meets the Undead. *The New York Times*, 18 September. Available at http://www.nytimes.com/1994/09/18/arts/pop-view-when-rap-meets-the-undead.html?sec=&spon.

PART III

Communities and their Contexts

CHAPTER 10

New Orleans, Food, Race and Gender on Television: *Frank's Place* and *Treme*

Robin Roberts

INTRODUCTION

This chapter focuses on the depiction of food in two US television shows set in New Orleans. While the shows appeared twenty years apart, their depictions of food's importance in New Orleans reveals how community is created through foodways. Analysing two representative episodes shows how central food is in defining and maintaining community. This chapter focuses on the representation of chefs in both series, as figures whose struggles highlight the importance of food as a cultural product. The televisual depiction of foodways as creative cultural expression reveals the city's long promotion and consumption of food as central to its identity. At the same time, the plots reveal the impact of race, gender and class on foodways. In both programmes specific cultural practices are shown in a fashion that promotes the desirability of respecting difference.

The award-winning US television show *Frank's Place* (1987–1988) has had a strong impact on critics and on television itself. Although decades have passed since it aired, *Frank's Place* deserves analysis not only

R. Roberts (✉)
University of Arkansas, Arkansas, USA
e-mail: roberts1@uark.edu

© The Author(s) 2017
R. Sanz Sabido (ed.), *Representing Communities*,
DOI 10.1007/978-3-319-65030-2_10

183

for its groundbreaking focus on a working-class black community and innovative 'dramedy' format (combination of drama and comedy), but also because the issues it raises remain relevant for televisual representation today. Critics and television professionals have long lauded the merits of *Frank's Place*—the series received Emmy awards and recognition from the NAACP—and one of the creators of *Treme*, HBO's twenty-first-century show set in New Orleans, David Simon, praises *Frank's Place* as "the first thing that argued for New Orleans intelligently. It was the first thing to argue for culture intelligently" (Rawls 2011: 85).

The critically acclaimed HBO series *Treme* (2010–2013) drew on *Frank's Place*, a relationship acknowledged by public events featuring the creators and cast members from both shows. In a wry instance of televisual intertextuality, lead star Tim Reid from *Frank's Place* appears as a judge on *Treme*. Joy Fuqua cites this example to claim that "at least this episode of *Treme* offers itself as televisual atonement for the economic (and ideological) decisions that cancelled the lease on *Frank's Place*" (Fuqua 2012: 237). Both programmes incorporate restaurant culture into their plot lines, and race and gender play an important role in these depictions. New Orleans' unique foodways are showcased in both series, highlighting the ways that television uses food culture to reflect and define a community. As Lois Eric Elie, a New Orleanian who served as story editor for *Treme*, explains, "food is central to identity" (Franklin 2011).

THE CINEMATIC CITY

Using folklore, race and gender theory, this chapter explores the depiction of New Orleans' food in each series, focusing on changes in cultural and televisual sensibilities in the twenty-five-year span that separates *Frank's Place* and *Treme*. Setting is central to both these shows, demonstrating that New Orleans has a significant place as a setting in television and film. While New Orleans is not one of the cities discussed in *Global Cinematic Cities: New Landscapes of Film and Media* (Andersson and Webb 2016), the book's emphasis on the importance of place for media provides some useful contexts for considering the 'Big Easy', as New Orleans is often called. As editors Johan Andersson and Lawrence Webb explain, "the digital turn has threatened the indexical link to geographic space" (Andersson and Webb 2016: 8). Television shows like *Frank's Place* and *Treme* (and many others, including *NCIS: New Orleans*, The Originals and *American Horror Story: Coven*) resist the digital turn by representing their settings in specific concrete ways and, in recent years, filming on location. While the generous state tax credits undoubtedly prompted many productions to film in New Orleans, many of them, like *Treme*, made the city itself integral to the narratives. New Orleans fits the authors' description of a cluster city, one that has achieved "unusual competitive success" according to economist Michael Porter (Andersson and Webb 2016: 29). A top-ten world tourist destination (*Travel and Leisure* 2016), New Orleans has achieved this status in part through the activities of its creative class, including that of its chefs. Elena Gorfinkel and John David Rhodes argue that "the cinema is instrumental in contributing to the circumvention of the homogenising tendencies of globalization" (Gorfinkel and Rhodes 2011: xii) and, as this chapter suggests, television shows like *Frank's Place* and *Treme* highlight specific cultural practices, including foodways, to portray the desirability of cultural specificity and difference. In particular, this specific city and its black and female residents produce food in a unique and location-bound manner. It is to experience these pleasures that tourists travel to the location, and viewers turn on the television programmes.

Televisual Culinary Tourism and Authenticity

These television programmes draw on the concept of culinary tourism, with food presented as entertainment. Both series represent behind-the-scenes perspectives of New Orleans' food culture, highlighting racial conflict and the stress between capitalism and food creation. As Lucy Long argues, culinary tourism "steps outside the normal routine to notice difference and the power of food to represent and negotiate that difference" (Long 2004: 20). As Barbara Kirshenblatt-Gimblett explains, "not authenticity but the *question* of authenticity, is essential to culinary tourism" (Kirshenblatt-Gimblett 2004: xii). In these television programmes, authenticity is cited in several ways, including the producers of *Frank's Place* doing research in New Orleans then flying Chef Leslie Austin (on whom the character of Big Arthur is based) to the set in Los Angeles to prepare food for the actors and crew (Walker 2011). Decades later, with a larger, cable channel, budget, *Treme* attested to its authenticity by filming on location in New Orleans, and including Susan Spicer, the real-life chef who inspired Janette's character, as a consultant, with Spicer appearing as herself in the finale to Season Two. For New Orleanians, both programmes' serious attempts to be accurate provided validation for their communities. Authenticity, in terms of these series, requires respecting the specificity of the local community. In both television series the representation of the food as authentically prepared is essential to the characters and to the narratives.

Significantly, the time period in which *Frank's Place* aired, the 1980s, was when, according to Sharon Zukin, changes in ideas about authenticity "reach[ed] a tipping point" (Zukin 2010: 222). The use of 'authenticity' as a concept, she explains, is central to the role of television and film in keeping the idea of the city alive (ibid.: 224). In its presentation of New Orleans' black working-class culture, the series was one of the first to portray it as valuable, at the same time that Cajun culture was being promoted nationally and internationally (and the show includes a Cajun character). As cities across the world became homogenised, taken over by international investors, New Orleans resisted this homogenisation, as the state of Louisiana began to market the Cajun culture as a tourist attraction. Parallel promotion of the state's black heritage, however, was not as strongly supported. *Frank's Place*, with its emphasis on a black neighbourhood, exposed this racist omission.[1]

A central issue in scholarship about New Orleans is a critique of neoliberal attitudes, leading to charges of exploitation and appropriation. The chefs on these two television shows not only expose different types of appropriation, but also present resistance to it, whether the oppressive mechanism is racism or capitalism. An acknowledgement of the city's history on television, as well as a more nuanced understanding of resistance to neoliberalist fatalism, shapes both programmes. The shows' creators have been quite explicit in detailing how the setting complements their series' political and cultural aims. Examining the ways the chef characters are used reveals that this figure is presented as an artist, a creative talent at odds with the homogenising, profit-seeking perspective of capitalism, especially in its neoliberal guise.

Herman Gray has written about both shows, and he warns of the dangers of a neoliberal position, "attacking an incompetent state, demonising clients of the state, privileging market transactions, and celebrating entrepreneurial subjects" (Gray 2012: 270). Yet, as the characters discussed here demonstrate, both *Frank's Place* and *Treme* highlight the dangers of embracing capitalism and its damaging effect on communities and individuals, as well as on creative endeavours. In both series, characters resist and deny profit making as the highest value, and their actions are validated and endorsed. This attitude connects the African American male chef in *Frank's Place* to the white female chef in *Treme*, in plots that could only be set in New Orleans.

Television, Place and the Representation of Community

The creators of *Frank's Place*, Tim Reid and Hugh Wilson, both from the South, were, as Reid explained, "never at ease with the portrayal of Southern characters. [Writers] would always go for a cliché, black or white" (Reid and Reid 2013). Their goal with *Frank's Place* was to create a programme that challenged conventional television norms in the 1980s. In Tim Reid's words, they wanted to explore "the unique richness of black culture … actual visuals and reality of black culture" (Reid and Reid 2013). The show's dramedy format, use of a single camera and extensive use of original music made the programme distinctive and memorable. Daphne Maxwell Reid, who co-starred in the series with her husband, confirmed that "we did a lot of research together based on actual [New Orleans] characters and settings" (Reid and Reid 2013). Basing the show on Chef Austin Leslie's famous restaurant, Chez Helene, the producers even flew the chef out to the set while they filmed the pilot. In addition, New Orleans native Don Yesso, at the time not an actor, was hired to play the bartender after Wilson met him on a plane. About the episode "Food Fight", which features black chef Big Arthur, Tim Reid said, "that's New Orleans: all about food and pride in your recipe" (Reid and Reid 2013). Eric Overmyer, another of *Treme*'s producers, explained that the series was created in part as a response to the terrible tragedy of the levees' failures and disastrous flooding after Hurricane Katrina. Overmyer, who had owned a house in the city since the 1980s, and who often spent time there, lamented that "as a result of Katrina, New Orleans had the attention of the country for a relatively brief time" (Overmyer, *Treme* Panel 2012). Lolis Eric Elie, a New Orleans newspaper columnist and writer for the show, described the series as trying to be radically different from other television drama. "*Treme*", he said, was "a new kind of storytelling [about] … how a culture rebuilt a city … not a documentary but captures culture through the eyes of a city" (Elie, *Treme* Panel 2012). Overmyer explained how the show drew on actual chefs, having them in scenes with actors, "We received nice respect from restaurant people" (Overmyer, *Treme* Panel 2012). The role of the series' main chef, Janette Desautel, was based on the award-winning chef of Bayonna, Susan Spicer, who appeared in a few scenes with Janette.

Research and consideration of cultural authenticity typifies both shows, and the incorporation of local residents provides one sign of the producers' focus. Yet place affects the programmes in other, less expected ways. One of the many unusual features of New Orleans is its femininity. The city's positioning as feminine shapes its culture and, consequently, the shows that draw on this setting. As many writers have noted, New Orleans functions as an exotic Other to the United States. Gender is, as this chapter suggests, integral to the use of race in this positioning. The creators and writers of *Frank's Place* and *Treme* used folklore to generate plots that reveal the intersection of gender, race and place in representation. On *Frank's Place*, the main character grew up in the northeast and inherited the restaurant from a father he never knew, in a city where he had never lived, which placed Frank in the same position as millions of viewers, similarly unaware of New Orleans' unique culture. As the protagonist Frank struggles to understand and appreciate what is depicted to him as "authentic" New Orleans, he and the viewers see the place as "plural, conflictual, and contested" (Gotham 2007: 164). A wide range of characters on *Treme* similarly wrestle with the concept of New Orleans.

Gender is central to both series' representation of New Orleans. Presented as outside the economy and the values of mainstream America (represented by corporations, efficiency and rationality), New Orleans is depicted as possessing an alternative culture, characterised through strong female figures and female-dominated voodoo. As William S. Woods explains in an article in *Modern Language Notes*, "etymologically the name *Orleans* should be masculine in French", "yet the name of the American city has apparently been feminine in French since its existence" (Woods 1951: 259, 260). This interesting linguistic fact underscores the city's feminisation relative to other cities and places. As the defeated region in the American Civil War, the South took on a subordinate, feminine role to the industrialised masculine North.

It is the use of gender, particularly through the performance of folklore, that characterises the city as feminised. As with their goal of accurately representing New Orleans' black working-class culture, *Frank's Place*'s co-creators explicitly worked to include more women in its development. While the absence of women is an ongoing problem within television (Lauzen 2011; Linshi 2015; Women's Agenda 2013), it was something the creators of *Frank's Place* were determined to avoid. Acknowledging the collaborative nature of the televisual process, Wilson and Reid stressed their debt not only to each other, but also to the city they researched, to other writers and directors, and to their actors. According to Wilson, he and Reid "set about hiring a racially mixed crew" (Campbell and Reeves 1990: 15). Campbell and Reeves cited Reid's description that "45–50% [of the 100 person crew] were black—and of that percentage, half were black women. Most significantly, as Reid is quick to point out, two of the show's directors were black women. That kind of hiring, according to Reid, 'is almost unheard of today in network television'" (ibid.: 16). Unfortunately, Reid's point, made in the late 1980s, is still true today. Looking at the impact that a mixed crew had on a television series, especially the involvement of more women, is informative. It can therefore be argued that feminising the workforce and setting the series in a feminised city can have a profound effect on the stories that are told. Two types of feminisation, the gender of place and the subordination, intermingle with the opportunity for female characters to have a space to perform as powerful agents. But that place has to be outside of the dominant culture—the city of New Orleans, with different priorities and historical traditions, enables this.

Conflict Between Communities: Race

Frank's Place follows the trajectory of the main character as he learns the customs and traditions of New Orleans. Although he was born in New Orleans, Frank left at the age of two and only returns after he inherits the restaurant from a father he never knew. Female characters, especially the restaurant's two waitresses, his girlfriend and his girlfriend's powerful mother, frequently school Frank in the ways of New Orleans. The episode "Food Fight" deals with a conflict between male chefs, but its interpretation comes through the presentation of a value system that is alternative to the practical Yankee culture (Boston) in which Frank was raised.

"Food Fight", written by Richard Dubin, first aired on 7 December 1987. In 2016, the significance of New Orleans' food to its identity and international reputation can hardly be overstated. The beginning of this burgconing reputation, started with the Cajun food craze of the mid-1980s, and is now fully realised in the emphasis on foodways, the cultural practices of producing and consuming food, on television and in tourist promotions. *Frank's Place* subordinated Cajun cooking to Creole cuisine, even through its portrayal of Big Arthur as the chef, with the

Cajun, called Shorty, serving under Big Arthur. In its portrayal of an African American restaurant, *Frank's Place* revealed that there was more to Louisiana cuisine than Cajun food. Even more importantly, this particular episode highlighted the unique features of Creole food, and exposed the appropriation of black food practices by white culture. While the episode is humorous in its tone, the issue it addresses is quite serious: the exploitation and theft of valuable products. It is also worth noting that the series' emphasis on food and chef-as-celebrity prefigured the Food Network (which began several years later, in 1993) and television's obsessive emphasis on food. Big Arthur's importance to the restaurant is stressed from the beginning of the series. A large, imposing man, he is respected by the restaurant's employees and its patrons. With many scenes filmed in the kitchen, the series demonstrated the importance of food in terms of both its cultural significance and its impact as a business. Food's feminine aspects are emphasised as Big Arthur stays in the kitchen, working behind the scenes.

The plot depicted a conflict within cultural traditions, with a white chef named Cyrus Litt, from a French Quarter establishment named Café Étoile, stealing recipes from Big Arthur. As the white chef and his white boss, a well-manicured lady, eat at Chez Louisiane, they chat amicably with Frank. But when Shorty alerts Big Arthur that not only is Cyrus in his restaurant but he is also taking away a doggie bag of food, Big Arthur erupts in anger. He chases the two French Quarter interlopers outside the restaurant, grabs the bag of food and warns them never to come back to Chez Louisiane. It is left to Shorty to explain to a befuddled Frank that Cyrus had not only stolen Big Arthur's recipes, but even published a cookbook in which "half the stuff is Big Arthur's". A classic example of white appropriation of black culture, this conflict moves to the venue of a boxing ring, in an illegal fight, with the winner being able to take credit for his food creations publicly. Although it takes place in a boxing ring, the conflict has all the hallmarks of a classic gentlemen's duel. As the two chefs assert their masculinity in the ring, the conflict spills out to a wider New Orleans, with a large audience assembled to view the fight. The spectacle provides a humorous, but also serious, exoneration for Big Arthur and, by implication, for African American culture. As a character named Sheriff and a bookie explain, "two chefs going toe-to-toe in New Orleans is a dream come true!" Reverend Deal, a minister known more for his entrepreneurial adventures than spirituality, orchestrates the fight, explaining that half the revenues will go to charity. Reverend Deal exclaims, "Gentlemen, this is the fight of the century, the soufflé melee, the battling chefs of New Orleans". Years before *Iron Chef* (2005–), *Frank's Place* had already seen the potential of a chef-to-chef conflict.

Although the boxing fight is otherwise depicted in classic form, the rounds are marked by a large frying pan being struck by a metal serving utensil. This feature signals the feminisation of the contest. Cyrus has previously belittled Big Arthur by dismissing him as "temperamental"—traditionally a word associated with the feminine being flamboyant and emotional—a word that presents Big Arthur as feminised by his lack of control over his emotions. Cyrus continues his attempts to goad Big Arthur, repeatedly and patronisingly telling him to "take it easy" ("Food Fight" 1987). Cyrus has been a professional fighter, and he is three inches taller and forty pounds heavier than Big Arthur. Arthur's position as underdog is also signalled when he tells Cyrus he will hit him with a slingshot. With Cyrus taller and much heavier than Big Arthur (as revealed in dialogue and by the visuals), the reference to a slingshot evokes the Biblical David battling the giant Goliath. The undercutting of the masculine and the association of the feminine are further reinforced by the match judges: one is a *Times-Picayune* sportswriter; the other the newspaper's food columnist. The camera pans to Big Arthur's female supporters, the waitresses Anna May and Miss Marie. Miss Marie, who previously evoked a voodoo spin to control Frank, calmly knits throughout the entire fight. The judges declare the fight a draw, but the crowd boos, and Big Arthur yells at Cyrus: "You're a thief! You're a thief!" They knock down the referee and Frank, and continue fighting, until Big Arthur knocks down Cyrus. Exhausted, Big Arthur still shouts out, "Listen up! I just want everyone to know that I was the first one to put vanilla in the bread pudding and the étouffée, the étouffée over at Café Étoile is my recipe!" ("Food Fight" 1987).

Throughout the episode Frank functions as a stand-in for the viewer, who is presumably without an awareness of white appropriation of black culture, the importance of food, or the specifics of New Orleans' codes of honour. Frank is perplexed at first and tries to stop the fight from being scheduled. He says repeatedly, "it's ridiculous", when it is clear that the conflict is quite serious to all the other characters. Frank also worries out loud that "somebody could get hurt here" ("Food Fight" 1987). Finally, when the actual fight winds down, Frank jumps in the ring to intervene and is knocked down for his pains. The nefarious Cyrus is forced to recant his thievery, and a victorious Big Arthur jumps in the air, frozen in time in his moment of victory.

The episode typifies the series' mixture of drama and comedy, with the exposé of white appropriation as a serious and significant struggle. At the same time, however, humour appears in the format of a boxing match, and in the perpetual outsider Frank, struggling to understand the importance of authorship of a recipe. His situation at the end of the fight, literally knocked down, positions him as the subordinate feminine. Other episodes reinforce the importance of Big Arthur and of food culture, for instance, in "I.O.U." (1987), a gangster manoeuvres to take over Frank's restaurant, but abandons the idea after Big Arthur explains he will refuse to cook for anyone besides Frank. In another episode, the Cajun cook Shorty explains to a perplexed Frank that he has insulted Big Arthur by referring to his cooking as Cajun. Big Arthur's culture, Shorty clarifies, is Creole, and the differences are significant. Understanding and respecting authentic local culture is one of the main lessons learnt by Frank throughout the series. Throughout the episodes, but especially in "Food Fight", African American foodways are shown as desirable and inextricably connected to their creators. The foodways are central enough to the community's identity that their theft is considered an outrage, and their defence essential. That Big Arthur wins the fight reifies the importance of his recipes not only to him, but also to his community, which turns out to watch the boxing match.

Conflict Between Communities: Gender and Class

This lesson is one that is also promoted throughout the show *Treme*, but with an emphasis on creative integrity and vision struggling against great odds. This series' main chef, Janette Desautel, a young white woman, is an outsider to the white-male-dominated food world. Having grown up in Alabama, Janette is also not a native New Orleanian, but has been drawn to the city. Although she leaves it after Katrina, her culinary profession and her love of the city eventually make her return. Her creativity appears in her fidelity to building on New Orleans's food traditions in original ways. In this way Janette preserves their authenticity and a high level of artistic expression. As Joy Fuqua explains, "the chef is [required] to perform … authenticity" (Fuqua 2012: 240) when a group of New York chefs come to her restaurant unannounced. Her successful creation "enforce[s] certain place-based conceptions of authenticity through mastery of the ingredients that give New Orleans meaning" (ibid.). Unlike the white chef in *Frank's Place*, Janette makes sacrifices for her art, and she demonstrates an artistic integrity that is compared to that of the show's musicians. Her gender is also integral to the plotlines, as she is one of the rare female chefs, and her conflicts involve battling male owners who would, as happens to Big Arthur, exploit her name and talent.

Treme is a larger, broader series than *Frank's Place*, reflecting the change from a network programme in the late 1980s to a pay-channel series in the twenty-first century. This is seen, for instance, in the fact that there are numerous main characters in *Treme*, with intersecting storylines. Curiously, much of the scholarship on the show deals only briefly with the chef; much more attention is given to the musicians, perhaps because they are mostly male. The series includes several musicians, but of the three major characters one is female. Yet the programme makes it clear that Janette's creativity and artistry is equal to that of the musicians. In this respect, Emily Nussbaum praises the series' "genuine payoff in the conversations among the show's many musicians and chefs, a sense of exploration—instead of lecturing—about tensions within the creative life" (Nussbaum 2012: 82). In Nussbaum's words, *Treme* depicts "a number of artists struggling to make something original, often by melding an older idea with something new" (ibid.). Nussbaum focuses her discussion on the musician Delmond Lambreaux, but her description applies just as well to Janette Desautel. In a conversation in a NYC bar, Delmond comments on Janette's profession: "odd thing you picked to do with your life". She responds, "You, me, both. People like us we just do a thing. We don't have a choice. Could you do anything else?" ("Santa Claus" 2011).

Treme abounds with loving close-ups of several of Janette's dishes, in shots designed by professional food raconteur (and chef) Anthony Bourdain (Gottlieb 2014: 30). The female chef's passion for her art is demonstrated in the admiration she receives not only from restaurant patrons, but also from the very best chefs in New York and New Orleans. In a rare acknowledgement of Janette's significance, Mike Miley describes the chef's success as key. He praises

the wordless sequence where she dazzles New York celebrity chefs with her unpretentious creole cooking ... her success in wowing the chefs reminds us that New Orleans has something that cannot be replicated, exported, or stolen, something that comes from the mixture of the people and the space. (Miley 2011: 98)

Despite her excellence as a chef Janette faces numerous obstacles. Her creativity in devising new and original dishes that nevertheless draw on traditional New Orleans cuisine reveals her to be an artist. The owner of a successful restaurant before the tragic flood, Janette at first struggles to maintain her business without adequate facilities. In a whimsical scene that evokes *Frank's Place*, Janette struggles to provide a dessert. Finally, she has an idea to dress up and serve a local commercial pie, a Hubig's pie, to her customer's great delight. Yet larger, more insurmountable obstacles arise, keeping her from practising her cooking to her own, and to the city's, high standards.

The first problem occurs with delayed insurance payments for her restaurant and her home, followed by problems with the gas line to her restaurant (ill-maintained by the city), and trouble finding staff and supplies. Like all of the characters, Janette faces tremendous obstacles to recovery, and these problems eventually lead to her selling her restaurant and moving to New York. But like many other New Orleanians, she eventually returns home. Only in New Orleans can she, as another chef advises her, find "a place where you can find your own style" ("Careless Love" 2012). Recruited by a successful owner of many restaurants, Janette agrees to a partnership for a restaurant with her name on it, with creative control acceded to her. The show depicts the inherent conflict that develops between capitalism and art, with the co-owner Feeny reneging on his promises, and holding her to a contract that strips her of the right to use her own name in another restaurant. While Janette works with her staff to create new and original dishes, she always insists, "make it beautiful" ("Careless Love" 2012). The co-owner Feeny has a different vision, describing Janette's dish of crawfish ravioli as "a money-maker" ("The Greatest Love" 2012). He even, horror of horrors, tells her that he will get her frozen (non-native) crawfish, so that she can make the dish year-round. This substitution indicates the owner's crass and deceptive ways, and Janette rejects the idea immediately, stating bluntly: "No fucking frozen crawfish, ever!" ("Promised Land" 2012). Her blunt rejection of artistic compromise presents the chef as parallel to the Mardi Gras Indian who similarly, in a New Orleans phrase, "Won't bow down. Don't know how." Janette's standards, like those of Big Arthur in *Frank's Place*, reveal that the creation of food is as important as that of the high arts. Both series present their chefs as artists, with uncompromising and compelling visions of their work. While race fuels the conflict in *Frank's Place*, in *Treme*, Janette's struggle is a feminist one. Both chefs have to deal with class as well, for neither owns the restaurant where they confront these artistic challenges.

The series also points to the exploitation of foodways on television, exposing how marketing results in deception and misrepresentation of cultural practice. In an awkward appearance on the *Today Show*, Janette manifests her discomfort with trying to prepare food in three minutes. The tension is emphasised by the fact the *Today Show* is a long-running and very popular programme, and its actual host appears in the episode of fictional *Treme*.

While host Al Roker plays with crawfish, talking to them, and asks about making a roux, we can see that his goal is entertainment, while Janette is far more serious. While Roker acknowledges the chef's excellence in his introduction of her as "turning heads with her new Southern cuisine", the presentation of food preparation is positioned as light entertainment, not as a creative enterprise ("Promised Land" 2012). Janette's appearance on the television show serves as marketing for the new restaurant, the idea of her financial partner. She resists Feeny's vision, which is "there's a time to cook and a time to sell" ("I Thought I Heard Buddy Bolden Say" 2012). *Treme* posits the possibility of finding a balance between commercialism and art in a conversation the chef has with Emeril Lagasse, a famous chef based in New Orleans. Emeril owns a number of restaurants and had his own eponymous popular cooking show. Emeril drives Janette to Uglisech's, a small but very popular neighbourhood restaurant, off the tourist track. There he praises the owners of the recently closed restaurant for working until they could cook no more. They "kept their hands on what they were serving", he tells Janette ("Promised Land" 2012). The series focuses primarily on Janette's difficulties as a chef, without suggesting an easy resolution. As the series ends, Janette's struggle continues; she runs out of champagne on New Year's Eve, so she closes the restaurant early. But this happenstance enables her to go out with her lover DJ Davis and her faithful sous-chef and former lover Jacques, to see in the New Year. Like *Frank's Place*, *Treme* suggests there is art and beauty in simply being in New Orleans. As Margaret Groarke characterises it, "*Treme* [...] presents the heart of the city in a way that leaves you no room to argue against its significance" (Groarke 2011: 266). That the city's significance is represented in large part by a chef points to the centrality of foodways to New Orleans' unique culture. Despite her difficulties, Janette will persevere, and the programme's positive characterisation of her vision reinforces the importance of specific cultural practices performed in a specific place.

CONCLUSION

Big Arthur in *Frank's Place* and Janette Desautel in *Treme* demonstrate the reason for the series' critical acclaim. A sophisticated and humorous portrait of popular culture, *Frank's Place* well deserves its reputation as an innovative, pioneering television show. Its mostly accurate and sensitive portrayal of New Orleans' ways of life, including practices of food and music, brought the city's African American heritage to the mass medium of television. Acknowledging New Orleans' unique culture, the series took steps to explain it, using the protagonist Frank, an outsider to the culture, as a stand-in for viewers with questions. Significantly, the show claims the status of artist for its chefs and musicians, with their power to move people and even to change lives. As individual creators with unique visions and creations, the chef and the artist stand on the margins of large-scale capitalism, with products like meals and performances that are ephemeral. Episodes from both series demonstrate the power and importance of food and music to people's everyday lives. In addition, the stories of New Orleans' food and music also explain the city's appeal to outsiders who, like Frank Parrish and Janette Desautel, come to New Orleans for what they plan as only a brief stay, and end up staying for life. Even more significantly, both characters show that not only is it possible for newcomers to contribute to the city's rich culture, but that their work can be critical to the maintenance of New Orleans' cultural traditions.

These episodes show the importance of considering race, class and gender in representing a specific profession in a city. The particularities of traditional foodways are what define the chefs in both programmes. The difficulties they face stem from a dismissal of their specific heritage and position. In Big Arthur's case, the issue is race, while Janette's situation is worsened by her situation as a female minority in a male-dominated industry. The plots and character development expose the injustice and dangers presented to the cultural heritage by racism and sexism. In both programmes, the values of authenticity and creative expression clash with those of profit-seeking capitalism. In both episodes, however, the chefs survive, bolstered by community support. The implications for the

African American community and the city at large are that it must support and value its foodways. The message for visitors and tourists is to appreciate the specific cultural features that constitute this unique city. Presenting these challenges in mass media allows a national and international community to see, in a highly personalised and compelling fashion, the elements that sustain community.

NOTE

1. For a detailed discussion of race and tourist promotion in the 1980s, see Kevin Gotham's *Authentic New Orleans.*

REFERENCES

Andersson, J. and Webb, L. (2016). "Introduction: Decentring the Cinematic City—Film and Media in the Digital Age". In: Andersson, J. and Webb, L. (Eds.) *Global Cinematic Cities: New Landscapes of Film and Media*, 1–16. New York: Columbia University Press.

Campbell, R. and Reeves, J.L. (1990). "Television Authors: The Case of Hugh Wilson". In: Thompson, R.J. and Burns, G. (Eds.) *Television: Authorship and the Production Process*, 3–18. New York: Praeger.

"Careless Love". (2012). *Treme*. HBO. 28 October.

Elie, Lolis Eric. (2012). *Treme* Panel, American Folklore Society Annual Meeting, October 25, Hotel Monteleone, New Orleans.

"Food Fight". (1987). *Frank's Place*. CBS. WAFB, Baton Rouge. 7 December.

Franklin, S.B. (2011). "Interview". *Southern Cultures*, 6: 35.

Fuqua, J.V. (2012). "In New Orleans, We Might Say it Like This … Authenticity, Place, and HBO's *Treme*". *Television and New Media*, 13(3), 235–242.

Gorfinkel, E. and Rhodes, J.D. (2011). "Introduction". In: Gorfinkel, E. and Rhodes, J.D. (Eds.) *Taking Place: Location and the Moving Image*, vii–xv. Minneapolis: University of Minnesota Press.

Gotham, K.F. (2007). *Authentic New Orleans: Tourism, Culture, and Race in The Big Easy*. New York: New York University Press.

Gottlieb, A. (2014). "An Artful Imbalance". *The Nation*, 298 (4), 28–31.

Gray, H. (2012). "Recovered, Reinvented, Reimagined: *Treme*, Television Studies and Writing New Orleans". *Television and New Media*, 13:3, 268–278.

Groarke, M. (2011). "Popular Culture Review". *New Political Science*, 33(2), 265–268.

"I.O.U." (1987). *Frank's Place*. CBS. WAFB, Baton Rouge. 30 November.

"I Thought I Heard Buddy Bolden Say". (2012). *Treme*. HBO. 21 October.

Kirshenblatt-Gimblett, B. (2004). "Forward". In: Long, L.M. (Ed.) *Culinary Tourism*, xi–xiv. Lexington: University of Kentucky Press.

Lauzen, M. (2011). "Boxed In: Employment of Behind-the-Scenes and On-Screen Women in the 2010–2011 Prime-time Television Season". http://womenintvfilm.sdsu.edu/files/2015-16-Boxed-In-Report.pdf.

Linshi, Jack. (2015). "See How Badly Television is Doing When It Comes to Diversity". www.tinme.com/3733692/tv-writers-diversity.

Long, L.M. (Ed.) (2004). *Culinary Tourism*. Lexington: University of Kentucky Press.

Miley, M. (2011). "*Treme* and the Battle for a Certified New Orleans". *New Orleans Review*, 37(1): 94–101.

Nussbaum, E. (2012). "Roux with a View: The flawed, seductive appeal of '*Treme*'". *New Yorker*, 88(30), 82–83.

Overmyer, Eric. (2012). *Treme* Panel, American Folklore Society Annual Meeting, October 25, Hotel Monteleone, New Orleans.

"Promised Land". (2012). *Treme*. HBO. 4 November.

Rawls, A. (2011). "David Simon Talks Back". *Offbeat*, April, 85–86.

Reid, T. and Reid, D.M. (2013). "Interview". By the author in Fayetteville, AR, 1 April.

"Santa Claus, Do You Ever Get the Blues?" (2011). *Treme*. HBO. 15 May.

"The Greatest Love". (2012). *Treme*. HBO. 14 October.

Travel and Leisure. (2016). "2016 World's Best Cities". Available at: www.travelandleisure.com/worlds-best/cities-in-us.

Walker, Dave. (2011). "We still know what it means to miss 'Frank's Place'". *The Times-Picayune*. 13 October, 1–4.

Women's Agenda. (2013). "Lack of Women on Top Jobs Reflected in Television Too". *Women's Agenda*, 20 May. Available at: http://www.womensagenda.com.au/talking-about/world-of-women/lack-of-women-in-top-jobs-is-reflected-on-television-too/201305202174#.U7SlErGooTA.

Woods, W.S. (1951). "L'Abbe Prevost and the Gender of New Orleans". *Modern Language Notes*, 66 (April): 259–261.

Zukin, S. (2010). *Naked City: The Life and Death of Authentic Urban Places*. Oxford: Oxford University Press.

CHAPTER 11

Partiality, Patriotism and Propaganda: Aggregating Local News Sources in Ukraine

Richard Pendry

INTRODUCTION

Russia annexed the Crimean peninsula in March 2014 after supporting a separatist uprising by local people who identified as Russian rather than Ukrainian. Such people are a majority in much of Eastern Ukraine and Crimea (Plokhy 2015: 337–354). The annexation was quickly followed by a positive vote in a hasty referendum organised by the separatists—but recognised by almost no outside actors—on whether to join Russia. War spread quickly across eastern Ukraine, as "spontaneous" uprisings followed in the Donbas region (Sakwa 2015: 148–237). Against the evidence, the Russian government denied its troops were supporting separatists to conduct a covert invasion. The Russian authorities mounted an online propaganda war using fake news published domestically (Khaldarova and Pantti 2016) and also via its international TV channel RT, formerly Russia Today, to spread the message that Russian troops were not involved. Some of the most compelling evidence that the Russian government was indeed sending troops to Ukraine came

R. Pendry (✉)
University of Kent, Canterbury, UK
e-mail: rp247@kent.ac.uk

© The Author(s) 2017   199
R. Sanz Sabido (ed.), *Representing Communities*,
DOI 10.1007/978-3-319-65030-2_11

from social media material collected by the citizen journalist website *Bellingcat*, run by Eliot Higgins (Sienkiewicz 2015: 9–11). This amateur collective verified and published material from social media that tracked the presence of Russian troops in Ukraine, including sightings of the Russian Buk-class missile launcher that destroyed Malaysian airliner MH17 in July 2014, killing all 298 people on board. Many international news organisations used *Bellingcat* as a source (Gordon 2015; Luhn 2016; Sharkov 2016; BBC 2016). Others conducted joint investigations with it (Borger and Higgins 2015; Ostrovsky 2015). In the film *Selfie Soldiers* (Ostrovsky 2015), *Vice News* reporter Simon Ostrovsky used selfies taken by a Russian soldier named Bato Dombayev during the journey from his base in Siberia to Ukraine. *Bellingcat* geolocated the images, so that Ostrovsky could find the same spot and stand in the soldier's position, in a neat conjunction of traditional journalistic techniques and online verification. The Russian authorities initially said that a Ukrainian Buk had shot down the plane and for months denied that they were sending troops across the border. Russian president Putin eventually admitted in December 2015: "We never said there were not people there who carried out certain tasks, including in the military sphere" (Walker 2015). This was understood to be an acknowledgement that the "little green men" (mysterious soldiers without insignia) who took over Crimea were, indeed, Russian troops, and that others had been fighting in Donbas (Sakwa 2015: 148–237).

Bellingcat uses online tools that are freely available, such as Google Maps, Facebook and Facebook's Russian equivalent, called v Kontakte (VK), to verify this information. Sienkiewicz sees *Bellingcat* as the leading example of an "interpreter tier" of individuals who are neither professional journalists nor producers of user-generated content (UGC), who analyse and interpret the flood of such material from contemporary conflicts (Sienkiewicz 2014: 696–698), which "vastly broadens" the opportunities for both news media and the news audience to hold the powerful to account (Matheson and Allan 2009: 102). Open source, a term borrowed from the computer world (Lewis and Usher 2013: 607), describes the process by which readers contribute to the development of a story. *Bellingcat* describes itself as a collective of investigative citizen journalists (Bellingcat n.d.). This chapter draws on interviews with *Bellingcat* investigators, their sources and other actors to clarify the sourcing strategies used by both *Bellingcat* investigators and the

Bellingcat sources themselves, in light of the latter's declared and undeclared allegiances to one or other side in the conflict.

THEORY

Throughout much of the history of war reporting, reporters not actually present at news events have relied heavily on those eyewitnesses who were (Williams 2012: 343). This is no longer the case. Now, numerous "accidental" sources post eyewitness material on social media, which is then remotely verified by reporters and others not at the scene (Allan 2013: 1–25). *Bellingcat* is an example of what Schudson (2003: 1) calls "the vast world of parajournalists", powerful sources who have learnt to act like reporters. Parajournalists are so ubiquitous in contemporary conflict reporting that, when Sambrook (2010) reviewed the greatly increased scope of their activities, it made him wonder whether they had made foreign correspondents redundant. The main reason professional journalists now have access to a larger number of diverse sources than ever before is the emergence of digital technologies. Parajournalists have exploited digital networks and interpret, share and publicise material in novel ways that news organisations then pick up and use in their news output (Sienkiewicz 2014: 695–698). However, as far as professional journalists are concerned, parajournalists and sources alike are all sources, whatever they call themselves and whatever types of relationship they have with reporters.

But the big question regarding such parajournalists is how seriously one can take their output—are they reliable as eyewitnesses or are they essentially propagandists? Plainly, war reporters have always used sources that are self-interested. This study examines the growing importance of parajournalists in light of their increased agency, compared to that displayed by sources active in the period before the appearance of digital technologies. Traditional sources do not aspire to undertake anything that resembles newsgathering. They simply respond to a journalist's questions and supply information. Parajournalists, on the other hand, play an active part in news production and display a variety of sourcing strategies, just like professional journalists. The way they work with sources in areas of conflict comes into focus when examined in the light of their partiality in relation to the protagonists in that conflict. The dilemma for war reporters whose country is a protagonist in a conflict is similar (Evans 2004: 38), but it is much harder for sources and parajournalists to report objectively on their own conflict.

In his studies of international reporters in the Spanish civil war of 1936–1939 David Deacon (2008a, 2008b) categorised the reporters according to how involved they were in their sources' political and military struggles, and whether they fulfilled their role as objective journalists. Deacon called the reporters' sympathy for—or involvement with—their sources their "elective affinity" (Deacon 2008a: 396). In this typology reporters' elective affinities could be propagandist, partisan, sympathetic or agnostic. Deacon distinguished the international reporters in Spain according to how they approached their work, on a continuum from absolute propaganda to absolute professionalism:

> Propagandists: These correspondents who were members or agents of a combatant force.
>
> [...]
>
> Partisans: those journalists who were passionately committed to one side, but had an associative rather than formal relationship with a cause or a party.
>
> [...]
>
> Sympathisers: those journalists who identified with particular protagonists, but whose ardour was more measured and conditional than the partisans.
>
> [...]
>
> Agnostics: The final category of foreign journalists in Spain, "agnostics", were those correspondents who did not connect to any significant extent with the politics of the conflict but focused instead on its intrinsic value as a news story. (Deacon 2008a: 400–403)

Neither parajournalists nor sources adhere to journalistic codes of ethics but, just like reporters, they can be truthful, dishonest or manipulative, depending in part on whether they have an agenda. As we shall see, when Deacon's categories are applied to *Bellingcat* and their sources, the results shed light on the changing relationship between sources and professional reporters—which is the "deep, dark secret" of journalism (Schudson 2003: 134).

Deacon (2008a: 398) modified the elective affinities of the reporters he studied by showing how a range of other practical factors affected their professional practice. These included: the shifting political allegiances of their editors and proprietors; changes in the readers' understanding of the war's political significance; and the diverse news management strategies by Republican and Nationalist forces. He called these external constraints on the reporters' work their "experiential affinities" (Deacon 2008a: 398). *Bellingcat* and their sources also have external factors—experiential affinities—that change their behaviour. As we shall see, the main question for the sources is to decide which is more important, fighting the information war or providing accurate information to their social networks.

METHODOLOGY

Sixteen different *Bellingcat* sources from social media were approached and, where possible, interviewed face to face in Kyiv. Lengthy interviews produced qualitative research that was rich in data. This is a research strategy by case study, defined by Yin (2003: 14) as an empirical enquiry that "investigates a contemporary phenomenon within its real-life context, especially when [...] the boundaries between phenomenon and context are not clearly evident". As far as possible the data from these interviews was also triangulated by talking to other actors, including *Bellingcat* investigators, reporters and the news organisations that published the stories, and other sources on the ground, such as conflict reporters and NGOs. The main intelligence agencies in Ukraine also provided written responses or interviews to questions about the way they work with informants on social media. In all, 35 interviews were conducted by phone, email, on social media and in person. The interviews were time coded, translated and transcribed. One shortcoming of the data is that interviewees come only from the Ukrainian side in the conflict—though the *Bellingcat* investigations use material from all protagonists. Another is that interviewees who see their role as protagonists in an information war have every incentive to aggrandise their true role. In this field, much information is hard to check. That is why this study focuses primarily on *Bellingcat* stories that crossed over to mainstream media outlets. Many of these draw on information that has been verified by the international police investigation report in September 2016 (JIT 2016).

The study used the most rigorous set of editorial guidelines available to ensure interviewee anonymity and the integrity of the data, drawing on the ethical codes used by the BBC Editorial Guidelines (n.d.) and the *New York Times* (Siegal and Connolly 1999: 22, 32). Each lays out rules that help writers "explain to the news audience what kind of understanding was actually reached by reporter and source and should shed light on the reasons" (Siegal and Connolly 1999). The identity of all the interviewees the researchers met in person was checked against the contributors' passports (two representatives of the hashtag #Ukraineatwar refused to show these on meeting, but one confirmed his identity in a later email).

[Field researcher: Mari Bastashevski]

FINDINGS

Sources can be classified into the following categories, whose membership overlaps: (1) civilians with friends and family who are trapped inside the occupied areas, who provide practical information to keep their friends and loved ones safe; (2) patriotic individuals who have set up online propaganda ventures on their own initiative to expose what they see as Russian wrongdoing; (3) individuals who are hoping to promote themselves as patriots while advancing their own political and financial advantage or to raise funds; and (4) individuals who want to help the military and security agencies target Russian and separatist forces.

It is no surprise that people may not be exactly what they seem to be online. In the theatre of war (Clausewitz 1949: 9), the guises that online sources assume often have a markedly performative element (Goffman 1971). It was notable that none of the *Bellingcat* sources whose Twitter handles featured actual locations in the battlefield were, in fact, located there. So, the owner of the Twitter handle "Luhansk Today" does come from Lugansk in the Donbas, but now lives in Poltava as a refugee. "Ukraine at War" is an amateur investigator located in the Netherlands. Two Twitter sources, "HuSnizhne" and "Wowihay" gave themselves online names that refer to locations near the site of the MH17 crash, are from Donbas, though both now live in Kyiv. "It was a trend on social media, especially on Twitter, to name your account after the city where you live", says HuSnizhne (2015). Wowihay's Twitter profile refers to the nearby town of Torez. In the absence of private conversations online or private meetings in person, it is difficult for outsiders to evaluate where such people are located. In their interviews, Wowihay and HuSnizhne said they are in constant touch with friends and family who are too scared to publish material online themselves.

Sources like this may be termed local aggregators since they pull together information from a variety of local sources. People they trust may simply look out of their kitchen window and make a phone call when they observe the movements of the separatists. Others with a small amount of technical knowledge may monitor open conversations on Zello or Viber, communications apps that are popular in Ukraine. The intelligence services are known to record conversations that take place in these open social networks, and so do local people. The joint police report into MH17 authenticated dozens of locally produced pictures, videos, audio or text descriptions of the Buk missile. International reporters do not always appreciate how difficult it is for local people on a battlefield that is controlled by armed men. Wowihay met a television crew from Germany that was led by an enthusiastic young correspondent who hoped to find the Buk launch site:

> Their understanding of the situation was, let's say, minimal. They thought they would come there with no questions asked, film what they need, talk to everyone, make their report and leave unperturbed. Their heads were in the clouds. What they were counting on, once they arrived, [was that] people will just start telling them everything. They did not understand that if today someone says something [to journalists], tomorrow he will be found dead. (Wowihay 2015)

Of course, local news aggregators are understandably not neutral when it comes to reporting the conflict. This does not necessarily imply that their posts are biased, misleading or untruthful. It just means it helps to understand what motivates the sources, to evaluate their credibility. Sources who have moved away from the battlefield re-post photos, videos and other news from friends and family who are still there. In effect, they are like professional reporters in areas of conflict, who, because of risk, also sub-contract newsgathering to their sources (Pendry 2011: 15).

Judging by the statements made by Ukrainian military intelligence (see below), the sources are right to be concerned. What the face-to-face interviews suggested was a distinction between a group of social media users—whose main declared aim was to help the Ukrainian side win the information war—and their humbler counterparts—who are more like eyewitnesses. All the interviewees in this study wanted the Ukrainian side to win and the separatists to relinquish control of the occupied territories.

Propagandists

According to Deacon, *propagandist* reporters in Spain were those who worked directly or indirectly for one of the protagonists. For example, Claud Cockburn and Arthur Koestler were both agents for the Comintern (Deacon 2008a: 401). Cockburn told fellow reporter Virginia Cowles in Spain: "I am not interested in watching revolutions; my job is making them" (Cowles 1941: 32). In Ukraine there are plenty of sources that also want to do their bit to win the war. Such people become active on social media for a variety of reasons. On the Ukrainian side propaganda ventures are ad hoc, provisional and utterly unlike the well-organised, top-down propaganda coming from Russia. Some interviewees think of themselves as information warriors. They proudly announce that their role is to pass on information to both the public and the Ukrainian military. Roman Burko runs one such site, Informnapalm. Burko says that, when the fighting was at its height in 2014, he passed on the location of a Russian and separatist unit to the military that was running the ATO (Area of Terrorist Operation, the Ukrainian government term for the occupied territories). "Our priority was to pass the exact coordinates of the enemy in order for army to react to that by capturing or bombarding them. Because I want this war to end, not simply to write about it" (Burko 2015). He supplied several examples of such cooperation, all of which were hard to check and, as outlined below, not part of this study. *Bellingcat* investigator Aric Toler has retweeted information from Burko, but says his strongly pro-Ukrainian stance calls his reliability into question (personal communication, 25 September 2015).

Other sources that were interviewed worked directly for the military. One of the volunteer military personnel who were such a feature of the conflict on the Ukrainian side is "Aeororazvedka", who operated reconnaissance drones for the military on the battlefield. *Bellingcat* republished one of their posts on a micro-site detailing apparent violations of the ceasefire agreement. The post showed what appeared to be a separatist armoured vehicle being blown up by a missile. In fact, the post was supposed to raise funds by demonstrating the unit's military effectiveness (Aerorazvdka 2015).

Ukrainian intelligence agencies, including the National Guard, the ATO, and the main state intelligence agency (SBU), supplied statements or agreed to on-the-record interviews with the researchers about their use of local people to gather intelligence in separatist-controlled areas. From what they said it is clear that news sources are right to be concerned for their security. A spokesman for the Ukrainian General Staff, Vladyslav Seleznyov, said that "opinion leaders" and bloggers were able, with the help of volunteers, to film events, gather information in plain sight and pass on data to the security services:

> People who provided us with information acted undercover. They did not publicise their activities. As private citizens they were able to openly document [...] events, remember them, make photos and videos—as opposed to the representatives of the intelligence agencies, who were also working in occupied territories. It is understandable that [the latter] had to follow protocols for their personal security and so they couldn't work openly. Local residents [on the other hand] did have the chance to do this. (Selyeznyov 2016)

It appears that the ATO intelligence officials are irritated by well-intentioned patriots on social networks, who provide incorrect and inaccurate information (Myronovych 2016). Activist Semyon Kabakaev coordinated a popular hashtag on Twitter, #Stopterror, that was supposed to inform the Ukrainian military with live information on the movements of separatist units, giving the latter crowd-sourced military intelligence provided by local people. Kabakayev was reluctant to explain how this works, but many of the *Bellingcat* sources that were interviewed used this hashtag when retweeting information from informants on the ground. One can speculate that people using social media could easily endanger Ukrainian forces when they publish information relating to ongoing operations.

Partisans

Other sources that are also politically partial, yet less focused on contributing to the information war, can be characterised as partisan. News sources in a war zone are in a complicated situation. They are trying to survive, to keep their friends and family safe—and some also want to play their part in winning the war. Most of the interviewees said they would publish fake news on social media if they thought it helped the war effort. Some of the propagandist sources claimed to have done so. All the interviewees were extremely patriotic. For its part, *Bellingcat* attempted to distinguish the ideological sympathies of the various actors that posted information on the day of the MH17 crash (Toler 2016), including intercepted audio of separatists, which was released by the SBU, and a plethora of comments from local people, both those who supported the separatists and others who supported the Ukrainian government. HuSnizhne had moved to Kyiv before the war, but her parents still lived there and were not active on Twitter. She live-tweeted news of the crash after a series of phone calls home, "I was like an interpreter", she says (HuSnizhne 2015). People in her wider social network locally were close enough to hear the Buk crew talk to each other:

> Everybody with whom I was communicating during that time knew exactly where that Buk was, and that it was Russian soldiers [who comprised its crew]. When we hear how people speak Russian, we hear their accent and [can distinguish] one from the Donbas, or the [style of] Russian [spoken in] different regions. (HuSnizhne 2015)

As the police investigators later showed, dozens of people like HuSnizhne were in a position to share similar eye witness testimony: "Those who saw the Buk SA-11 moving, those who saw the rocket being fired—this was all in open view. Here is the village, there is the field where the rocket was shot from" (HuSnizhne 2015).

Some contributors to the study stated that the security services try to control what is tweeted from the battlefield. One interviewee, who wanted to remain anonymous because they feared being targeted by separatists if their identity became known, claimed to have been approached by a man on Skype, who showed a medal he had received from the SBU, the Ukrainian intelligence agency, to reinforce his request that the interviewee not live-tweet the movements of a Russian convoy. The interviewee was told that once alerted, the column might change direction and be harder to track. It is outside the scope of this research to definitively evaluate interviewees' claims that they had helped the Ukrainian military to target Russian and separatist units.

Sources usually only tweet once or twice from the battlefield because others inevitably assume they are working for either side's military and intimidate them. All interviewees agreed it is dangerous to live-tweet sensitive information directly from the battlefield. Wowihay, for instance, had had his home set on fire by separatists looking for him after he posted photographs of the Buk missile smoke plume that had been taken by a close friend. Two police detectives from the JIT later said (in a face-to-face interview in Antwerp, Holland, 19 September 2016) that they believed the pictures showed what Wowihay said they did. Realising the photograph contained all the metadata from his friend's camera, and that a simple online search would reveal its owner, Wowihay hurriedly deleted it and substituted it with a screenshot (so as to conceal the metadata). A furious argument broke out online, during which he was accused of falsifying information. In the end, Wowihay made the data available to *Bellingcat*, who vouched for its authenticity. This failed to convince separatist supporters online, and there were consequences in the real world: "My parents' house was already searched twice. They [the pro-Russian fighters] were looking for me [laughing]. Then my house was set on fire" (Wowihay 2015).

For professional journalists, the location and status of sources are significant considerations. From the reporter's point of view, an authoritative source is an identifiable eyewitness who responds honestly to a reporter's questions, whose propagandistic, partisan, sympathiser or agnostic attitudes are unconcealed and transparent, and whose information is checkable.

SYMPATHISERS

No doubt part of *Bellingcat*'s success is that it selects stories that coincide with those that international news media are also interested in pursuing. Inevitably, many of the *Bellingcat* investigations focus on providing counter-claims to Russian propaganda. Accordingly, it must be said that the *Bellingcat* investigators fall into the category of sympathisers. However, is debunking of propaganda genuinely possible if the organisation tasked with debunking only debunks the propaganda of one antagonist? *Bellingcat*'s brief attempt to monitor ceasefire violations only addressed those committed by one side—the separatists. Furthermore, the fact that *Bellingcat* now receives funding from Google and has worked with the Atlantic Council (Czuperski et al. 2015), a US think tank that promotes a stronger relationship between NATO and the EU, has been held up as evidence that *Bellingcat* is partial. But reports by the joint police investigation (Bellingcat 2016) and the Dutch air safety board both support *Bellingcat*'s claims relating to MH17, the former being confirmed by detectives from the Dutch-led Joint Investigation Team (face-to-face interview in Antwerp, 19 September 2016). Impartiality does not have to lead to covering each side 50%. This is an important point that news organisations also struggle with. A BBC guide for its journalists on how to represent all ranges of opinion while maintaining impartiality concluded that a seesaw, or 50-50, approach to balance does not always work well (BBC Trust 2007). Such an approach can accord both sides equivalence, when that may not be the case. The sheer volume of fake news and propaganda coming from the Russian side means that outside investigators end up defining themselves in opposition to it. So *Bellingcat* has spent a lot of time trying to catch out the Russian state actors in Ukraine who said one thing and did another. *Bellingcat* has since come under cyber attack, apparently from the Russian authorities.

AGNOSTICS

It is hard to find Ukrainians who can be said to be agnostic about the conflict. Of the news sources used by *Bellingcat*, there is only one that investigates propaganda and disinformation used by both sides, a website called *Stop Fake*, which was set up by academics based at Mohyla School of Journalism. They conduct simple checks to verify material for the benefit of the news audience:

> *Bellingcat* […] talks to expert groups and [they] do all these magic tweaks. We [on the other hand] call sources, check information, [and take] some easy steps to explain [things] to the very average media consumer. (Fedchenko 2015)

Local people are not neutral but, as in many areas of conflict, many wish the armed men that appeared in their neighbourhoods would go away and leave them in peace. HuSnizhne (2015) points out: "What people agree among themselves is that they genuinely want the people with machine guns off the streets, nobody wants them there […] Everybody is sick and tired of it".

The interviews revealed some of the *Bellingcat* source's other motivations for their work on social media. Dmitry Tymchuk is an occasional *Bellingcat* source and a Ukrainian MP. He was in the military during the Soviet period and serves on the parliamentary defence committee. As he puts it, he "curates" defence contracts. When asked what social media was good for, he related how he was able to use his large following on Facebook to put pressure on the government to pay up on one of his defence contracts when it was late (Tymchuk 2016).

Discussion: Experiential Affinities of Journalists and Parajournalists in Ukraine

The practical considerations affecting the work of reporters and sources—their *experiential affinities*—in Ukraine relate to transparency, the chaotic Ukrainian response to Russian propaganda, and the value that professional reporters add to amateur newsgathering. All these factors affect how Bellingcat collaborators, their sources and the professional journalists they work with understand their respective roles (Deacon 2008a). Dmitry Kisilyov runs the Russia Today news agency, which is part of RT. "Objectivity is an outdated concept", he claims. "Objectivity does not exist. There's not one publication in the world that's objective. Is CNN objective? No. Is the BBC objective? No. Objectivity is a myth" (Kisilyov 2013). Others have long argued that objectivity is essentially bogus. So, while Michael Schudson (1978) says that the journalist's job consists of reporting something called news, without commenting on it or shaping its formation, Gaye Tuchman (1972) describes objectivity as a "strategic ritual" in which reporters sidestep their responsibility to interpret a story by simply attributing news accurately. However, Keeble and Reeves (2015: 153–154) suggest that transparency works better for modern online news gathering than objectivity. "Facts always support particular points of view [...] The very notion of objectivity discourages audience participation because it is presented as something that could not be challenged". According to this view, transparency is more about the process of working through the evidence, while objectivity tends to stress the result. With objectivity, journalists are supposed to trust some sources more than others because they have more credibility. When sourcing is transparent, members of the news audience make their own mind up. Some say objectivity is the new transparency (Ingram 2009; Goodman 2014; Kovach and Rosenstiel 2007). International news organisations may believe propaganda sites lack credibility, and quickly lose interest when trying to evaluate the claims and counter claims of hard-to-check self-appointed 'news' sources online. But perhaps the election of US President Donald Trump shows that news audiences prefer not to have their beliefs challenged. The current research does not address whether the audiences of Ukrainian propagandist websites are dissatisfied with the narrowness or poor quality of the information they are being offered.

How does open source investigation in areas of conflict change journalism? The online news audience is saturated with amateur analysis. Simon Ostrovsky from *Vice News* says that if investigators on social media want to have an impact, they have to bring it to the real world in some way. If someone takes a screen grab of a photograph of a soldier, and circles some key elements on the photograph that they want other people to pay attention to, it is not sufficient to put it up on Twitter and think their job is done. If that fact goes against the person's belief, the person will discard it as fake. Ostrovsky says that applying long-established journalistic principles is what makes the difference:

> You [...] have to follow the traditional rules of journalism, whether that is trying to track down the person who the photograph is about, to get their version of the events, or to verify their identity, speak with them on the phone, talk to their friends, meet them in person, see some real photographs. A lot of people [...] from social media [...] don't really know the rules. So it is not instinctual to them to do something besides taking the screen grab and distributing it: "This guy is a soldier from such and such a division in Russia" and write a caption. [...] The right of reply is dressed up as something that is a right of a person who is being investigated but it is so much more than that. We call it the right of reply, but really it's a verification step. (Ostrovsky 2015)

The reporting of the war in Ukraine is an example of a "pop-up news ecology" (Wall and Zahed 2015: 720) that relies on ever more curation to focus attention on what is worthwhile in the "cacophony of alternative voices" (Wall and Zahed 2015: 731). The main differences between the news ecology in Spain examined by Deacon and that in Ukraine are that more news sources are now available to professional reporters, and we know more about them. "The citizen, the amateur, the individual, the passionately partisan and the victim caught up in events all became categories of value, associated with claims to authenticity, the authority of personal experience and independence", according to Matheson and Allan (2009: 107). There is no longer any meaningful distinction between 'traditional' newsgathering techniques and open source verification. The techniques of online verification have become part of the repertoire of modern journalists, and it would be peculiar now for modern conflict reporters not to make use of social media to gather news.

When asked about their first contact with *Bellingcat*, sources unanimously said that *Bellingcat* first retweeted them, and only contacted them later. As one of the local aggregators put it: "This is the problem with open source: first we post, then we check" (Wowihay 2015). This is something that news organisations have also struggled with. Is it more important to be first with the news, or hold off publication to verify a story properly (Gowing 1994: 27)? *Bellingcat* acknowledges that their sources are not completely trustworthy, but argues that it is important that they are diverse: "If they tweet something in tandem, it is more likely to be true rather than an organised disinformation campaign [like that conducted by the Russians]" (Toler 2016).

Finally, the fact that a parajournalist acts like a journalist, or is commissioned by a journalist to gather information, also raises the question about what is distinctive about the role of the journalist in an information environment where the differences between journalists and other participants are blurred. This way of working tends to flatten out some of the distinctions between witnesses and reporters. "It's very hard to find anything without a hand from locals", says a *Bellingcat* researcher who is a Russian native speaker, based in Kyiv (Mortis 2015). He points out that in one of the posts from an aggregator, only a local person was in a position to confirm that 'Cheryoma' is a neighbourhood slang term for the Cheryomyshki area near the Buk missile launch site. Journalists who are reluctant to expose themselves to the dangers of contemporary conflict reporting on the ground increasingly cover war from a distance. Professional international journalists use all types of locally hired newsgatherers, activists and parajournalists to report on their behalf (Palmer and Fontan 2007; Murrell 2015; Pendry 2011: 14–20; Pendry 2015: 12). Some of the most effective interpreters of material on social media are people who are just far enough removed to be safe, yet have the necessary language skills and understanding of the local ways, like Bellingcat's aggregators.

REFERENCES

Aerorazvedka. (2015). Face-to-face interview, 11 September.
Allan, S. (2013). *Citizen Witnessing: Revisioning Journalism in Times of Crisis.* Cambridge; Malden, Mass.: Polity Press.

BBC. (2016). "MH17 Ukraine Disaster: Report Names Suspected Russian Soldiers". *BBC*, 24 February. Available from: http://www.bbc.co.uk/news/world-europe-35654692.

BBC Editorial Guidelines. (n.d.) Section 3.4.13 *Avoiding Misleading Audiences* in Section 3 (Accuracy). Available from: http://www.bbc.co.uk/editorialguidelines/guidelines/accuracy/avoiding-misleading-audiences.

BBC Trust. (2007). "From Seesaw to Wagon Wheel: Safeguarding Impartiality in the 21st Century". *BBC*, 18 June. Available from: http://news.bbc.co.uk/1/shared/bsp/hi/pdfs/18_06_07impartialitybbc.pdf.

Bellingcat. (n.d.). Home page: "*By and for citizen investigative journalists*". https://www.bellingcat.com.

Bellingcat. (2016). "Revelations and Confirmations from the MH17 JIT Press Conference". *Bellingcat*, 30 September. Available from: https://www.bellingcat.com/news/uk-and-europe/2016/09/30/revelations-confirmations-mh17-jit-press-conference/.

Borger, J. and Higgins, E. (2015). "Russia shelled Ukrainians from within its own territory, says study". *Guardian*, 17 February. Available from: https://www.theguardian.com/world/2015/feb/17/russia-shelled-ukrainians-from-within-its-own-territory-says-study.

Burko, R. (2015). Face-to-face interview, 11 September.

Clausewitz, C.V. (1949). *On War*. Vol. 1. London: Routledge & Kegan Paul.

Cowles, V. (1941). *Looking for Trouble*. London: Hamish Hamilton.

Czuperski, M., J. Herbst, E. Higgins, A. Polyakova and D. Wilson. (2015). "Hiding in Plain Sight". *Atlantic Council*, 15 October. Available from: http://www.atlanticcouncil.org/publications/reports/hiding-in-plain-sight-putin-s-war-in-ukraine-and-boris-nemtsov-s-putin-war.

Deacon, D. (2008a). Elective and experiential affinities. *Journalism Studies*, 9(3): 392–408.

Deacon, D. (2008b.). *British News Media and the Spanish Civil War: Tomorrow may be Too Late*. Edinburgh: Edinburgh University Press.

Evans, H. (2004). Propaganda versus professionalism. *British Journalism Review*. 15(1): 35–42.

Fedchenko. (2015). Face-to-face interview, 10 September.

Goffman, E. (1971). *The Presentation of Self in Everyday Life*. Harmondsworth: Penguin.

Goodman, E. (2014). "Eric Newton, Advocating for Transparent Objectivity in the Digital Age". *Knight Foundation*, 24 March. Available from: http://www.knightfoundation.org/articles/eric-newton-advocating-transparent-objectivity-digital-age.

Gordon, M. (2015). "Armed With Google and YouTube, Analysts Gauge Russia's Presence in Ukraine". *New York Times*, 28 May. Available from:

https://www.nytimes.com/2015/05/28/world/europe/videos-and-google-help-researchers-gauge-russias-presence-in-ukraine.html.

Gowing, N. (1994). *Real-Time Television Coverage of Armed Conflicts and Diplomatic Crises: Does it Pressure Or Distort Foreign Policy Decisions?* Cambridge, MA: Joan Shorenstein Barone Center on the Press, Politics, and Public Policy, John F. Kennedy School of Government, Harvard University.

HuSnizhne. (2015). Face-to-face interview, 11 September.

Ingram, M. (2009). "Is Transparency the New Objectivity? 2 Visions of Journos on Social Media". *Nieman Lab*, 28 September. Available from: http://www.niemanlab.org/2009/09/is-transparency-the-new-objectivity-2-visions-of-journos-on-social-media/.

JIT. (2016). "Flight MH17 was Shot Down by a BUK Missile from Farmland Near Pervomaiskyi". *Openbaar Ministerie*, 28 September. Available from: https://www.om.nl/onderwerpen/mh17-crash/@96068/jit-flight-mh17-shot/.

Keeble, R. and Reeves, I. (2015). *The Newspapers Handbook*. Abingdon, New York: Routledge.

Khaldarova, I. and Pantti, M. (2016). "Fake News". *Journalism Practice*, 10(7): 891–901.

Kisilyov, D. (2013). "Video of Dimitry Kisilyov's First Speech at RIA Novosti". *The Interpreter*, 13 December. Available from: http://www.interpretermag.com/video-of-dmitry-kiselyovs-first-speech-at-ria-novosti%e2%80%8f/.

Kovach, B. and Rosenstiel, T. (2007). *The Elements of Journalism: What Newspeople should Know and the Public should Expect*. California: Three Rivers Press.

Lewis, S.C. and Usher, N. (2013). "Open source and journalism: toward new frameworks for imagining news innovation". *Media, Culture and Society*, 35(5): 602–619.

Luhn, A. (2016). "MH17 report identifies Russian soldiers suspected of downing Russian plane in Ukraine". *Guardian*, 24 February. Available from: https://www.theguardian.com/world/2016/feb/24/mh17-report-identifies-russian-soldiers-suspected-of-downing-plane-in-ukraine.

Matheson, D. and Allan, S. (2009). *Digital War Reporting*. Cambridge: Polity.

Mortis, R. (2015). Face-to-face interview, 11 September.

Murrell, C. (2015). *Foreign Correspondents and International Newsgathering: The Role of Fixers*. London: Routledge.

Myronovych, A. (2016) Interview by email, 31 May.

Ostrovsky, S. (2015). "Selfie Soldiers". *Vice News*. Available from: https://news.vice.com/video/selfie-soldiers-russia-checks-in-to-ukraine.

Palmer, J. and Fontan, V. (2007). "'Our ears and our eyes': Journalists and fixers in Iraq". *Journalism*, 8(1): 5–24.

Pendry, R. (2011). "Sub-Contracting Newsgathering in Iraq". *Ethical Space*, 8(3/4): 14–20.

Pendry, R. (2015). "Reporter power: News organisations, duty of care and the use of locally-hired news gatherers in Syria". *Ethical Space*, 12(2): 4–13.

Plokhy, S. (2015). *The Gates of Europe: A History of Ukraine*. London: Allen Lane.

Sakwa, R. (2015). *Frontline Ukraine : Crisis in the Borderlands*. London: I.B. Tauris.

Sambrook, R. (2010). *Are Foreign Correspondents Redundant? The Changing Face of International News*. Oxford: Reuters Institute for the Study of Journalism.

Schudson, M. (1978). *Discovering the News: A Social History of American Newspapers*. New York: Basic Books.

Schudson, M. (2003). *The Sociology of News*. New York; London: Norton.

Selyeznyov, V. (2016). Phone interview, 7 June.

Sharkov, D. (2016). "Russian Awards For Combat Surge Since Ukraine Conflict: Report". *Newsweek*, 1 September. Available from: http://europe.newsweek.com/russian-awards-combat-surge-ukraine-conflict-report-494937.

Siegal, A.M. and Connolly, W.G. (1999). *The New York Times Manual of Style and Usage*. New York: Times Books.

Sienkiewicz, M. (2014). "Start making sense: a three-tier approach to citizen journalism". *Media, Culture and Society*, 36(5): 691–701.

Sienkiewicz, M. (2015). "Open BUK: Digital Labor, Media Investigation and the Downing of MH17". *Critical Studies in Media Communication*, 32(3): 208–223.

Tymchuk, D. (2016). Face-to-face interview, 10 September.

Toler, A. (2015) "MH17 in their Own Words: Witness Testimonies on Social Media from July 17th, 2014". *Bellingcat*, 16 July. Available from: https://www.bellingcat.com/news/uk-and-europe/2015/07/16/in-their-own-words/.

Toler, A. (2016). Personal communications, 24 June and 25 September 2016.

Tuchman, G. (1972). "Objectivity as Strategic Ritual: An Examination of Newsmen's Notions of Objectivity". *American Journal of Sociology*, 77(4): 660–679.

Walker, S. (2015). "Putin admits Russian military presence in Ukraine for first time". *Guardian*, 17 December. Available from: https://www.theguardian.com/world/2015/dec/17/vladimir-putin-admits-russian-military-presence-ukraine.

Wall, M. and Zahed, S. (2015). "Syrian Citizen Journalism". *Digital Journalism*, 3(5): 720–736.

Williams, K. (2012). "War correspondents as sources for history". *Media History*, 18(3–4): 341–360.

Wowihay. (2015). Face-to-face interview, 12 September.

Yin, R.K. (2003). *Case Study Research: Design and Methods*. Thousand Oaks, California; London: Sage.

CHAPTER 12

Constructing "Ordinary People" on British Television: Notes on the Politics of Representation

Rosalind Brunt

It is February 1971. Seven men are sitting round a table during their lunch break at the London Guinness factory. Three women canteen workers listen to them for a while. For nearly fifty minutes they give their opinions on the current state of British television. It is a wide-ranging discussion, covering sport, current affairs and entertainment programmes. They think the programme formats are rather stale, there is too much repetition and too little variety and choice. Occasionally, an eighth man, writer and film critic, Tony Bilbow, throws in the odd comment or brief question. But it is the men who hold the floor. They get on to the popular *Frost Programme*, a talk show on topical issues that had introduced the 'trial by TV' format to British commercial television:

> First man: David Frost—he has some good programmes but they're very bad conducted... too many people butting in and you don't get the point.

R. Brunt (✉)
Sheffield Hallam University, Sheffield, UK
e-mail: R.Brunt@shu.ac.uk

R. Sanz Sabido (ed.), *Representing Communities*,
DOI 10.1007/978-3-319-65030-2_12

217

... Frost hasn't got the mannerism, I think, or the knowhow, to hold a crowd and put them in their place to ask questions at the proper time—

Bilbow: You aren't saying he's biased? You're just saying he doesn't handle it well?

First man: No, I don't think he handles the job well. Er... I don't know if he's bigheaded or he can't do that part of it. He's not a bad talker, but he can't control a crowd of people (*Late Night Line-Up* 1971).

Bilbow then asks about a recent controversial *Frost Programme* that had discussed the power workers' action against the current Conservative Government:

Second man: I think that was disgusting. ... He didn't even step in to stop that chap being slapped. But I don't think he gave each individual a fair chance to outline their case. I mean there was a man there trying to outline his case who'd been there for *years*. But he never got as much speech as a certain man from the newspapers. Did you see that? He had most say. He was a learned chap and he could speak well but just because he's like that I don't think he should have most say.

Bilbow: I think the man on the newspaper was from the *Guardian*, wasn't he? And in fact he was *in favour* of the power workers?

Second man: Yes, he was. But they gave him a lot of space. They never brought out the actual workers' ins and outs and their problems. That chap was a good chap for 'em. He was an educated man. But unless you do the job yourself, you don't know the intimate problems that they were having, do you? He only knows the technical side of it, and the financial side of it, doesn't he? That's all. ...

Third man: Can I come in there? Don't you think that commentators or people like Frost browbeat people like myself and these gentlemen sitting here? We are not with words. We are with our hands. ... If you was Frost, I could be lost with words. Because you could bamboozle me with words and I would—

Bilbow: [laughter] I haven't said a word!—

Third man: No, what I'm trying to do is give an example. If you [TB] was Frost, all I thought of saying, you could say something and browbeat me and I'd forget all I was saying. And I can talk more than most people can talk. ... I think he really insults people and pulls them down if it ain't going his way.

Bilbow: You're not just talking about Frost are you? You're talking about television in general. (*Late Night Line-Up* 1971)

This discussion was transmitted on BBC 2's *Late Night Line-Up*, a regular weekday commentary on the arts and cultural politics that had come out of a nightly promotion for the then new channel in 1964. The programme had maintained its interest in examining broadcasting, but this was the first time it had left the studio to talk to audience members at a workplace. Broadcasters were astounded at the breadth and depth of the workers' criticism of television output and, despite all the participants' strongly held beliefs that their discussion would be "cut to blazes", the decision was taken to run the entire recording unedited, including the clapperboard in the final shot. But not before the Guinness men had emphatically told the always-affable Bilbow that the scheduling—being transmitted at 10.50pm on a Friday night on a minority channel—was entirely wrong: this was when "most people" would be down at the pub.

In the programme Bilbow defends the scheduling by assuming an audience that might exclude the workers: "If we put it out on a Friday night and other sections of the community are watching, they are hearing, perhaps, your point of view for the first time". To which the riposte from several voices is: "We've got to have the *size* of the audience, haven't we? What is the television medium? To communicate to the masses, isn't it? *Therefore* you need to put it on at the right time to masses of people!" (*Late Night Line-Up* 1971).

I have started by quoting extracts from what rapidly became an influential television landmark in the early 1970s, because it highlights a number of themes about class and community that I want to consider in this concluding chapter. What is striking throughout the *Late Night Line-Up* broadcast is both the strong class consciousness it conveys together with a repeatedly signalled sense of inadequacy and powerlessness 'up against' television, particularly as represented by the actions and words of its studio anchors. Repeatedly the Guinness workers refer to themselves as representing "the average man", "the working man" or "ordinary working class people" (*Late Night Line-Up* 1971). They emphasise a solid identification with a community that wants to better itself, particularly through education. For instance, aware that in asking for more 'live' sport on television, they might have appeared "just all football maniacs", they initiate a long discussion on the need for a range of good, *practical* education programmes "that appeal to working people" on, say, cost-effective holiday destinations, the variety of trade jobs still available for school-leavers, how the exam system works and tracing family history.

However, for all the quite militant class solidarity conveyed in the programme, there is an ever-present sense that television represents the sort of cultural capital that can "bamboozle" and "browbeat" at any time, both through the content it transmits *to* "ordinary people" and the way it represents them when they themselves appear *on* television. Because it is always "the educated", those "with words", who will define their experience *for* them.

It is this contradiction that is explored further with reference to some of British television's other pioneering programmes that have sought to engage with ordinary people. Before doing so, here is an indication of how the Guinness workers implied their sense of marginalisation and exclusion relative to the broadcasting world—and how Bilbow responded to it—with a final extract from the *Late Night Line-Up* programme. During a lengthy exchange about entertainment shows, Bilbow asks about the popular quirky sketch show, *Monty Python's Flying Circus*, which had been running on BBC 1 since 1969 and featured a team of young, mainly male, actor-writers, the central five of whom were all Oxbridge educated:

> Bilbow: You're talking about the old-established favourites, if you like. What about the *Monty Python* lot? Now, what do you think about them?
>
> First man: Good. Sometimes exceedingly good. The humour is, er, you know, on the ball. But other times it's a little bit sick. Yes.
>
> Bilbow: Do you mind that?
>
> First man: No–No that's all right. It goes down—(pause)
>
> Bilbow: What would you rather have? That kind of humour, which, as you say, sometimes you don't find funny, or would you rather have something you *know* you're going to like? (*Late Night Line-Up* 1971)

The group then expresses a strong preference for the original and unexpected, and complains again about unadventurous established formats:

> Bilbow: I mean, you wouldn't call the *Monty Python* lot establishment figures would you?

Several replies: No, No! They haven't been around long enough. Are you trying to promote them?! [Laughter and banter.]

Bilbow: I've got a note under here that says: 'I love Monty Python'!

Second man: [Serious, breaking the mood] Now you see what I mean. We've all been having a say. Now you're [TB] a person that does this regular. And *straight away* the text went on to what *you* were thinking. Now let's get this back to my whole argument. It's the same people that can *outdo* the working class man trying to give his point of view. He's bamboozled and made to look a fool.

Bilbow: [incredulous but still genial] *I'm* bamboozling you?

General dissent: No, no, no!

Second man: I'm talking about the way you brought out *Monty Python*—the way it all came from what you were thinking. Not what we—You were trying to interview *us*. But straightaway it came to what *you* were thinking. ... And that's the way it goes—*every* interview regarding the government, wages, union disputes—

Bilbow: No, no! I must say something. In fact, generally speaking I try to sit on the fence. I don't want to influence you one way or the other.

[Continued good-humoured protest from Bilbow and some acknowledgement from the participants that he is by no means the worst offender. But still the point is pressed.]

Third man: Every interviewer on telly—he wants his way and he's got the experience, in words, so he'll have it his way...

Fourth man: The interviewer who says, "it's now time to move on". Or "we must change the subject". Yes, yes.

Fifth man: We see *all* of the game. [But] on telly it doesn't appear. We see exactly what's happening and what's being talked about. But we can't put it in words. And we can't express ourselves. We're not glib-tongued. (*Late Night Line-Up* 1971)

Again, there is the concern and anxiety about inadequate means of expression, but this time the group is probing further into the implications of apparently lacking the 'right' cultural capital. They suggest that 'ordinary people' will inevitably be at a disadvantage in any discussion mediated by television presenters, however friendly, impartial and "fence-sitting" they may be. Because, it is implied, it is they, with their elite education and glib tongues, that set the agenda and frame the debate.

It was the group's almost taken-for-granted perception that a power disparity, which was ultimately based on class, existed in broadcasting, that so shocked the broadcasters themselves. Especially coming as it did from a group so vehemently expressing their sense of powerlessness, both as the subjects of television documentaries and current affairs and as audiences of these programmes. The Guinness workers' discussion galvanised *Line-Up*'s editor Rowan Ayers, to follow up with several programmes examining the state of British television and to seek, in 1972, a willing management's approval for a 13-part 'community access' experiment called *Open Door*.

The early 1970s proved a propitious time for 'openness' and access. The industrial action mentioned in the Guinness discussion was attaining unprecedented levels of militancy against a Conservative government's attempts to restrict wages and rights. A newly confident section of power and manufacturing workers were using the novel grassroots tactics of the work-in and mass picket under local shop-steward leadership. Post-1968 ideas about creating 'alternative' and more democratically 'participatory' politics were widespread amongst all classes, including those working in the media. Stuart Hood, a controller of BBC 1 in the 1960s and now an 'out' Marxist, coined the formulation "access, accountability and participation" (Brunt 1975: 467), and was a leading activist in the Free Communications Group (FCG) of mainstream broadcasters, journalists and media academics, which was set up in 1969 with a programme aiming for workers' control of the media industry, "opening up the possibilities of alternative means of communication" and "working towards … more participation by the audience, too often the mute, manipulated recipients of the communications industry" (FCG 1971; see Ascherson and Brunt 1972). FCG's main publication was entitled *Open Secret*, and one of its editors also produced *Open Night*, a weekly series for Granada Television in the UK's northwest region, where local people took on the broadcasters to discuss current television output.

The immediate success of the BBC's *Open Door* series led directly to the establishment of the Community Programme Unit (CPU) in 1973, with its invitation to any community groups or individuals "to have your own say in your own way", encouraging particularly those feeling under- or un-represented by mainstream television, and promising to cede as much editorial control as possible to "accessees", as was consistent with broadcasting guidelines and UK law.

The establishment of the CPU was paralleled at local and regional levels by the growth of 'alternative' political papers, grassroots community presses and radical bookshops. Meanwhile, a community television experiment, based in five urban locations, was licensed by the government in 1972. It used existing cable systems and the new mobile technologies, such as Super8 film cameras and video portapaks that non-professional "volunteers" could handle (Lewis 1978). All these developments were enthusiastically supported by national groups such as ComCom (The Community Communications Association), which consisted of both paid and unpaid media practitioners and radical theorists.

However, most of these local and regional community media initiatives had foundered long before the end of the decade, mainly owing to difficulties in sustaining grassroots activism in a worsening political and economic climate. However, at the national mainstream level, the BBC's CPU was able to continue until, after nearly thirty years, its department was eventually restructured out of existence as one of the consequences of the marketing and management-led 'efficiency' priorities of the Director-General, John Birt, a one-time supporter of FCG.

In its time CPU never made peak viewing. It was not allowed the budgets nor the sort of shooting to editing ratios enjoyed by big-rating television departments, which often distrusted them for working with 'amateurs'. Yet, it developed a fierce loyalty to what they saw as unheard voices or dissenting viewpoints, and a commitment to challenging stereotypes through representing a group's own definition of the situation. The most risk-taking of the resulting programmes offered a direct challenge to the mainstream media, including the BBC itself. As an indication, the three which caused most controversy were: first, *Why Their News is Bad News* (1982), which was produced in conjunction with the Campaign for Press and Broadcasting Freedom. Secondly, *Taking Liberties* (1984), in the new *Open Space* slot with Sheffield Police Watch. This clearly showed that the *police themselves* initiated the violent intimidation they had been blaming on the 'rioting' strikers, based on film shot *not* from behind police lines as the mainstream news broadcasters had done, but from the side of picketing miners during their prolonged national strike. And thirdly, also in 1984, the Gay and Lesbian Media Group's *A Plague On You*, which challenged "gay plague" stigmatisation by the tabloid press, while also implicating more 'respectable' channels, including the BBC, for their negative reporting of HIV/AIDS.

The new availability of the hand-held camcorder in the 1990s encouraged CPU to promote a more individualised approach, with the ambitious *Video Diaries* and *Video Nation* projects created in 1993. In a recently published joint account of CPU by two of its senior production team, Giles Oakley and Peter Lee-Wright (2016) expressed widely divergent views on these developments. Oakley saw them as providing "something of a golden age" for CPU, as they gained new audiences and awards for their wide-ranging and varied content. However, for Lee-Wright, the new diary format represented the loss of "a broadcast space dedicated to the articulation of popular voices and views", and he now regretted an inexorable shift towards personal views and a "first person modality" that excludes issues of class and community (Oakley and Lee-Wright 2016: 224).

I am with Lee-Wright on this. Although *Video Nation Shorts* won a prestige regular two-minute slot just before BBC 2's current affairs flagship, *Newsnight*, and was much admired for the heterogeneous originality of its diarists, its format invited only a sort of fascinated celebration of what would now be called diversity. An individualised type of diversity, however, without context or consequence, which, as I will later note, turned out to prefigure many of the reality-television formats of the twenty-first century.

The second pioneering programme from the 1970s that I want to discuss is *The Family*, a 'documentary serial' shown on BBC 1 in 1974. Despite some apparent similarities with early CPU output, I would suggest that *The Family* actually comes closer to the later CPU 'diary' output in that it represents a move away from a concern with community contexts towards focusing on more privatised, often domestic settings. But unlike *all* CPU productions, where participants always retained some meaningful editorial control, the settings filmed in *The Family* are spaces where 'ordinary people', although drawing on their own everyday life experiences and speaking and behaving spontaneously and unprompted, are never, in any adequate way, 'in charge' of how they are represented.

What was novel about *The Family* was its intense observational detail, an approach inspired by the previous year's broadcast of *An American Family*. Shown over twelve thirty-minute episodes on the United States' public broadcasting network, and based on seven months of filming in 1971, *An American Family* had featured a well-off Californian family, the Louds, who owned an engineering company and had five teenage children. During the filming, the Louds' marriage had broken up and their eldest son, Lance, aged 19, had been filmed living an openly gay bohemian life in New York.

Adopting the same episodic structure and similar close-up camera scrutiny, BBC's *The Family* chose a working class family, the Wilkins, who lived in Reading, a town favoured by opinion pollsters for its 'average' Englishness. In the opening sequence it is described by the producer, Paul Watson, with a brief claim to typicality: "Situated 40 miles west of London, famous for seeds and biscuits, Reading has all the problems of any town" (*The Family* 1974). Over melancholic music, the camera then pulls back from overhead shots of the town, in through the window of the Wilkins' flat above a greengrocer's, to focus on a series of framed family photos as if on a living room mantelpiece. The first episode starts in the Wilkins' kitchen as they all eat a fish and chips supper:

> Paul Watson: [off camera, shots panning round the kitchen] As you can see, we're filming. It is going to be a tremendous intrusion into your life. Because we *will* film everything. And there's no lights, so you're not going to be in a position to think when they turn the lights off we can talk in secret. ... We are here *all* the time and we can film you *anytime, anywhere.*

> Margaret Wilkins (mother/greengrocer): We've all talked it over. We know that that much would be involved. So, therefore, in for a penny in for a pound. We're either not going to do it or we *are* going to do it.

> Paul Watson: [jocularly] There're not *that* many pounds in it! [Dissenting voices.]

> Margaret Wilkins: No, no, we know. We're not interested in money in that respect. I mean, all right, fair enough, so we get paid. That is by the way: a nice bonus, so to speak. It gives us the chance to portray ordinary people, if you like, instead of actors and actresses on the screen...

> Paul Watson: [now in shot at the table; clean unused plate in his place] There will be people who object to your behaviour. There will be people who object to your political views, your moral views—

> Tom (lodger/fiancé of daughter Marion): [interrupting] Well, people don't have to listen to us. They can always turn the volume down. Or just use the on–off button.

> Margaret Wilkins: Our opinions are what probably 60% of the people in this country think. But can't put it over. They've got no media to put it over. This is an opportunity, you see. I mean, whether people'll agree with

us or not is beside the point. We're the ones who are doing it. (*The Family* 1974)

Paul Watson goes on to stress both the experimental nature of the project and the "public pressure" the family is likely to be under when the programmes are aired, but he offers no back-up apart from complimenting the family on its own resilience: "We're going to have to rely on you... because you're used to it" (through having lived with the camera crew already in preparation for the documentary).

This 'establishing' episode demonstrates the producer's intention to prove his good faith in the light of his undoubted knowledge of the fierce controversy surrounding *An American Family*, particularly the portrayal of the Louds' lifestyles and what they apparently 'said' about being American, and the family's own widely publicised and often ambivalent responses, as when all five children declared on *The Dick Cavett Show* (1973) that they would be happy to do it all again, after voicing strong objections to the programme having reductively categorised each of them as uni-dimensional types ("just *one* thing: the future builder, the dancer, the schoolgirl, etc."). This was, indeed, the sort of accusation that producer Craig Gilbert had sought to avoid when he appeared in shot in the opening sequence of *An American Family*, high above Santa Barbara, to issue this statement:

> For seven months, the family were filmed as they went about their daily routine. There is no question that the presence of our camera crews and their equipment had an effect on the Louds. One which is impossible to evaluate. It is equally true that the Louds had an effect on us, the film-makers, for this was a cooperative venture in every sense of the word. The Louds are neither average nor typical. No family is. They are not *the* American family. They are simply *an* American family. (*An American Family* 1973)

This introduction contains a number of disclaimers designed to pre-empt any criticism that the family were unfit representatives of the American way of life, because they weren't 'types' to start with, and to stress the collaborative nature of the experiment. In a similar fashion, Paul Watson seeks to demonstrate his own filmmaker's credentials for *The Family* when he concludes the introductory discussion about the likely effects of the camera crews' continual presence by seeking the whole family's consent to the project:

Paul Watson: Does anybody have any real objections to our filming?

Terry Wilkins (father/bus driver–conductor): No. We've talked it over—*thoroughly*. And we've no objections whatsoever—we're all interested to get stuck in, actually.

When Watson revisits the Wilkins ten years later for *The Family: The After Years*, the tone is much less compliant. During an amiable discussion filmed between Margaret and her elder daughter Marion, both now remarried, about wanting to talk to the Royal Family, Margaret suddenly breaks off and asks quite truculently: "Why did he, Paul Watson, pick us?". Watson, suddenly revealed leaning in a corner of the newly refurbished flat, is clearly taken aback, but smilingly seeks to deflect the question:

Paul Watson: I don't know. I mean, I picked you because you seemed to me a very good, loving, caring family. You all supported each other. You all rallied round each other—

Margaret Wilkins: [interrupting] I know why you picked us! You were bloody lucky! You had everything in one family, didn't you? Girl [Marion] living with her boyfriend; a couple who was pregnant when they got married [son Gary and wife Karen, married at 16], Heather [younger daughter, 15] a teenage young woman, very difficult, going with a coloured fellow. And then there was Christopher [aged 9]. So what else did you want? You had it all, didn't you? (*The Family: The After Years 1983*)

Watson's response is not recorded, as the programme then inserts the original sequence where Margaret reveals in interview that Christopher is "not his [Terry's] son". The controversy surrounding *The Family* mainly picked up on the very issues of sexual relations that Margaret outlines—which shocked sections of the audience and press at the time. The question was repeatedly raised, whether in hostile tones of moral indignation, or in a more neutral spirit of sociological enquiry, about who or what the Wilkins *really* represented: British people today? Reading people? (the local press ran a smear campaign feverishly distancing the town from any association with the family). The working class? Changing social and cultural attitudes?

On various phone-in and talkback shows, Paul Watson repeatedly defended his documentary in the same way Craig Gilbert had before him, on the grounds of its *non* representativeness:

Reading journalist on BBC's *Speakeasy*: People were upset at the beginning of the programme about them being a "typical family".

Paul Watson: They're *not* typical. We *never* said this. How can *any* family be typical? Typical of *what*? (*Speakeasy* 1974)

He goes on to say that people are judging the programme too early, because "by the end of the serial it will be a *whole* statement. I will do a piece on marriage. I will try and provide a statement about housing, morality, etc.". Jimmy Savile, the *Speakeasy* presenter, then asks him to define the purpose of the documentary: "Was it just a pointless peep-show?" Watson replies with passion that he was attempting to make films about "people contending in an urban society and to follow it through with *trust* [between filmmaker and subject]. We wanted to show how the ordinary family—or *a* family—coped with these pressures" (*Speakeasy* 1974).

Despite the disclaimers it is apparent that Watson does have some idea of representativeness in his filmmaking approach, and his voice-over 'statements' do indeed provide a generalising, socially aware context about the difficulties of working-class life. There are numerous instances of a strong community-access ethos in *The Family*. One of the most striking is the story of Gary and Karen, which highlights the economic pressures on their daily lives. Both 18, and bringing up son Scott in one room in the cramped flat, they argue over money and domestic chores, with other family members joining in and taking sides. Karen feels isolated and stranded in the Wilkins' home, while Gary feels entitled to his leisure time in pubs and clubs without her, after a long day's work on the buses. The programme then follows their difficult struggle to get a council house. Similarly, daughter Heather's disaffection with school is sympathetically explored and the programme is manifestly on her side in an encounter with a non-comprehending careers teacher.

It is clear that, for all the rather disingenuous denials, much is being said here through the portrayal of one unique family about, particularly, class and gender in 1970s Britain. Furthermore, alongside Watson's voice-over and occasional interview questions, the Wilkins are the ones saying it, directly, volubly, forcefully. The Wilkins women, especially, come across as strong and independent-minded, unafraid to express frank opinions about their everyday experience and the state of the country.

However, although the Wilkins' voices are powerful and frequently given a social and economic context, I would argue that the programme does not give voice to the family in the community-access sense. They have only *apparent* agency, which is why current television history has it right when both *The Family*, and the earlier American documentary, are described as the first examples of "reality television" (Creeber 2015). Although this term only comes into widespread usage in the twenty-first century, particularly through the global spread of the *Big Brother* franchise, I suggest that *The Family* displays a number of aspects that do indeed make it the progenitor of present-day reality television, and which have served, in effect, to crowd out community-access approaches.

First, there is the question of the nature of the 'contract' between programme makers and the 'ordinary people' they feature. Besides the formal legal and financial signed agreements between them, what is the real deal here? And who is in charge? Whilst Craig Gilbert placed emphasis on "a cooperative venture in every sense", Paul Watson goes further in seeking an *on-camera* agreement from the whole family to proceed with filming. While he is honest enough to show that Heather, not eating with the family but silently fuming in the kitchen corner with her arms folded, has offered only the faintest of nods, the general display of consent serves to mask where the power actually lies in the filming process—for all that Watson goes out of his way to stress its unpleasant, even coercive, consequences. For consent is only required once; thereafter, as everyone must feel honour-bound to stick in there to see the project through (if for no other reason than the broadcasting resources expended on it), the ensuing process is unlikely to be cooperative in the important sense of any kind of ongoing collaboration between equal parties.

Of course, it could be said of the Wilkins, as of any subsequent reality stars, that they freely chose to participate in the filming and, to some extent, enjoyed the publicity. But they certainly never had, as in the strongest traditions of access broadcasting, any kind of ownership or control of the end result. As Watson said subsequently, though apparently not at the time, "When I made *The Family*, I had my own voice, a point of view. ... I made the films with a clear idea of the story I wanted to tell" (cited in Bruzzi 2000: 79). Thus, once the choice is made, the consent given, the documentary becomes Watson's property, his take on the family, his story, his voice—and he has the equipment, and, above all, the edit suite.

In this situation, the best the Wilkins can do is *collude* with the camera and the editorial pressure for a story arc leading to a conclusion.

Of all the family, daughter Marion sees the opportunity from the start for active collusion with Watson to effect a narrative resolution to the programme. She repeatedly demands that Tom must marry her before filming ends in the June. While Tom resists—"I'm marrying you, love. Not the bloody cameraman"—the family puts increasing pressure on Tom for the televised fairy-tale ending. Finally, Tom's resistance is worn down after Watson interviews him, separately in the pub, on his intentions and later intervenes on an argument from behind the camera:

> Tom: I've *said* I *will* marry you and that. But in *private*. I just don't want to get married on television.
>
> Paul Watson: [off-screen] But Tom, the camera's here *now*. (*The Family* 1974)

While the always poshly reasonable voice of Watson serves to subdue Tom's doubts, his editor's eye is inclined to trump any ethical considerations. To give just two examples: first, the youngest child, Christopher, is repeatedly shown in humiliating situations, shouted at or slapped for not "hurrying up", having his mother wash him "like a baby", or being told off for his school report. Invariably, he cries, trying to shield his face from the camera's gaze, or hides under the bed as the only protection from the crew. It was stressed at the time that Christopher already knew the details of his paternity before Margaret revealed it in interview with Watson, giving praise to Terry for "accepting him as his son". But never mind that child safeguarding guidelines were not much in evidence in 1974, Watson is still prepared, in the interests of *his* story, to put distressing and salacious details above any professional duty of care for family members.

Another example appears when, in another scene, Karen is shown struggling to fill in the council housing application. Sitting beside her on the sofa amidst toddler's toys, Gary is casually reading whilst answering Karen's questions about spelling and grammar. The camera homes in on what Gary is reading; it is the men's magazine *Climax*, a most telling encapsulation of the interrelationship of class and gender from a production point of view, and thus a scene that deserves its place in the weekly half-hour slot, edited down from up to 18 hours-a-day filming. But to point out that the scene risks showing up a young man, obviously unaware of how it could be interpreted, and humiliating his wife in the process, is immediately to bump up against the issues of free consent—after all, the couple are both 18—and accusations of patronising ordinary people who have, anyway, chosen to appear on television.

In more recent times, Watson has appeared at film festivals or written in the press to defend the integrity of his documentary vision against the new forms of reality television. Writing in the *Daily Mail* in 1998, he observed:

> I despair of what's happening, for this rash of docu-soaps sums up the very worst of programme-making. This is television at its cheapest and laziest ... not much better than moving wallpaper ... Why ... invest in a serious investigative documentary when you can get away with a cheap series simply by pointing a camera at someone wanting self-promotion. (cited in Corner 2004: 294)

Whilst there is obviously a qualitative difference from the type of observational documentary that Watson pioneered with *The Family*, I would also contend that there are undoubted continuities in terms of televised perspectives and the treatment of 'ordinary people' in the sorts of modern television genres that Watson dismisses as "moving wallpaper".

I will briefly take *The Jeremy Kyle Show* as an example of the type of series that Watson would doubtless most deprecate. Started on ITV in 2004, it runs for periods throughout each year at 65 minutes every weekday morning. It developed out of the presenter's commercial radio show *Jezza's Confessions*, and adapts the confrontational format of the American *Jerry Springer Show*, inviting various parties to a contentious personal relationship problem to argue it out, in front of the presenter, an audience encouraged to take sides, and security men poised to restrain any too-aggressive guests.

The Jeremy Kyle Show has tended to escape much critical scrutiny, perhaps because it is seen as so self-evidently gross that it requires no evaluation, or because analysing it would risk passing judgement on its participants. It has also acquired a cult status that inhibits taking the show seriously and encourages a sort of ironic fascination, particularly among a young (student) audience—an attitude that may conceal class-contempt. Such views apart, my interest here is to indicate how the show's ethos might reverberate with that of *The Family*.

The daily format of the show presents several confrontational scenarios. Each requires an intense outline of the problem before moving to a speedy resolution, which is usually suspended until "after the break—so *don't* go anywhere!". The narrative reveal then typically involves the results of a DNA test (for paternity), a lie detector test (for affairs), or an unexpected guest with a new confession. Each scenario is continuously framed with a tabloid-style caption, as if said by the main protagonist. Here is a summary of one such scenario. It is headlined: "Who's the father of my baby? You or your brother?" Charlotte, aged 20, is brought on stage to insist Jake, aged 18, is her baby's father, which he is denying. Kyle announces Jake's appearance as a "first" for the series, as he has just participated in one of the day's earlier scenarios: "He's the one who slept with his *father's* girlfriend and *now* his *brother's* girlfriend!" Charlotte sums up her story: "I slept with Jake in May, and then I missed my period in June. And then I slept with Kelvin in July" (*The Jeremy Kyle Show* 2017). Denying Kyle's accusation of having sex with both brothers at the same time, she says she turned to Jake when boyfriend Kelvin "wasn't treating me well". There is then a fierce argument between Jake and Kelvin, with Kyle shouting at them to "sit down! Stop lying! Shut up! Talk to each other!" After the break the DNA test reveals that Jake is indeed the father. Kyle admonishes him to grow up, get a job and "use your brain and not your bits", as he and Charlotte are ushered off stage to receive couple counselling. The emphasis on therapy and 'aftercare' is presumably what keeps the show within the regulatory body Ofcom's reality television protocol. It allows Jeremy Kyle to claim that he is helping people who have been failed by social services and that the show preserves "solid family values" (Burrell 2013). Although he has no formal therapeutic training, Kyle cites his previous gambling addiction and his ongoing OCD as evidence that he can identify with other people's problems (Kyle 2009).

The people who appear on his stage for judgement are almost invariably unemployed or working-poor, and often very young adults. However, the likely economic stress and material circumstances that have doubtless served to exacerbate their personal crises are not for the programme to explore, nor does the routine format allow it. Their scenarios are represented as simple morality tales, with Kyle as the final arbiter of who is a good or bad person—as confirmed by the studio audience's applause or boos. So the social context of Charlotte's story remains unexamined, although the hints are certainly there about why Kelvin might have mistreated her, and why jobless Jake convinced himself that she was lying about their child: "I thought I was being used for money after I'd paid for the baby's pushchair. And then she was expecting me to go on paying her" (*The Jeremy Kyle Show* 2017).

It is by no means inevitable that having considerable wealth and an early life frequenting royal palaces (Kyle's father was personal secretary to the Queen Mother) would produce an inability to acknowledge socioeconomic disadvantage. But Kyle's public allegiance to the Conservative Party, and his belief in the erstwhile nostrums of Prime Minister Cameron's Broken Britain, make empathetic awareness of class realities unlikely, and serve only to highlight the disparity between presenter and presented on the show. It is, after all, *The Jeremy Kyle*, not *The People's, Show*. The participants must fit the format and understand the 'contract', that is, be prepared to allow an invasion of their privacy in exchange for the reveal, to win the hopefully redemptive conclusion by first engaging in the verbal and physical abuse that Kyle will then loudly and aggressively condemn.

The term 'humilitainment' has recently been coined by media psychologists to express concern about the trend towards increasing aggression and bullying on reality television (Booker 2004). However, there is also a significantly emerging counter-trend that draws entirely on people's capacity for wit, fun and quick acuity. It is best exemplified by Channel 4's most popular and highest-rated programme, *Gogglebox*. Running since 2013, the hour-long programme consists entirely of extracts from the past week's broadcasts commented on by a regular cross section of the British public, who are shown in their own living rooms as they watch the selected programmes. The commentary comes only from them, apart from a lightly humorous linking voice-over introducing the extracts and the people.

What is immediately striking about *Gogglebox* is the very wide range of domestic settings, friendships, sexual and family groupings that are represented from across the regions, classes and ethnicities of Britain. Its appeal to an audience is not only to suggest that the people we are watching watching television are 'just like us', but also that they make the self-same sort of comments that we would make as television viewers. Thus the *Gogglebox* tone tends to the exclamatory, the cynical and the jokey, as it well might in anyone's home: "Oh. My. God!/ He's the Sigmund Freud of film directors/That's *so* fucking weird!/ It's so bad it's brilliant!/They should have brought back *Eldorado*— or *Crossroads*!" (individual comments on the return of *Twin Peaks*; *Gogglebox* 2017)

Unmediated as they are by any presenter, academic expert or interviewer, the *Gogglebox* voices invite enjoyable and immediate audience identification. However, they remain tightly constrained by the edit and the format. For all the sharpness of their remarks, the quick cutting, attention-grabbing juxtapositioning of different living-room settings pre-empts much dialogue beyond a speedy exchange of one-liners and bantering soundbites. Hence the welcome display of diversity on the programme remains merely that: it has a primarily *performative* function that serves to mask the absence of any elaborated critique, or any reflective evaluation of mainstream television by its viewers. Similarly, given the current lack of any serious investment in community-access programming by the major British channels, the reductive recourse to street vox-pops and brief common-sense opinion in news and current affairs coverage inevitably confirms the impression that, when it comes right down to it, ordinary people have little interest, imagination or useful knowledge to communicate.

The promise of the 1971 *Line-Up* programme described at the beginning is still to be fulfilled. Namely, that in less professionally mediated spaces, people are quite capable of developing the sort of deliberative arguments that adequately represent their experiences of the world—and, indeed, of the media. To conclude, I am therefore suggesting the need for continual analytical scrutiny of all mainstream media discourses from the perspective of a politics of representation.

This could start by recognising the disparities of cultural capital between the makers of television and those they 'cast' in the 'ordinary person' role. How do they see this role as representative or typical? And of whom and what? Constantly aware of dynamics of power in all fields, it would also ask who and what governs the resources that ultimately control the edit and the format. Finally, it could acknowledge what might be called the relations of representation; an approach that understands the notions of community, class and, yes, the current one of diversity, to have a material context altogether more profound, creative and exciting than television's current construction of ordinary people.

REFERENCES

An American Family. (1973). PBS, 11 January.

Ascherson, N. and Brunt, R. (1972). "The FCG's AGM: Two views". *Open Secret*, 9: 28–31.

Booker, S.M. (2004) *Lessons from Temptation Island: A Reality Television Content Analysis.* Unpublished doctoral dissertation, Central Connecticut University.

Brunt, R. (1975). "Postscript: Mass Communications in Britain". In: Ford, B. (ed.) *The Pelican Guide to English Literature: Vol. 7 The Modern Age*, 465–470. London: Penguin.

Bruzzi, S. (2000). *New Documentary: A Critical Introduction.* London and New York: Routledge.

Burrell, I. (2013). "Jeremy Kyle, Judge, Jury, Exploiter?". *Independent*, 5 April. Available at: http://www.independent.co.uk/news/people/profiles/jeremy-kyle-judge-jury-and-exploiter-8562459.html.

Corner, J. (2004). "Afterword: Framing the new". In: Holmes, S. and Jermyn, D. (eds.) *Understanding Reality Television*, 290–299. London: Routledge.

Creeber, G. (ed.) (2015). *The Television Genre Book.* London: British Film Institute/Palgrave.

FCG (1971). Programme and Aims agreed at FCG Annual General Meeting. Personal notes, 4 April.

Gogglebox. (2017). C4, 26 May.

Kyle, J. (2009). *I'm Only Being Honest.* London: Hodder and Stoughton.

Late Night Line-Up. (1971). "Guinness workers give opinion about the quality and content of television programmes". BBC 2, 19 February.

Lewis, P.M. (1978). *Community Television and Cable in Britain.* London: British Film Institute.

Oakley, G. and Lee-Wright, P. (2016). "Opening Doors: the BBC's Community Programme Unit 1973–2002". *History Workshop Journal*, 82(1): 213–234.

Speakeasy. (1974). BBC 1, 16 June.

The Dick Cavett Show. (1973). ABC, 20 February.

The Family. (1974). BBC 1, 3–26 April.

The Family: The After Years. (1983). BBC 1, 10 December.

The Jeremy Kyle Show. (2017). ITV, 22 May.

INDEX

© The Editor(s) (if applicable) and The Author(s) 2017
R. Sanz Sabido (ed.), *Representing Communities*,
DOI 10.1007/978-3-319-65030-2

Printed by Printforce, the Netherlands